Cooperation and Conflict between Europe and Russia

When thinking about relations between Europe and Russia, International Relations scholars focus on why conflict has replaced cooperation. The "geostrategic debate" excludes the possible coexistence of cooperation and conflict. This edited volume argues that, although the standard narrative remains compelling, local patterns of cooperation and conflict are partly autonomous from the geostrategic level. Tracking the evolution of conflict and cooperation patterns in three zones of contact (Estonia, Kaliningrad, and Moldova) between 1991 and 2016, the first chapter elaborates a theoretical proposition distinguishing fluid, rigid, and disputed symbolic boundaries, which have different impacts on the ground. The subsequent chapters address distinct dimensions of Euro-Russian relations, paying attention to local reality in Estonia, Moldova, Ukraine, or Kaliningrad, different sectors from energy to peoples' movement, and across institutional contexts such as the EU and NATO. They confirm that the standard narrative holds in most cases, but also that Euro-Russian relations vary in crucial ways according to the interests and representations of actors immersed in specific geopolitical fields.

Despite a deterioration of geostrategic relations between Europe and Russia since the end of the Soviet Union, *Cooperation and Conflict between Europe and Russia* explores the intriguing coexistence of conflict and cooperation at the local level and across sectors and institutions.

The chapters in this book were originally published as a special issue of the journal *East European Politics*.

Magdalena Dembińska is Professor of Political Science and Academic Director of CÉRIUM, the Centre for International Studies at Université de Montréal.

Frédéric Mérand is Professor of Political Science and Scientific Director of CÉRIUM, the Centre for International Studies at Université de Montréal.

Cooperation and Conflict between Europe and Russia

Edited by
Magdalena Dembińska and Frédéric Mérand

LONDON AND NEW YORK

First published 2022
by Routledge
2 Park Square, Milton Park, Abingdon, Oxon OX14 4RN

and by Routledge
605 Third Avenue, New York, NY 10158

Routledge is an imprint of the Taylor & Francis Group, an informa business

© 2022 Taylor & Francis

All rights reserved. No part of this book may be reprinted or reproduced or utilised in any form or by any electronic, mechanical, or other means, now known or hereafter invented, including photocopying and recording, or in any information storage or retrieval system, without permission in writing from the publishers.

Trademark notice: Product or corporate names may be trademarks or registered trademarks, and are used only for identification and explanation without intent to infringe.

British Library Cataloguing in Publication Data
A catalogue record for this book is available from the British Library

ISBN: 978-1-032-06438-3 (hbk)
ISBN: 978-1-032-06440-6 (pbk)
ISBN: 978-1-003-20234-9 (ebk)

Typeset in Myriad Pro
by Newgen Publishing UK

Publisher's Note
The publisher accepts responsibility for any inconsistencies that may have arisen during the conversion of this book from journal articles to book chapters, namely the inclusion of journal terminology.

Disclaimer
Every effort has been made to contact copyright holders for their permission to reprint material in this book. The publishers would be grateful to hear from any copyright holder who is not here acknowledged and will undertake to rectify any errors or omissions in future editions of this book.

Contents

Citation Information	vi
Notes on Contributors	viii

1 Theorising cooperation and conflict in Euro-Russian relations 1
Frédéric Mérand, Magdalena Dembińska and Dominika Kunertova

2 Conflict and cooperation between Europe and Russia: the autonomy of the local 13
Magdalena Dembińska, Frédéric Mérand and Anastasiya Shtaltovna

3 Hybrid geopolitics in EU-Russia relations: understanding the persistence of
conflict and cooperation 35
Cristian Nitoiu and Florin Pasatoiu

4 Kaliningrad: a dual shift in cooperation and conflict 51
Anna-Sophie Maass

5 Not on speaking terms, but business as usual: the ambiguous coexistence of
conflict and cooperation in EU-Russia relations 65
Tom Casier

6 Theorising conflict and cooperation in EU-Russia energy relations: ideas,
identities and material factors in the Nord Stream 2 debate 80
Marco Siddi

7 Crisis response, path dependence, and the joint decision trap: the EU's
eastern and Russia policies after the Ukraine crisis 100
Joan DeBardeleben

Index 122

Citation Information

The chapters in this book were originally published in *East European Politics*, volume 36, issue 4 (2020). When citing this material, please use the original page numbering for each article, as follows:

Chapter 1

Theorising cooperation and conflict in Euro-Russian relations
Frédéric Mérand, Magdalena Dembińska and Dominika Kunertova
East European Politics, volume 36, issue 4 (2020), pp. 465–476

Chapter 2

Conflict and cooperation between Europe and Russia: the autonomy of the local
Magdalena Dembińska, Frédéric Mérand and Anastasiya Shtaltovna
East European Politics, volume 36, issue 4 (2020), pp. 477–498

Chapter 3

Hybrid geopolitics in EU-Russia relations: understanding the persistence of conflict and cooperation
Cristian Nitoiu and Florin Pasatoiu
East European Politics, volume 36, issue 4 (2020), pp. 499–514

Chapter 4

Kaliningrad: a dual shift in cooperation and conflict
Anna-Sophie Maass
East European Politics, volume 36, issue 4 (2020), pp. 515–528

Chapter 5

Not on speaking terms, but business as usual: the ambiguous coexistence of conflict and cooperation in EU-Russia relations
Tom Casier
East European Politics, volume 36, issue 4 (2020), pp. 529–543

Chapter 6

Theorising conflict and cooperation in EU-Russia energy relations: ideas, identities and material factors in the Nord Stream 2 debate
Marco Siddi
East European Politics, volume 36, issue 4 (2020), pp. 544–563

Chapter 7

Crisis response, path dependence, and the joint decision trap: the EU's eastern and Russia policies after the Ukraine crisis
Joan DeBardeleben
East European Politics, volume 36, issue 4 (2020), pp. 564–585

For any permission-related enquiries please visit:
www.tandfonline.com/page/help/permissions

Notes on Contributors

Tom Casier is Jean Monnet Chair and Reader in International Relations at the University of Kent's "Brussels School of International Studies" (BSIS), Belgium. He has provided policy advice for different institutions and organisations, including the European Parliament, House of Lords and the US State Department.

Joan DeBardeleben is Chancellor's Professor in the Institute of European, Russian and Eurasian Studies and Co-Director of the Centre for European Studies, Carleton University, Ottawa, Canada.

Magdalena Dembińska is Professor of Political Science and Academic Director of CÉRIUM, the Centre for International Studies at Université de Montréal, Canada.

Dominika Kunertova is Senior Researcher in the Global Security Team at the Center for Security Studies, ETH Zürich, Switzerland.

Anna-Sophie Maass is Lecturer in International Relations and Diplomacy in the Department of Politics, Philosophy and Religion at Lancaster University, UK.

Frédéric Mérand is Professor of Political Science and Scientific Director of CÉRIUM, the Centre for International Studies at Université de Montréal, Canada.

Cristian Nitoiu is Associate Fellow at LSE IDEAS and Lecturer in Diplomacy and International Governance at the Institute for Diplomacy and International Governance at Loughborough University, London, UK.

Florin Pasatoiu is Lecturer in International Relations, president and director of the Center for Foreign Policy and Security Studies (CFPSS), Romania.

Anastasiya Shtaltovna is researcher at University of Montreal in Canada. She holds a PhD in development studies from the University of Bonn, Germany.

Marco Siddi is Senior Research Fellow at the Finnish Institute of International Affairs, Finland.

Theorising cooperation and conflict in Euro-Russian relations

Frédéric Mérand, Magdalena Dembińska and Dominika Kunertova

ABSTRACT
When thinking about Euro-Russian relations, IR scholars focus on why conflict has replaced cooperation. The "geostrategic debate" excludes the possible coexistence of cooperation and conflict. In this Introduction to the special issue, we track the evolution of conflict and cooperation patterns in three zones of contact (Estonia, Kaliningrad, Moldova) between 1991 and 2016. Our findings show that, although the standard narrative remains compelling, in several cases patterns of cooperation/conflict are largely autonomous from the geostrategic level. This diversity justifies the elaboration of theoretical propositions distinguishing fluid, rigid, and disputed symbolic boundaries which are constructed in and through geopolitical fields.

Introduction

The standard narrative about Euro-Russian relations is told along geostrategic lines: While the early post-Cold War years were a honeymoon between former enemies, strategic competition resurfaced in the late 1990s, culminating in open rivalry since the Ukrainian crisis. To be sure, Russia agreed to the formation of the NATO-Russia Council and, after 11 September 2001, joined the coalition against terrorism. But the Kosovo war (1999), the expansion of NATO and the EU to former Soviet satellites in 1999–2004, the US missile defense plan (2007–09), the Georgian war (2008), the 2009 energy crisis, the conflict in Ukraine and the annexation of Crimea (2014) all contributed to a significant deterioration of geostrategic relations. The literature in International Relations focuses on why such divisions cracked open. Although realists, liberals and constructivists debate the causes, they agree that the story is one of uniform and unilinear deterioration. There is a zero-sum relationship between cooperation and conflict: as the former went down, the latter went up.

What if things were not so simple? Although relations between Europe and Russia do look bad in general, they have resisted cooling on several issues, namely energy relations, Arctic cooperation, migration in Kaliningrad or environmental management in the Baltic sea. This diversity of situations constitutes a puzzle for mainstream IR theories that focus on the macro level. Revisiting the assumption that conflict has *entirely replaced* cooperation, the articles collected in this special issue aim at understanding whether and how cooperation and conflict *coexist* in Euro-Russian relations (Haukkala 2015;

Nitoiu 2017). Contributors embed and contextualise geostrategic relations by taking a close look at comparative empirical cases, either geographical, sectoral, or institutional. Eschewing the reification of heterogeneous actors and interests, they argue that there is not a single Europe-Russia *relationship* but, rather, multiple *relations*.

Theoretically, this special issue on Theorising Cooperation and Conflict in Euro-Russian Relations is eclectic: contributors freely adopt a realist, a liberal or a constructivist approach. Empirically, the objective is open-ended: we do not seek to show that cooperation trumps conflict, but rather to explore the extent to which cooperation and conflict coexist, how, and why. To do so, contributors analyse zones of contact between the two blocs, "geopolitical fields" that state leaders and international organisation summits often obfuscate. These zones of contact can be geographical, sector-based, or institutional. Through nuanced empirical analysis and complementary theoretical angles, each article deepens our understanding of the interplay of cooperation and conflict in Euro-Russian relations.

In this Introduction, we justify the importance of analysing the coexistence of cooperation and conflict. This coexistence is shown with a quantitative measure of the evolution of Euro-Russian relations in three geographical flashpoints, i.e. Estonia, Moldova and Kaliningrad, over a period covering from 1991 to 2016. We select these three cases because they shared common traits when the Soviet Union collapsed but have since gone through contrasted dynamics of conflict and cooperation. Then, we elaborate a common conceptual vocabulary, formulating theoretical propositions that contrast the dynamics of fluid, rigid, and disputed (also "contested" in this issue) symbolic boundaries constructed in and through geopolitical fields. Finally, we summarise the main findings of this special issue.

The geostrategic debate

As already mentioned, the IR literature focuses on why, since the early years of the post-Cold War era, conflict replaced cooperation in Euro-Russian relations. This is what we call the geostrategic debate, or standard narrative.

For realists, NATO enlargement and the EU's vigorous promotion of its norms in the post-Soviet space threatened a declining state's sphere of influence. Mankoff (2009) and Trenin (2014) explain growing tensions by the disregard for Russian interests and the humiliation felt in Moscow during the 1990s, both of which continue to feed nationalism and nostalgia for "Great Russia" (Cross 2015). For the Kremlin, the West broke the commitment it made in 1990, when Gorbachev was promised that German reunification would be the end of enlargement. While this interpretation is challenged by scholars from a historical point of view (Kramer 2009), it shapes Russian foreign policy and explains the influence of *Realpolitik* thinking in Moscow, leading to a conflictual attitude (Averre 1998).

Realists point to the "rebirth of geopolitics" in Russia: in this line of thought, Russia must remain at the centre of the Eurasian strategic arc, which gives great power status and the right to veto the foreign policy of its former satellites (Lynch 2001). Because Ukraine cuts across this "geopolitical fault line" (Berryman 2012, 538), Mearsheimer argues for instance that this country should be turned into a buffer state between Russia and the West. Oblivious to the strategic importance of Russian naval bases in Crimea, NATO and the EU made the mistake of trying to get Ukraine out of Russia's orbit. For Mearsheimer (2014:, 84), "the United States and its allies have, unwillingly, provoked a major crisis with Ukraine." According to this reading, taken up by Kissinger (2014), Götz (2015) and Wolff (2015), the EU and NATO must recognise the specific character of countries of special interest to Russia, such as Ukraine or Georgia, which should have never been promised accession. The West's open-arms policy is not shaped by a sound reading of national interest but instrumentalized by domestic groups that demonise Putin. While they criticise Washington, realists are even harsher on the EU, whose norm and value promotion is seen as a counterproductive "theology" (Lindley-French 2014, 36).

For liberals, by contrast, the cause of conflict is found less in NATO and EU activism than in their *moderation vis-à-vis* an increasingly authoritarian regime and political culture. Russia seeks to challenge the West with an alternative political model. According to Dunnett (2014), Putin is a "short-sighted autocrat" whose aggressive actions have nothing to do with his country's security. Rather, they are explained by a desire to strengthen his regime. The role of the orthodox church and of the military is fundamental in the development of an imperial imaginary that looks beyond Russia's physical borders (Lomagin 2012; Barany 2007). In the face of this powerful imaginary, Europeans failed to create a regional security architecture that would have strengthened liberal forces in Russia (Charap 2014; Karasek 2014). After 20 years of Putinism, the second-best solution is to contain Russia and extend security guarantees to countries on the geopolitical fault line, like Ukraine (Motyl 2014).

Occupying the middle ground between realists and liberals, constructivists argue that Euro-Russian conflict is embedded in misunderstandings between powers with divergent values and identities. Over the past two decades, Russian identity has grown apart from Europe (Casier 2013; Tsygankov 2012). This intersubjective gap, of which the Ukraine crisis may either be a symptom or an accelerator (Haukkala 2016), is striking with regards to notions of sovereignty (Haukkala 2010; Ziegler 2012). While sovereignty is limited and fluid for Europeans who view their Neighborhood Policy as a win-win partnership, it is absolute for the Russians, for whom sovereignty cannot be shared and influence is a zero-sum game (Haukkala 2009; Emerson 2011; DeBardeleben 2012). The problem is a lack of mutual understanding and trust.

In a 2018 book, Tom Casier and Joan DeBardeleben argue that the EU and Russia went from a period of cooperation (1993–2003) to pragmatic competition (2004–2013) to confrontation (2014- …). They focus on the mutual perceptions and images held in European capital cities and Moscow during this period, as Russia went from being treated as a pupil to being called a revisionist actor by the EU, and the EU moved from partner to declining power in Russia's eyes. During the 2004–2013 period, tensions rose but pragmatism continued to rule. In their view, the Ukraine crisis was a defining moment that worsened an already deteriorating situation, which they call the "dynamics of dwindling trust". The relationship turned negative in several areas, notably trade relations, the visa regime, security policy, and human rights cooperation. Casier (2017) argues that Russia started to challenge the EU's superior institutional, structural and productive power with the best resources Moscow had: compulsory power, hence the growing aggressiveness.

In contrast to the realist literature but in a more nuanced way than liberals, Casier and DeBardeleben (2018) view Moscow as the main culprit. Not all constructivists agree. Neumann and Pouliot (2011) as well as Larson and Schevchenko (2014) observe a source of tension in the fact that Russia's quest for great power status is not acknowledged by the EU and NATO. Far from benign, the way the West treated Russia's identity in the 1990s was considered as an affront (Averre 2009, Pouliot 2011). Now, *déclassement* in the international normative order feeds victimisation (Sakwa 2013). It also explains, according to Feklyunina (2008), the Kremlin's desire to upgrade the country as a great power. Of course, as Hopf (2005) and Tsygankov et Tsygankov (2010) remind us, it is crucial not to reify Russian identity, which consists of different ideological tendencies. But, for conservatives who dominate the foreign policy establishment, Russia's prestige is now crucially at stake in the post-Soviet space (Tsygankov and Tarver-Wahlquist 2009; Tsygankov 2012; Morozov 2015).

Can cooperation and conflict coexist?

Centred on the macro level, the geostrategic debate seems to exclude the possible coexistence of cooperation and conflict. There are partial exceptions of course, such as Casier and DeBardeleben (2018) who acknowledge the coexistence of tension and pragmatism. Nevertheless, the assumption remains that the Euro-Russia relationship, centred on leadership in capital cities, is fairly unidimensional. To question this assumption, we track the evolution of conflict and cooperation patterns in three zones of contact (Estonia, Kaliningrad, Moldova) between 1991 and 2016. This allows us to measure the extent to which conflict has replaced cooperation, as the standard narrative predicts, and contextualise the patterns we observe. To do so, we plot the frequency of conflict and cooperation "events" as they were recorded in Russian (*Isvestia*) and European (*Financial Times*) media. We focus on four "boundary issues": the mobility of people and goods; energy and natural resources; security; and the protection of minorities. In this Introduction, we only present the elements that help us track the extent to which patterns of cooperation and conflict fit with the standard narrative. Dembińska, Mérand and Shtaltovna (this issue) elaborate on the research design and empirical findings.

Consider Figure 1, which depicts the total number of conflictual events between Russia and Europe captured by the media in the three zones of contact. In contrast to many geostrategic analyses, the period between 1994 and 2005, and not 1991–1994, is the least conflictual. Immediately after the Cold War, when Estonia and Moldova were leaving Russia, there were many boundary issues to deal with, which probably explains a fairly high degree of conflict. This dropped when some of these issues were either settled (Estonia) or frozen (Moldova). Conflict is on the rise after the 2004 enlargement, when the EU gets geographically closer to Russia. Euro-Russian relations go through a bout of fever in Estonia in 2007, but the situation along that particular border actually calms down during the major geostrategic deterioration of Euro-Russian relations which begins with the Georgian war in 2008. Relations around Moldova also have their ups and downs (the downs being 1992, 2006, 2007, and 2014): some conflictual periods map well onto geostrategic tensions (2014), but not all. As for Kaliningrad, the most conflictual period is around 2002, a few years before it became encircled by EU members – by all accounts not a low point in macro Euro-Russian relations, when Putin joined Chirac and Schröder to oppose the Iraq war.

The comparison with Figure 2, which graphs the total frequency of cooperative events over the same period, is instructive. First, it shows that the highest degree of cooperation occurred between 1991 and 1994, concomitantly with the fairly high conflict levels seen in

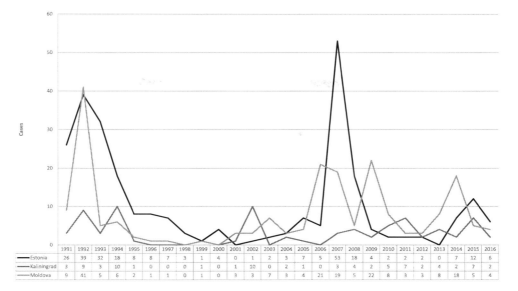

Figure 1. Conflict 1991–2016.

Figure 1. This suggests that the standard narrative about the honeymoon of the early 1990s is not entirely wrong: although there was conflict, there was also a great deal of cooperation going on. Second, Figure 2 shows that there is no zero-sum relationship between conflict and cooperation. Kaliningrad, to take one example, goes through its highest period of cooperation and conflict simultaneously. The 1994–2005 period is as quiet on the cooperation side as it was on the conflict front. During this period Russia accepts the rather symbolic title of "strategic partner" but rejects being included in the EU's neighbourhood policy. This suggests that relations can be intense or not, irrespective or their quality.

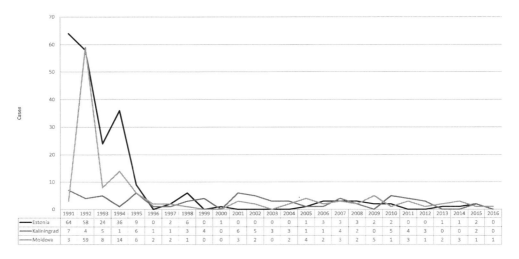

Figure 2. Cooperation 1991–2016.

Overall, this brief comparative analysis of the three zones of contact leads to two tentative conclusions. First, cooperation and conflict often coexist at the local level. Second, although they often map onto the standard narrative, local patterns of cooperation sometimes contradict conflict at the geostrategic level, and vice versa. Thus, zones of contact represent a challenge for IR perspectives which have constructed a binary opposition between analytical positions containing strong policy prescriptions, namely to antagonise Russia for some, and to abandon former satellites to Russian domination for others. Overtime, it is true that there is less cooperation over time, but conflict was far from absent in the early post-Cold War years, and there are instances of cooperation today.

Symbolic boundaries and geopolitical fields

In order to explain how cooperation and conflict coexist in Euro-Russian relations, we focus on symbolic boundaries, defined as "principles of vision and division" (Bourdieu 1993) that distinguish the self from the other, the neighbour from the alien, and the allied form the enemy. Unlike physical borders, symbolic boundaries are not fixed in political geography but constructed through symbolic interaction, shifting configurations of interests, and the institutionalisation of practices (Lamont and Molnár 2002; Newman 2003; Brubaker 2006; Parker and Vaughan-Williams 2009). Working as social representations that categorise, classify and differentiate actors, symbolic boundaries structure schemes of thought and action that shape the odds of cooperation or conflict (Paasi 1996; Kolossov 2005; Cooper and Perkins 2012). In our view, many symbolic boundaries can coexist under a single geostrategic relationship: they may vary according to sector, institution, or local geographical reality. And of course, they may shift over time.

To analyse Euro-Russian relations, we conceptualise three types of symbolic boundary. Tacit agreement on what distinguishes the European side from the Russian side, geographically, politically and culturally, defines a *solid* boundary; symbolic interaction is sparse but stable, producing well-defined principles of vision and division on both sides; relatively little cooperation and little conflict is expected to occur around solid boundaries. The decoupling of geographical, political and cultural identities in a context of intense and multilayered interactions defines a *fluid* boundary; here, interests tend to shift, and symbolic categories are unstable, blurring social representations; in such a case, we expect patterns of cooperation to dominate conflict. Finally, the absence of agreement on how political or cultural identity maps onto a territory defines a *disputed* (or contested) boundary; competing claims are made on where the boundary lies, producing conflicting principles of vision and division.

Symbolic boundaries, we argue, are constructed in and through geopolitical fields, which are "spaces and places, territories and landscapes, environments and social agents. (…) [They are] both a sociospatial context of statecraft and the social players, rules, and special dynamics constituting the arena" (Toal 2017, 9). Our working hypothesis in this special issue is that patterns of cooperation and conflict in a discrete geopolitical field of Euro-Russian relations are partly autonomous from patterns in other fields. Using the geopolitical field as a unit of analysis enables us to disaggregate the macro "Euro-Russian relationship" into its constituent parts, which are more manageable empirically because they involve real actors and tangible rules, inserted in sociospatial dynamics that cannot be captured in bird's eye approaches. Each field generates its own symbolic boundaries which may reproduce, refract or challenge macro dynamics. In other words, there is not one single relationship but several Euro-Russian relations.

This working hypothesis can be tested in two ways. Vertically, it leads to the empirical expectation that local patterns of cooperation and conflict are partly autonomous from the geostrategic level. While critical, the macro level is refracted through local geopolitical fields, wherein symbolic boundaries are constructed from the bottom up. Departing from IR theories, we expect that cooperation and conflict on the ground will not be tightly coupled with the geostrategic level but partly shaped by the local dynamics of symbolic boundary making. The opposite is also possible, as some significant local conflicts may fail to alter the geostrategic level.

Horizontally, we expect that patterns of cooperation and conflict in one sector or one institution are partly autonomous from patterns in others. For instance, there may be conflict on security but cooperation on energy and natural resources. As the standard narrative predicts, there will be interferences and contagion among sectors or regions, but the relative autonomy of geopolitical fields makes it possible for cooperation and conflict to coexist. In some cases, actors may even try to compensate for a conflictual pattern in one field by doubling down on cooperation efforts in another, insulating for example the EU from NATO, even though most of the member states are the same. Disaggregating the Euro-Russian relationship into several geopolitical fields, vertical or horizontal, allows us to explain the puzzle of conflict/cooperation coexistence.

Findings

All the contributions in this special issue take up and engage with our working hypothesis, which predicts the differentiated impact of three types of symbolic boundary (solid, fluid, and contested), either in the vertical (local vs macro) or horizontal (across institutions or sectors) dimension of geopolitical fields. By and large, they confirm that the standard narrative holds in most cases, but also that Euro-Russian relations vary in crucial ways according to the interests and representations of actors immersed in specific geopolitical fields.

The first article, by Dembińska, Mérand, and Shtaltovna, explores the autonomy of local actors from the geostrategic level. Through fieldwork and semi-structured interviews conducted in Estonia, Kaliningrad, and Moldova, it zooms in on the practitioners in charge of the boundary issues that emerged with and since the end of the Cold War: the mobility of people and goods, energy and natural resources, security, and protection of minorities. The authors find substantial evidence of vertical decoupling: local geopolitical fields developing dynamics that are partly autonomous from the geostrategic level in zones of contact. Departing from IR theories, they conclude that cooperation and conflict are largely shaped by the local dynamics of symbolic boundary making.

Taking on the macro perspective, Cristian Nitoiu shows how, despite strong Euro-Russian tensions, a set of fluid symbolic boundaries operate to avoid a breakdown, leading to the chronic coexistence of cooperation and conflict. He analyses the way in which the rise of what he calls "hybrid geopolitics" has affected these European and Russian perceptions of conflict and cooperation. Following the dissolution of the Soviet Union, and the subsequent evolution of a new European security architecture, cooperation coexisted with competition and conflict between the two actors. The end of the Cold War created a series of lingering contradictions in EU-Russia relations, which neither had the willingness nor the ability to resolve. As a result, a complex dynamic has emerged that hinders the development of genuine cooperation but also inhibits open conflict.

By looking at a specific zone of contact, it is possible to see more concretely the interplay of symbolic boundaries. Anna-Sophie Maas analyses Kaliningrad as a zone of contact where cooperation and conflict fluctuate between the EU, Russia and NATO. Challenging the proposition that a fluid boundary necessarily leads to more cooperation, she suggests that conflict may simply be pushed from one institution to another. Her article shows that while EU-Russia relations over Kaliningrad shifted from a contested boundary to a fluid boundary after the issues raised by the 2004 enlargement were solved, the NATO-Russia boundary became more solid after the stationing of Iskander missiles in 2013. Kaliningrad is no longer on the EU-Russian agenda as a source of conflict but it has become a security concern for the Atlantic Alliance. The evolution of the geopolitical field around this enclave shows that while some symbolic boundaries may become fluid and ease cooperation, this process can go alongside a hardening of other boundaries.

Tom Casier makes a similar argument by looking at complex trade-offs between energy, trade, people's movement, and security in the broader Euro-Russian relationship. Despite the deterioration of Euro-Russian relations, he notes that in specific sectors, business seems to continue as usual: trade has largely recovered, the import of natural gas has peaked, and educational exchanges still reach high levels between the EU and Russia. In order to explain this paradox, Casier situates the issues of conflict and cooperation along the spectrum of low politics *versus* high politics. While relations are based on multi-actor structures with diffuse interests in low politics, they are characterised by a limited number of actors and strong paradigmatic positioning in high politics. Daily practices in the energy field are constituted by millions of acts and decisions by a huge number of public and private actors. As a result, Casier argues, interests are diffuse and driven by dispersed commercial interests, not by geostrategic interests. This confirms that patterns of cooperation and conflict in specific geopolitical fields are partly autonomous from each other.

The coexistence of cooperation and conflict can be explained by shifting symbolic boundaries across geopolitical fields but also by competing views on the nature of the boundary inside one geopolitical field. By comparing how symbolic boundaries are perceived in one institution, the EU, it is possible to observe the coexistence of cooperation and conflict. In his contribution, Marco Siddi focuses on German and Polish official discourses which epitomise distinct European approaches to the EU-Russia energy relationship. For him, the role and centrality of the "Russian Other" in national identity construction influences foreign and energy policy debates concerning Russia. The key question is whether the Russian Other is perceived as antagonistic or cooperative. In the German case, the Russian Other is partly conceptualised in non-antagonistic terms based on the *Ostpolitik* tradition and long-standing economic cooperation. This conceptualisation results in a fluid symbolic boundary between the German Self and the Russian Other. In the Polish case, the Russian Other is constructed as threatening and aggressive, which generates a solid symbolic boundary between the Polish Self and the Russian Other.

Most contributions to this special issue take a *moyenne durée* perspective on Euro-Russian relations, comparing the early 1990s or turn of the 2000s with today. Perhaps less surprisingly, the one article that focuses on the short-term aftermath of the 2014 Ukraine crisis finds much less evidence for the proposition that geopolitical fields are decoupled from the geostrategic debate. Examining the EU's response to a cascade of foreign policy crises that followed the Ukrainian affair, Joan DeBardeleben explores whether the EU's stark reaction to Russian actions in Ukraine has been accompanied by a paradigm shift in EU policy or only by smaller-scale adjustments that reflect a combination of conflict and cooperation. She argues that, so long as the EU, the West and Russia have not softened their geostrategic differences, little cooperation can be expected at the local level. Although she uses the same vocabulary as ours, DeBardeleben thus harbours doubt on our working hypothesis, at least as far as the post-2014 period is concerned. Her article is a sober reminder that the autonomy of geopolitical fields may change over time, and sometimes shrink in the face of great geostrategic challenges.

Conclusion

In this Introduction, we have argued that the geostrategic debate portrays Euro-Russian relations as a zero-sum game. It is either a narrative of cooperation or one of a conflict, the latter being assumed to have replaced the former. Providing quantitative evidence on three zones of contact, Estonia, Kaliningrad and Moldova, we have argued that cooperation actually coexists with conflict in patterned ways. To explain this coexistence, we have proposed to look at the construction of symbolic boundaries in and through geopolitical fields, which may be centred on regions, sectors, or institutions. This offers a more nuanced picture of the ways in which geostrategic dynamics are refracted in multiple fields, producing patterns that range from geostrategic overdetermination (the "standard narrative") to possible decoupling.

Acknowledgements

We would like to thank all the participants in the workshop "Theorizing Relations Between Europe, North America and Russia", held at the Montréal Jean Monnet Centre on November 17, 2017, for their contribution and feedback on a first version of the articles included in this special issue. In particular, we thank Anastasiya Shtaltovna, Tringa Bytyqi, Emma Smeyers and Félix-Antoine Cloutier who have provided invaluable research assistance. We acknowledge funding from the Social Science and Humanities Research Council (Insight Grant #CF133847) as well as the European Commission (Erasmus+ program).

Disclosure statement

No potential conflict of interest was reported by the author(s).

Funding

This work was supported by Social Sciences and Humanities Research Council of Canada: [Grant Number CF133847].

References

Averre, Derek. 1998. "NATO Expansion and Russian National Interests." *European Security* 7 (1): 10–54.

Averre, Derek. 2009. "Competing Rationalities: Russia, the EU, and the Shared Neighbourhood." *Europe-Asia Studies* 61 (10): 1689–1713.

Barany, Zoltan. 2007. *Democratic Breakdown and the Decline of the Russian Military*. Princeton, NJ: Princeton University Press.

Berryman, John. 2012. "Geopolitics and Russian Foreign Policy." *International Politics* 49 (4): 530–544.

Bourdieu, Pierre. 1993. *Language and Symbolic Power*. Cambridge: Harvard University Press.

Brubaker, Rogers. 2006. *Ethnicity without Groups*. Cambridge, MA: Harvard University Press.

Casier, Tom. 2013. "The EU-Russia Strategic Partnership: Challenging the Normative Argument." *Europe-Asia Studies* 65 (7): 1377–1395.

Casier, Tom. 2017. ""The Different Faces of Power in European Union—Russia Relations."." *Cooperation and Conflict* 53 (1): 101–117. doi:10.1177/0010836717729179.

Casier, Tom, and Joan DeBardeleben. 2018. *EU-Russia Relations in Crisis: Understanding Diverging Perspectives*. London and New York: Routledge.

Charap, Samuel. 2014. "The Ukraine Impasse." *Survival* 56 (5): 225–232.

Cooper, Anthony, and Chris Perkins. 2012. "Borders and Status-Functions: An Institutional Approach to the Study of Borders." *European Journal of Social Theory* 15 (1): 55–71. doi:10.1177/1368431011423578.

Cross, Sharyl. 2015. "NATO–Russia Security Challenges in the Aftermath of Ukraine Conflict: Managing Black Sea Security and Beyond." *Southeast European and Black Sea Studies* 15 (2): 151–177.

DeBardeleben, Joan. 2012. "Applying Constructivism to Understanding EU-Russian Relations." *International Politics* 49 (4): 418–433.

Dunnett, Chris. 2014. "A Reply to John Mearsheimer: Putin is Not a Realist." *Ukraine Crisis Media Center*, September 11. Accessed September 12 2015. http://uacrisis.org/9283-reply john-mearsheimer-putin-realist.

Emerson, Michael. 2011. "Just Good Friends? The European Union's Multiple Neighbourhood Policies." *The International Spectator* 46 (4): 45–62.

Feklyunina, Valentina. 2008. "Battle for Perceptions: Projecting Russia in the West." *Europe-Asia Studies* 6 (4): 605–629.

Forsberg, Tuomas. 2013. "The Power of the European Union: What Explains the EU's (Lack of) Influence on Russia?" *Politique Européenne* 1 (39): 22–42. doi:10.3917/poeu.039.0022.

Götz, Elias. 2015. "It's Geopolitics, Stupid: Explaining Russia's Ukraine Policy." *Global Affairs* 1 (1): 3–10. doi:10.1080/23340460.2015.960184.

Haukkala, Hiski. 2009. "Lost in Translation? Why the EU has Failed to Influence Russia's Development." *Europe-Asia Studies* 61 (10): 1757–1775.

Haukkala, Hiski. 2010. *The EU–Russia Strategic Partnership: The Limits of Post-Sovereignty in International Relations*. London: Routledge.

Haukkala, Hiski. 2015. "From Cooperative to Contested Europe? The Conflict in Ukraine as a Culmination of a Long-Term Crisis in EU-Russia Relations." *Journal of Contemporary European Studies* 23 (1): 25–40. doi:10.1080/14782804.2014.1001822.

Haukkala, Hiski. 2016. "A Perfect Storm; Or What Went Wrong and What Went Right for the EU in Ukraine." *Europe-Asia Studies* 68 (4): 653–664. doi:10.1080/09668136.2016.1156055.

Hopf, Ted. 2005. "Identity, Legitimacy, and the use of Military Force: Russia's Great Power Identities and Military Intervention in Abkhazia." *Review of International Studies* 31 (225): 243.

Karasek, Tomas. 2014. "NATO and Russia after Crimea: From Failed Socialization to Renewed Containment." Policy Paper 1/2014, March. *Association for International Affairs*.

Kissinger, Henri A. 2014. "To Settle the Ukraine crisis, start at the end." *The Washington Post*, March 5. Accessed September 8 2015. https://www.washingtonpost.com/opinions/henry kissinger-to-settle-the-ukraine-crisis-start-at-the-end/2014/03/05/46dad868-a496-11e3 8466-d34c451760b9_story.html.

Kolossov, Vladimir. 2005. "Border Studies: Changing Perspectives and Theoretical Approaches." *Geopolitics* 10 (4): 606–632. doi:10.1080/14650040500318415.

Kramer, Mark. 2009. "The Myth of a No-NATO-Enlargement Pledge to Russia." *The Washington Quarterly* 32 (2): 39–61.

Lamont, Michèle, and Virág Molnár. 2002. "The Study of Boundaries in the Social Sciences." *Annual Review of Sociology* 28 (1): 167–195. doi:10.1016/j.postcomstud.2014.09.003.

Larson, Deborah Welch, and Alexei Schevchenko. 2014. "Russia Says no: Power, Status, and Emotions in Foreign Policy." *Communist and Post-Communist Studies* 47 (3–4): 269–279.

Lindley-French, Julian. 2014. "Ukraine: Understanding Russia." *The RUSI Journal* 159 (3): 36–39.

Lomagin, Nikita. 2012. "Interest Groups in Russian Foreign Policy: The Invisible Hand of the Russian Orthodox Church." *International Politics* 49 (4): 498–516.

Lynch, Allen. 2001. "The Realism of Russia's Foreign Policy." *Europe-Asia Studies* 53 (1): 7–31.

Mankoff, Jeffrey. 2009. *Russian Foreign Policy: The Return of Great Power Politics*. Lanham, Maryland: Rowman & Littlefield Publishers.

Mearsheimer, John. 2014. "Why the Ukraine Crisis is the West Fault." *Foreign Affairs* 93 (5): 77–89.

Morozov, Viacheslav. 2015. *Russia's Postcolonial Identity: A Subaltern Empire in a Eurocentric World*. Berlin: Springer.

Motyl, Alexander J. 2014. "Putin's Zugzwang: The Russia-Ukraine Standoff." *World Affairs* 177 (2): 58–65.

Neumann, Iver B., and Vincent Pouliot. 2011. "Untimely Russia: Hysteresis in Russian-Western Relations Over the Past Millenium." *Security Studies* 20 (1): 105–137. doi:10.1080/09636412.2011.549021.

Newman, David. 2003. "On Borders and Power: A Theoretical Framework." *Journal of Borderlands Studies* 18 (1): 13–25.

Nitoiu, Cristian. 2017. "Still Entrenched in the Conflict/Cooperation Dichotomy? EU-Russia Relations and the Ukraine Crisis." *European Politics and Society* 18 (2): 148–165. doi:10.1080/23745118.2016.1197875.

Paasi, Anssi. 1996. "Inclusion, Exclusion and Territorial Identities. The Meanings of Boundaries in the Globalizing Geopolitical Landscape." *Nordisk samhällsgeografisk tidskrift* 23: 3–17.

Parker, Noël, and Nick Vaughan-Williams. 2009. "Lines in the Sand? Towards an Agenda for Critical Border Studies." *Geopolitics* 14 (3): 582–587.

Pouliot, Vincent. 2011. "The Year NATO Lost Russia." In *European Security Since the Fall of the Berlin Wall*, edited by Frédéric Mérand, Martial Foucault, and Bastien Irondelle, 239–259. Toronto: University of Toronto Press.

Sakwa, Richard. 2013. "The Cold Peace: Russo-Western Relations as a Mimetic Cold war." *Cambridge Review of International Affairs* 26 (1): 203–224.

Toal, Gerard. 2017. *Near Abroad: Putin, the West, and the Contest Over Ukraine and the Caucasus*. Oxford: Oxford University Press.

Trenin, Dimitri. 2014b. "Russia's Breakout From the Post-Cold War System: The Drivers of Putin's Course." *Carnegie Moscow Center*, December 22. Accessed September 13 2015. http://carnegie.ru/2014/12/22/russia-s-breakout-from-post-cold-war-system-drivers-of-putin-s-course.

Tsygankov, Andrei P. 2012. *Honor in International Relations: Russia and the West from Alexander to Putin. Cambridge*. RU: Cambridge University Press.

Tsygankov, Andrei, and Matthew Tarver-Wahlquist. 2009. "Dueling Honors: Power, Identity, and the Russia-Georgia Divide." *Foreign Policy Analysis* 5 (4): 307–326.

Tsygankov, Andrei P., and Pavel A. Tsygankov. 2010. "National Ideology and IR Theory: Three Incarnations of the 'Russian Idea'." *European Journal of International Relations* 16 (4): 663–686.

Wolff, Andrew T. 2015. "The Future of NATO Enlargement After the Ukraine Crisis." *International Affairs* 91 (5): 1103–1121. doi:10.1111/1468-2346.12400.

Ziegler, Charles E. 2012. "Conceptualizing Sovereignty in Russian Foreign Policy: Realist and Constructivist Perspectives." *International Politics* 49 (4): 400–417.

Conflict and cooperation between Europe and Russia: the autonomy of the local

Magdalena Dembińska, Frédéric Mérand and Anastasiya Shtaltovna ⓘ

ABSTRACT
This paper takes a bottom-up perspective on the "boundary issues" that emerged between the EU and Russia with and since the end of the Cold War: the mobility of people and goods, energy and natural resources, security, and protection of minorities. This paper compares three zones of contact: Estonia, Moldova and Kaliningrad. Our starting point is that there is not a European-Russian relationship, but Russian European relations that vary according to interests and representations on the ground. We argue that cooperation and conflict are not tightly coupled with the geopolitical level but also shaped by the local dynamics of symbolic boundary making.

Introduction

Taking up the challenge laid out in the Introduction to this Special Issue, this article analyses how cooperation and conflict coexist in Russian-European relations (Nitoiu 2017). How can the geostrategic deterioration of Euro-Russian relations, which began with the Georgian war in 2008, coincide with an improving situation on the ground in Estonia, where Euro-Russian relations went through their worst period in 2007? Why is it that Kaliningrad no longer seems to pose a major problem to the EU and Russia, while Moldova still does?

Liberalism, realism and constructivism suggest macro-level hypotheses to explain the deterioration of Euro-Russian relations. We, by contrast, argue that political-strategic relations are refracted through local geopolitical fields (Toal 2017). While conventional explanations focus on conflict and cooperation over territorial borders (as an aspect of state sovereignty in a state-centred international system), we contend that the degree of conflict and cooperation between Russia and Europe is partly autonomous from the political-strategic level because it also depends on the symbolic boundaries constructed at the local level.

To ascertain that Euro-Russian relations are not solely shaped at the macro-level, there is a need to investigate them from the bottom-up. This article seeks messy, contextualised answers to the coexistence of cooperation and conflict in local symbolic boundaries –

"principles of vision and division" which distinguish the "self" from the "other", the "neighbour" of the "stranger", the "ally" of the "enemy" (Bourdieu 1994). While they can be coterminous with physical borders, symbolic boundaries are not fixed by geography but are enacted through symbolic interaction, past experience, the configuration of interests and the institutionalisation of practices (Lamont and Molnar 2002; Newman 2003; Brubaker 2002; Parker and others 2009). Symbolic boundaries are produced and reproduced by elites, the education system or mass media that propose and impose "geopolitical frames" (Toal 2017, 747). They organise and delineate the world's political map into convenient categories and recognisable spaces, constructing stereotypes and working largely as dichotomising performatives (O'Loughlin, Toal, and Kolosov 2016, 747). Performing a function of categorisation, classification and differentiation, symbolic boundaries structure patterns of thought and action in a way that can increase the frequency of cooperation or conflict (Paasi 1996; Kolossov 2005; Cooper and Perkins 2012; Neumann 2016).

In this perspective, there is not a Russian-European relationship, but contingent Russian-European relations that vary according to these symbolic boundaries. Specifically, we explore the following propositions:

(1) Where the symbolic boundary is *solid*, cooperation around issues of common interest is difficult but open conflict is not frequent.
(2) Where the symbolic boundary is *fluid*, cooperation is frequent around the management of economic, cultural and social flux, even in times of geopolitical tensions.
(3) Where the symbolic boundary is *disputed*, cooperation is difficult and the likelihood of conflict is great, with more or less acute phases depending on the international context.

A solid symbolic boundary refers to contexts where public manifestations (discourses, policies, announced objectives) clearly define who the "other" is, here in reference to Europe and/or Russia. Where the nature of the "other" is debated in the public sphere, we speak of a disputed symbolic boundary. Fluid symbolic boundaries correspond to situations where representations and interests vary according to the issues at stake. Compared with the explanations offered by realism, liberalism and constructivism (discussed in the Introduction to this Special Issue), these propositions predict variation in the degrees of cooperation and conflict according to the evolution of symbolic boundaries at the local level. In arguing so, we do not deny that the state of the international system, the economic and institutional relations between Russia and Europe, or the intersubjective relationship between Russian and Western identities all exert an influence. But we qualify these macro-variables to explain the coexistence of cooperation and conflict.

Instead of objectifying "Russia" and "Europe" and looking at them as fixed and homogeneous, our research strategy is to compare local practices, interests and representations in three "zones of contact" that are characterised by a different and changing degree of conflictuality: Estonia, Moldova and Kaliningrad. Although Kaliningrad is a region of Russia, we include it here in order to disintegrate "Russia" and see if and how locally constructed symbolic boundaries may account for conflict and cooperation between Europe and Russia. The cases are chosen according to (1) the similarity of military, economic and identity issues at stake in the aftermath of the disintegration of the USSR; (2) varying degree of local sovereignty (fully independent Estonia, independent Moldova with two regions backed by Russia, and Russian region of Kaliningrad); and (3) the varying degree of conflict / cooperation over time (this allows us to track the co-evolution of conflictual and cooperative patterns without prejudging that there is a trend).

In other words, this article juxtaposes macro- and micro-level variation in Euro-Russian conflict and cooperation. Our three cases represent "playgrounds" where the evolution of relations between Russia and Europe can be tested *in situ* (Topaloglou et al. 2005). Symbolic boundaries, we surmise, are shaped and may transform over time in response to endogeneous and exogeneous, past and present experiences, as well as the degree of local sovereignty. Depicted in the graphs included in the Introduction and the appendix section, this variation is identified by compiling the frequency of conflictual and cooperation "events" recorded in Russian (*Izvestiya*) and European (*Financial Times*) media. Events are identified through a systematic survey of all newspaper articles during the period between 1991 and 2016, using a list of codewords "Moldova/Estonia/ Kaliningrad [and] EU/Europe/NATO [and] Russia". As the next step, we coded data using QDA Miner. The qualitative nature of the relation is classified manually as "conflictual", "cooperative" or "neutral". In each case, we focus on four border issues: mobility of people and goods, energy and natural resources, security and protection of the Russian and Russian-speaking population. The result we seek to explain is the variation in cooperation and conflict between Russia and Europe on the ground. The study covers the period from the disintegration of the USSR in 1991–2016. This allows us to (1) report the complexity of interrelated factors between the Russian-European relationship at the politico-strategic level and local contexts; (2) see these relationships in terms of processes and sequences over time and space.

To explore the validity of our propositions, we reconstruct the story of Euro-Russian relations in each zone of contact. As we show, Euro-Russian relations around Estonia experience little cooperation *or* episodes of tension. Since it acquired sovereignty in 1991, Estonia aims at "returning to Europe" by minimising its links with Russia. But despite its accession to the EU and NATO in 2004, the country is still dependent on Russian energy (Galbreth and Ainius 2011; Stratfor 2012) and the question of Russians and Russian-speakers (almost 25% of the population, now largely EU citizens) remains a sensitive subject (Onken 2007; Mälksoo 2009; Hurt 2015). In the case of Kaliningrad, a Russian exclave surrounded by the EU and NATO since 2004 and a "geopolitical anomaly" (Diener and Hagen 2011) enclaved within "Schengenland" (Vitunic 2003), the EU and Russia cooperate on the issues of the border control regime, trade and investment, as well as the environment in the Baltic Sea (Oldberg 2009; Archer and Etzold 2010; Palmowski 2010), but with its military base, the region is a source of potential instability for Europe. At the same time it is vulnerable economically since isolated from its motherland (Horris 2014). In the Moldovan case, Euro-Russia relations display recurring conflicts. Rapprochement with the EU and with NATO through a number of projects and agreements ("Common Spaces" in the 1990s, North Atlantic Cooperation Council in 1992, Partnership for Peace in 1994, Association Agreement in 2014; Smith 2005; Korosteleva 2011) is thwarted by Russian policies towards its "near abroad", including sanctions and military support to the separatist region of Transnistria (Lynch 2001; Tolstrup 2009; Orttung and Walker 2015; Malling 2015; Skala and Miklasova 2015).

In the following sections, we reconstruct the story, trace and identify local symbolic boundaries in three empirical cases illustrating the coexistence of conflict and cooperation between Russia and EU. We capture the local symbolic boundaries by looking at their public manifestations, that is, discourses, policies and objectives announced by local elites who personify local institutions (similarly to Michael Mann's conception of "states as actors, in the person of state elites", 1984, 201). The analysis of symbolic boundaries is based on two sets of sources: (1) qualitative-interpretive media analysis of articles gathered while tracking the evolution of conflict and cooperation in the three cases; (2) semi-structured interviews conducted in Estonia and in Kaliningrad in 2018, as well as in Moldova in 2011 and in 2019. The interviews have been cross-checked with media analysis, communiqués and official documents.

Estonia: solidly in Europe

The graph in Appendix 1 shows the occurrence of conflict and of cooperation in Estonia between 1991 and 2016. From 1991 to 1995, the degree of conflict and of cooperation is similar, whereas in the following years we observe almost no cooperation and very little conflict, with a significant conflictual event in 2007. What kind of symbolic boundary is erected in Estonia? In the following, we tell the story paying attention to local representations of and interests with Europe and Russia.

Since Estonia became independent in 1991, its strategic objective has been unambiguous: to make a clean break with the Soviet past and to reintegrate Western economic and political systems. But Russia saw its dovorce with Estonia differently. The withdrawal of Russian troops, the rapprochement of Tallinn with NATO and the treatment of the ethnic Russian minority constituted the main sources of conflict between Estonia and Russia throughout the post-Soviet period. All these problems stem from the forced integration of Estonia into the Soviet Union in 1940/44 (pictured as "liberation" in Soviet and now Russian narrative), a Sovietisation/Russification campaign, and the stationing of large military contingents on the Baltic coast (Munuera 1994). As we show in this section, local symbolic boundaries quickly solidified, and remained so, as it became evident that local actors saw Estonia as belonging to Europe and Russia as the "other". With such a clearcutting alignment, it was clear for both Brussels and Moscow that Estonia is solidly in Europe. It also meant that cooperation on common interests in this zone of contact would be difficult but, at the same time, open conflict would be attenuated at the macro level between the EU and Russia.

Security: demilitarisation of Estonia

The clearest illustration of Estonia's solid boundary, where cooperation around issues of common interest is difficult but open conflict is not frequent, is the withdrawal of the Russian army in the early 1990s. Soviet occupation between 1944 and 1991 was an era of extensive militarisation. Military ports and airfields, garrisons, missile and radar stations, 160 Soviet military bases covered a total area of 85,175 ha (Varu 1995; Jauhiainen 1997). Immediately after independence, Estonia began negotiations with Russia for a speedy withdrawal of Soviet troops from its territory (Interview with an Estonian defence official, Tallinn, May 2018). At that time, foreign minister Lennhart Meri said: "It is not a comfortable situation when our parliament can be reached in less than 15 minutes by Soviet paratroopers" (*Financial Times*, March 7, 1992). According to Juri Luik, who replaced Meri in 1994,

Russian interests were different [from those of the Baltics] because they wanted to achieve an agreement that would legitimize the presence of the troops. At least temporarily. It boiled down to the fact that the Russian aim was to prolong the process as long as they could. Our aim was to speed it up as much as possible. For us, the main issue was the date – when will the troops leave. (Interview with Juri Luik, February 21, 1996 in Beyrle 1996)

From the Russian perspective, expressed by then Russian Minister of Foreign Affairs Andrei Kozyrev, a complete pullout of Russian forces from former Soviet republics would cause "a security vacuum" into which forces hostile to Russian interests would step in: "We should not withdraw from those regions which have been the sphere of Russian interests for centuries and we should not fear these words" (quoted by Itar-Tass, *The Moscow Times* 19.01.1994; Beyrle 1996). From the Baltic perspective, Soviet/ Russian troops have always been in Estonia illegally since the region was under occupation forces (Beyrle 1996).

In September 1993, two years after independence, 26,000 ha of Estonian territory was still occupied by the Russian military (Varu 1995; Jauhiainen 1997; *Izvestiya*, July 31, 1992). As the negotiations dragged on, Estonia and the two Baltic countries gained international support. The final 1992 CSCE summit in Helsinki communiqué called on Russia to act "without delay for the early, orderly and complete withdrawal of foreign troops from the Baltic States". Estonian officials came to rely on support from Europe and the United States to make up for the leverage they themselves lacked in their dealings with Moscow. The Russian declaration that it was pulling the August 31 withdrawal date off the table provoked a good deal of international criticism. The Nordic Council, the EU, and the US State Department all issued statements reiterating they expected Moscow would honour its commitment to the August deadline (Beyrle 1996), which it finally did. In July 1994, President Yeltsin admitted: "Estonia succeeded in agitating the West. I received letters from Bill Clinton and Helmut Kohl. They all had a slant toward the troop withdrawal." He added: "But Russia took a tough stand on the human rights issue. We managed to ensure that Russian pensioners are granted equal rights with Estonian citizens" (in Beyrle 1996 *ITAR-TASS*, July 27, 1994). Indeed the issue of the treatment of ethnic Russians and the Russian-speaking population in the Baltics was put as a condition for the withdrawal of Russian troops right from the start (Munuera 1994). Referring to the delays of the withdrawal in Estonia as compared to Lithuania, President Yeltsin stated,

We are completing the withdrawal of troops from Lithuania, as Lithuania does not violate human rights and treats the Russian-speaking population with respect. As Latvia and Estonia violate human rights, since according to their national legislation national minorities, mostly Russians, are persecuted, and that involves basically Russians, we will link the withdrawal schedule with the human rights situation there, although we have adopted a political decision to pull the troops out of the republics. (*ITAR-TASS*, April 5, 1993 as quoted in Beyrle 1996)

Russian speakers

With one-quarter of the Estonian population belonging to the Russian-speaking community, the establishment of a solid boundary was not self-evident. 37–40% of Russian speakers supported the independence of Estonia in the 1991 referendum (Melvin 2000). By 1994, only 2% of Estonia's Russian speakers declared their willingness to leave (Kirch and Kirch 1995), and by 2003, 84% self-identified as inhabitants of Estonia (Vihalemm and Masso 2007, 79). Although cultural and linguistic identification with Russia remains strong, "surveys testify to a strong territorial identification with Estonia among Estonian-Russians where the overwhelming majority of them identify Estonia as their only homeland" (Kallas 2016, 13). The enduring controversies about minority rights are about integration and accommodation policies rather than about Estonia's interests with Europe and its European choice.

The Russian policy of "near abroad", which legitimates a sphere of influence for the protection of Russian minorities, contributes to the solidification of the local symbolic boundary between Europe and Russia. Although research shows that Russian speakers in Estonia are not necesseraly responsive to it (Kallas 2016), the fear of Russia attempting to exploit the minorities by threatening or implying territorial secession in North Eastern Estonia, the region of Narva, populated mostly by Russian-speakers, was and – still is – palpable (Interview with an Estonian journalist, Tallinn, May 2018; Kauppila 1999).

Migration of, among others, managers, officials, military personnel and their families account for ethno-demographic changes during the Soviet period. According to Melvin (2000), if in 1934 Estonians constituted 88.1% of the population and Russians 8.1%, by 1989 the respective percentages are 61.4% and 30.3%. To these numbers one has to add non-ethnic Russian Russian-speakers (Poles and Belarussians, for example) adding up to a total of 40% non-Estonian-speakers in the beginning of 1990s (Kolstø and Edemsky 1995, 109). Moreover, Russian was the language of social mobility, and Russians lived mostly in urban areas, whereas Estonians in rural areas. In parallel, tens of thousands of Baltic citizens were forced to exile to Siberia (Beyrle 1996).

In that context, with the 1991 independence, came politics among at restoring the status of the Estonian language and culture together with a resentment towards the "colonizers". Citizenship and language laws put Estonian-Russians at a disadvantage. In February 1992, Estonia laid down its new citizenship policy, under which most of the country's ethnic Russian minority were declared non-citizens. Eventually, the law was slightly modified after critics from and consultations with expert international organisations (OSCE, Council of Europe) (Kauppila 1999; Dembinska 2012). The fact that the laws at some point were handed to international organisations for revision reduced the level of hostile rhetoric emanating from Moscow (Munuera 1994). "6.7% of the population is now 'stateless', down from more than 32% twenty years ago, and 53% of the Russian-speaking Estonians are now also Estonian citizens" (Winnerstig 2014, 13). This does not preclude internal controversies concerning minority rights or "memory wars" (Mälksoo 2009) around the narrative of liberation versus occupation of Estonia, around the Victory Day and all symbols of and history writing on the Soviet period, where external actors may interfere or be dragged into.

Minority issues and the removal of the Bronze statue

In 2007, what had been a fairly cooperative relationship between the EU and Russia turned into a conflictual one. This is shown in a peak in media reporting (see Appendix 1). The cause was the removal of the so-called Bronze Soldier and the consequent riots, siege of the Estonian Embassy in Moscow, and cyber attacks of government websites in Estonia (Liik 2007;

Roth 2009; Interview with an Estonian defence official, Tallinn, April 2018). The troublesome monument had been erected in 1947 to honour the Soviet troops that entered Tallinn, as liberators according to the Soviet view, as occupiers according to the Estonian view (Liik 2007). The Bronze Soldier occupied a square in central Tallinn. Whereas many Estonians came to regard the monument as a symbol of Soviet repression, it represented wartime sacrifice to many Red Army veterans. During Victory Day commemorations on 9 May 2006, a serious clash occurred at the site. This prompted the Estonian prime minister, Andrus Ansip, to argue for relocating the monument, which in his view had become a site of confrontation exacerbating societal divisions. In January 2007, the Estonian parliament passed the War Graves Protection Act to create a legal basis for relocating the monument (Roth 2009). Besides parts of Estonia's Russian-speaking community, the planned relocation to a Russian military cemetery in Tallinn evoked fierce protests from "Russian politicians, who levelled vociferous accusations of glorifying fascism at Estonia" (Roth 2009, 13). On 23 April 2007, the Russian foreign ministry issued an official protest, warning of "most serious consequences for relations between Russia and Estonia" (quoted in Roth 2009, 13), the latter in the EU by then. The crisis started on 26 April, when excavation preparations at the site sparked a series of demonstrations and violent riots that lasted for two nights and resulted in over 1000 persons detained, more than 150 injured and one dead.

The response in Russia was immediate. A weeklong blockade of the Estonian Embassy in Moscow took place. Estonia faced economic pressure referred to as "hidden sanctions". Apart from boycott calls against Estonian products by Russian officials, Estonian sales contracts were abruptly cancelled and planned Russian investments suspended. Truck traffic at the main bridge into Estonia was blocked temporarily and the Russian railways halted deliveries of oil, petroleum products and coal (Ruus 2008; Herzog 2011). In the cyber attacks that followed, it is estimated that a million computers were hijacked (Ruus 2008).

In response, Estonia requested EU support. Minister of Foreign Affairs Urmas Paet issued a dramatic declaration stating that "the European Union is under attack, as Russia is attacking Estonia" (Republic of Estonia 2007 as quoted in Roth 2009). Yet, despite these flaring tensions, the Bronze Soldier statue case is an example of the likely impact of a solid symbolic boundary. While a solid boundary allows occasional conflict to happen, it is characterised more by the absence of cooperation than by open, long-lasting conflict. From the very beginning, support coming from the EU was mostly declarative. Eventually, German foreign minister Frank-Walter Steinmeier mediated a compromise to end the blockade of the Embassy in Moscow (Wetzel 2007 as quoted in Roth 2009). Angela Merkel was instrumental in talking to Moscow (Interview with an independent journalist, Tallinn, May 2018). At the Samara summit, the EU presidency and the European Commission raised the issues of the embassy blockade, sanctions and cyber attacks. While Commission President Barroso called for mutual dialogue over sensitive historical issues, he expressed the EU's solidarity with Tallinn and asserted during the press conference that Estonian problems were problems for all of Europe.

Energy security: Nord Stream 2

A final example is the construction of Nord Stream, which is a central element of Gazprom's international expansion strategy (*Financial Times,* October 17, 2007). Here again, we see that a solid symbolic boundary produces little cooperation and conflict that is occasional but peacefully treated. The project was controversial from the very beginning. Most Baltic Sea states feared that the Russian gas giant Gazprom, and its main shareholder, the Russian Federation, would misuse the construction of the pipeline for geopolitical purposes. Besides environmental concerns voiced mostly by Scandinavian states, Estonia, Latvia, Lithuania and Poland also drew attention to its potential political, economic and military risks (Whist 2008; Interview with Estonia's defence officials, Tallinn, April 2018). Proponents of Nord Stream, (Germany, Russia and the Nord Stream consortium), dismiss the concerns and argue that the pipeline is a common European project benefitting "an increasingly energy thirsty union" (Whist 2008; German Foreign Minister Frank-Walter Steinmeier, *Izvestiya*, July 11, 2007). Contrary to countries, such as Germany, where representations of Russia are more fluid (as argued by Siddi in this Special Issue), Estonia, Latvia, Lithuania and Poland have maintained their critical line pointing to the *naïveté* of Western Europe (*Financial Times,* October, 17, 2007; *Izvestiya*, July 11, 2007). As argued in a note for for the European Parliament by Fraser Cameron, The Nord Stream Gas Pipeline (NSGP) project "highlights the problem of bilateral deals undermining a common EU approach towards Russia" (Cameron 2007). With Nord Stream, Ukraine, Belarus, the Baltic countries and Poland also risk losing transit money and counter-leverage on Russia (Larsson 2007).

Together with the Nord Stream issue, Russia's annexation of Crimea in 2014 and its involvement in the Donbas conflict in Ukraine, under the pretext of protecting Russia's compatriots, solidified the symbolic boundary even further. As Agnia Grigas puts it:

> On the one hand, as NATO members, the Baltic states have the security of Article V not afforded to Ukraine. On the other hand, Moscow's ability to conduct a shadow war in Ukraine, the increasing Russian military activity in the Baltic sea region, and Vladimir Putin's insistence of protecting Russian 'compatriots' abroad are all legitimate red flags for the Balts. (Grigas 2014, 3)

On Tallinn's request, NATO is now semi-permanently stationed in Estonia. Our interviews in Estonia show that right from the beginning everything was done to reduce relations with Russia to a strict functional minimum (for example, construction of energy plants to undermine dependency on Russian gas). Also, and contrary to what we found in Kaliningrad, there was a quasi-total lack of cooperation at grass-roots level. In sum, in Estonia, the symbolic boundary is solid, cooperation is difficult but open conflict is not frequent.

Kaliningrad: a fluid boundary

Although Kaliningrad is part of Russia, local symbolic boundaries with Europe are more fluid than one might think. Cooperation and conflict coexist (see Appendix 2); the former on soft issues of common interest, the latter on hard issues related to military security.

Kaliningrad is a Russian enclave in Europe, which after the end of Soviet Union turned from the strategic fort post of Russia to an isolated island in Europe. In the early 1990s, there were hopes for the future of Kaliningrad: Yurii Matochkin, its first governor, recognised that "Kaliningrad could only prosper as a 'bridge' between Russia and Europe – not a secluded 'island'", a "Baltic Hong Kong" where civilisations would meet (Sukhankin

2016, 2). In an interview with the authors, a former politician confesses that "[w]e thought Kaliningrad would be a pilot region to develop relationships between Russia and Europe".

The collapse of the Soviet Union left the entire Kaliningrad region in limbo, a no man's land caught between its neighbouring states of Poland, Lithuania and Belarus, with no direct links to Russia, and its only real historical ties to Germany (*Financial Times*, May, 25, 1993). Around the turn of the century, the double EU and NATO enlargement encircled Kaliningrad, which became a geopolitical hotspot, especially around the movement of people for the EU and military security for NATO. Fifteen years later, the situation has changed. Although reports in the Western media point to a "black hole or garrison" region, Kaliningrad has, to some extent, locally remained a fluid zone of contact between the EU and Russia. As Maas shows in her article in this Special Issue, most of the conflict between Kaliningrad and its neighbours shifted to NATO, while the relationship with the EU is largely cooperative.

Security: conflictual (de)militarisation

Extremely militarised during the Soviet period, Kaliningrad was a strategic outpost directed against NATO that also allowed to monitor the Baltic region and to exert pressure on Poland (Chillaud and Tetart 2007). As a consequence of the dislocation of the Soviet army from Eastern Germany, the Baltic states and Poland, and increasing numbers of former Soviet military forces moved to Kaliningrad (up to 300,000 according to some accounts; *Financial Times*, December, 16, 1992). At the same time, Kaliningrad had grown in the 1990s into a market for weapons (*Financial Times*, January 12, 1994). Preoccupied, the neighbouring countries – Poland, Estonia and Lithuania – requested a demilitarisation of Kaliningrad, a request that drew a response from Moscow that outsiders should not interfere in Russia's internal affairs (Fairlie 1996). Even if the military presence was eventually reduced (by the end of 1990s, estimates of Russian troops on the ground ran from a low of 24,000 to a high of 40,000; Laurinavicius 2002; Hoff and Timmermann 1993; Krickus 1998), Kaliningrad retains many characteristics of a military base.

Security disputes characterise the post-Soviet period and became acute starting with the year 2004, which marked a shift in the geopolitical situation of the area when the Kaliningrad region became a "Russian island" within the enlarged EU and NATO. With the instability in the Middle East and in Ukraine as of 2013, the number of military manoeuvres by both Russia and NATO in and around Kaliningrad have significantly increased. Since the annexation of Crimea in 2014, security issues between Europe and Russia are at its worst. While Moscow launched military manoeuvres in Kaliningrad, NATO began its own war games near the Russian border. The Baltic states and Poland asked for permanent presence from NATO (*Radio Free Europe*, June 2015). Clearly, security issues on the ground are highly contentious between Western allies and Russia.

Cooperation on mobility issues

Instead of being the region of cooperation, mounting tensions between NATO and Russia suggest that Kaliningrad has become an increasingly contested zone of contact, with a more solid symbolic boundary around military security. This picture is not complete, however. The projects of Kaliningrad as a military outpost of strategic importance or, on the contrary, of Kaliningrad as an economic bridge between the Europe and Russia (Laurinavicius 2002), have been in tension since it became a Russian exclave "enclaved" in Europe, when its neighbours joined the EU (Archer and Etzold 2010, 330). On the one hand, its geographic position is used by Moscow in its geopolitical game, on the other hand, local actors from the beginning push – with some success if with difficulties (Fairlie 1996) – for economic and cultural cooperation with Europeans. Questions of economic development, tourism, cross-border trade and mobility of goods and persons are discussed and to some extent solved despite the overall climate of security conflict. While contested at the geopolitical level, the symbolic boundary around people and trade remained fluid at the local level, easing tensions between the EU, Kaliningrad's neighbours and the Russian enclave.

In an effort to revitalise and integrate Kaliningrad into the economic life of the Baltic, Russian and European regions, it was granted the status of a free (1991) and then special economic zone (SEZ in 1996) (which was amended and prolonged in 2006; Ivanova et al. 2015; Fedorov, Gorodkov, and Zhukovsky 2011, 23). The open zone was initiated bottom-up and sustained throughout the whole period by the local administration, starting with the first governor of Kaliningrad, Yurii Matochkin, convinced that Kaliningrad could prosper only as a "bridge" between Russia and Europe (Sukhankin 2016). Aleksander Barinov, Director of the Institute of Economics and Management, who was on Matochkin's team developing the SEZ, confirms in our interview that the initiative and conceptualisation "came bottom up, from here [Kaliningrad] ... Matochkin developed this idea, he went to Moscow to discuss it. Eventually, Eltsin has sighed a law on the open economic zone". Local interests and representations of Europe did not necessarily coincide with those in Moscow. For many officials in Kaliningrad, the symbolic boundary is fluid and it is possible to initiate cooperation despite the macro-level conflicts between Europe and Russia.

Our interviews show an active agency exercised by Kaliningrad actors. Returning from Lithuania were she was negotiating border crossing for FIFA teams and fans, an official in the Government of Kaliningrad Region explains: "There are a lot of unique points about Kaliningrad due to its special geographic location (on the border, transit, etc.). Thus we have quite an intense contact with the Ministry of Transportation, Ministry of Foreign Affairs, etc. [in Moscow]." According to Yuriy Rozhkov-Yurevsky, former state official, Kaliningrad is at the forefront of creating Russia-Europe relations:

> The project of inter-regional cooperation had to be agreed with the Ministry of foreign affairs. We made agreements on the local level before the law was created on cooperation amongst regions with parties of other countries. In a way, we were an example to the rest of Russia and to our government by signing those agreements. We had to do it as we did not have a choice. If we didn't have friendly relationships with neighbours, the border would have been closed. (Interview, Kaliningrad, April 2018)

After all, an official from the Kaliningrad government affirms,

> we very much depend on the neighbouring countries. To reach Kaliningrad you have to cross six borders: Russia, Belarus, Belarus, Lithuanian two times, Russian again .... Goods are more expensive than in Russia .... The main task of Kaliningrad government is to demand from central government either for compensations or let us alone run the business here.

The main mechanism of the SEZ is a tax relief for large domestic and international investors, which gives incentives for foreign business and joint ventures (such as AvtoVAZ and General Motors; *Radio Free Europe*, June 12, 2006; *Financial Times*, May 30, 2006). The SEZ in Kaliningrad was designed to develop not only import substitution but also export-oriented production units, which implies the transformation of the Kaliningrad region from an "unsinkable aircraft carrier into an assembly shop" (Fedorov, Gorodkov, and Zhukovsky 2011). While the European Commission spent nearly €100 million up to 2006 for technical assistance in Kaliningrad (Archer and Etzold 2010, 336) and Lithuanian and Polish governments sent humanitarian aid to Kaliningrad when Kaliningrad was seriously hit by the Russian financial crisis in 1998 (Vitunic 2003, 16), by the mid-2000s, Kaliningrad enjoyed a new flow of foreign direct investments as its "regional economy in 2004 was exposed to the international markets" (Horris 2014, 29). According to Horris, EU enlargement had a profound impact on the structure of Kaliningrad's economic activities: "prior to 2004, 40% of regional trade was with the EU-15. After 2004, the EU has accounted for between 75% and 80% of Kaliningrad's foreign trade" (Horris 2014, 30). In fact, the SEZ has turned Kaliningrad into the main entry point for the EU-Russian trade.

For the SEZ to prosper, access to Kaliningrad had to be ensured. Kaliningrad cooperates with Germany, Poland, Baltic and Scandinavian countries to incorporate it into the sea, rail and road infrastructures. In 2007, Russia and Lithuania signed an agreement on navigation in the Kurshsky gulf, which regulates the passage of vessels of international communication on inland waterways of the Kaliningrad region and the Republic of Lithuania (*RIA News*, December 4, 2007).

That being said, and despite the best efforts from local actors, the functioning of the SEZ is affected by the geopolitical environment. A local governmental official sums it up:

> Our economy develops according to the rules of SEZ … . Poles came to sell herring, vodka, whatever you want; joint enterprises opened up; there was a general euphoria here; everybody thought it would be Hong Kong here. Poles are very good tradesmen. By the number of joint ventures, Poland was in the first place in Kaliningrad region; invested capital in the economy of Kaliningrad region– Germany, but a number of enterprises – Poland. [But] now [since 2014 more or less] almost nothing is left from those times. Everywhere you could see a joint enterprise for example on the production of metal-plastic windows, etc … Poles help us a lot in developing agriculture, developing apple gardens; … . So half measures are introduced towards Kaliningrad. Kaliningrad to be an economically open zone and at the same time to have military stationed there - those two do not come together. Thus, SEZ was announced and has not been implemented at full scale up to now. (Interview with the governmental official, Kaliningrad, April 2018)

Apart from trade issues, the mobility of persons proved to be a challenging issue, particularly when the new visa regime between Russia and the EU countries came into force on June 1, 2007, with Lithuania and Poland entering the Schengen zone (Vitunic 2003). Residents of the Kaliningrad region were among the first victims of the new visa regulations. Previously, they received visas for free, for a long period, with the possibility of multiple visits to these two neighbouring countries (Interview with state official, Kaliningrad, April 2018). Kaliningraders have lost this advantage but, as a tourist agent in Kaliningrad explains:

> You open a Schengen visa and go wherever you want. Before, to go to Hungary, we had to get the Polish visa first, then get a Hungarian. No, it's much better now. If you have a 2-3 year visa,

travel wherever you want! There are no more borders between the Schengen countries. So it's so much easier to cross countries. (Interview, Kaliningrad, April 2018)

One of the respondents even pointed out that Kalingraders apply for Spanish or Portuguese visas because it is easier and then they have access to all Europe.

In the context of Schengen, the 2012 Small Border Traffic (SBT) agreement between Kaliningrad and Poland's northern regions represents one of the recent successes of EU-Russia diplomacy. "Loosening of the border crossing regime reduced the social and functional distance between Poland and Kaliningrad, and in a broader sense between EU and Kaliningrad" (Domaniewski and Studzińska 2016, 538). It allowed "Kaliningraders soon [to] grew accustomed to buying sprees in cheap Polish shops without needing a visa. [However,] now that guns and fighters are seeping through Ukraine's porous eastern border with Russia" (*Forbes*, June 6, 2014), Warsaw closed its border.

That being said, small economic cooperation and cooperation in education and culture are continuing almost unaffected by the strategic macro considerations (Interviews with the employees of Kant Federal University, Kaliningrad, April 2018). At the university, a team under Dr. Anna Belova, implements projects between EU and Kaliningrad since 1992, first as partners to projects from European universities or NGOs but since 2005, "we can officially apply and receive money for the projects".

In the words of one of our respondents, "the relationships are difficult. The EU doesn't like Russia, Russia doesn't like the EU" but "the human relationships amongst Kaliningrad, Poland, and Lithuania are good despite geopolitics. Business is rational. It is good for both of us to cooperate" (Interviews with a local official and with a reseracher, Kaliningrad, April 2018). As a legal expert and researcher sums up:

> The difficulties of being disconnected do not disturb a normal life, but rather it is seen as a special feature of the region … . Energy is being supplied through Lithuania from Russia; no problem with transit. Maybe there were issues with the transit of military, but not with gas … . In overall, the question of the transit of goods and people is solved. It can be improved. … . There are serious problems in relations. … We do not feel some geopolitical tension. … you have heard a lot about Kaliningrad and Poland relations. We have very good relations with Poles, amongst people and politicians. Very warm and good relations … .. There are problems with Soviet monuments [in Poland]. On May 9 [Soviet/Russian Victory of the Great Patriotic War in 1945], he [the Polish Consul] will go together with the Governor of Kaliningrad oblast to put flowers to the monument of Unknown Soldier in Poland. It is always a big official delegation with participants from Poland and Kaliningrad oblast. It still takes place. (Interview, Kaliningrad, April 2018)

Despite the contested nature of the symbolic security boundary between Europe and Russia, around Kaliningrad, local representations of Europe and the alignment of interests with Europe are much more fluid when it comes to the mobility of goods and persons, accounting for numerous initiatives of cooperation. Cooperation is frequent however difficult because often overrun by geopolitical considerations.

Moldova: a disputed boundary

As presented in the graph in Appendix 3, cooperation between Europe and Russia on the Moldovan ground is difficult and there are recurrent outbursts of conflict. Since the end of the Soviet Union, Moldova is literally torn up between Europe/Romania and Russia. On the one hand, there are separatist regions, Transnistria – with its Russian military base still on the ground – and Gagauzia, willing to join or at least to stay within the Russia's sphere of influence. Moldova lost control over the former after a civil war that took place in 1992–1993 and eventually granted to the latter territorial autonomy in 1995. On the other hand, Moldovan identity *per se* is a disputed issue, oscillating between Romanianism and Russophile Moldovanism with heated public debates on national history and on the geopolitical projects Chisinau should enter into. Symptomatically, between 2016 and 2019, the executive is divided: the government issued from the legislative elections is pro-European, whereas the directly elected President, Ion Dodon, is pro-Russia. European and Eurasian integration projects are in constant competition accounting for a "stable instability" (Volovoj 2017). Part of Moldovan people would prefer integration to the EU, part are pro-Russian and support the project of the Eurasian Economic Union. Put differently, Moldova is crisscrossed with disputed symbolic boundaries, which create conflicts.

Such domestic tensions are related to the historically formed dual identity of the country. The old Moldovanist and Romanianist narratives started to play an important role within the societal and political spheres of the newly found state of Moldova. "Romanianism emphasises the shared ethnic, cultural, and linguistic background between citizens of Moldova and Romania. Romanianism contends that Moldova is culturally part of the larger Romanian nation, and some believe that reunification with Romania is desirable" (Worden 2011, 235). Moldovanism, based on the Soviet Moldovanist identity doctrine, which appeared in the 1920s, stresses that Moldovans are ethnically, culturally, and linguistically distinct from Romanians. Being a highly politicised issue, every regime change brought its own vision over the history teaching in schools, and thus, around 40 different history textbooks have been published in Moldova between 1991 and 2009 alone. This situation reinforced the divisions in the Moldovan society, deepening the identity crisis and thus the symbolic boundary is disputed.

Security, Russian speakers and disputed territory

These competing understandings of "who are we", and of the status of languages and alternative projects, is at the basis of the territorial separatism within Moldova. Transnistria's population is Russian-speaking but ethnically heterogeneous. An industrial region with a strong military presence, Transnistria's residents were well connected to Soviet institutions. When, in 1989, Chisinau introduced Moldovan/Romanian as the state language and established close relations with Romania (Kaufman and Bowers 1998), Russain-speaking managers and military personnel took control of institutions in Tiraspol and proclaimed independence (King 2001, 532–533). Thus, the conflict in Transnistria was about two opposed identities, pro-Romanian and pro-Soviet (Dembinska 2019).

Since it "won" the 1992–1993 civil war with Chisinau and entered the category of "frozen conflicts" and de facto states, Transnistria regularly calls upon its patron state Russia for integration. The 2006 referendum showed an overwhelming majority of Transnistrians ready to join Russia (with a voter turnout of 78.6%, 94.6% voted against re-joining the Republic of Moldova, 97.1% voted for independence with the possibility of joining Russia). With Western countries' recognition of Kosovo, followed by Russian recognition of Abkhazia and South Ossetia in 2008, and finally with the annexation of Crimea in

2014 (recognised by Transnistria immediately), Tiraspol hoped for similar treatment (Dembinska and Mérand 2019). The picture of disputed symbolic boundary and projects in Moldova is further emphasised when looking into Gagauzia, a region in the Southern part of Moldova inhabited by Orthodox turcophone people, the Gagauzs, who speak Gagauz and Russian rather than Moldovan/Romanian. Gaugauzia's separatist aspirations, in the wake of the disintegration of the USSR, have cooled after it was granted territorial autonomy in 1995. However, in the context of the upcoming March 2014 referendum in Crimea, Gagauzia organised its own referendum on February 2: with a turnout of some 70%, 98.5% of voters favoured the Russian-sponsored Customs Union, 97.2% were against closer EU integration and 98.9% of voters supported Gagauzia's right to declare independence if ever Moldova is to re-unify with Romania (Calus 2014, 59).

EU-Russia contest over Moldova

Although unrecognised by the international community, Transnistria survives thanks to Russia's patronage. Russia assures Transnistria's socio-economic survival and military security. Even though overall the number of Russian military deceased, together the 14th Army and the Russian peacekeeping mission (part of the trilateral Moldova-Russia-Transnistria mission) constitute Transnistria's security guarantee against Chisinau. In 2008, there were some 25,000 tons of armament and around 1500 Russian troops (400 by 2016; Lungu 2016) in Transnistria (Quinlan 2008, 133). According to Volovoj (2017), Russia's interest to keep Moldova in its sphere of influence is motivated mainly by the desire to show the West "red line" in the post-soviet area.

The EU has been involved in the Transnistrian frozen conflict resolution diplomatically (5+2 format negotiations and the presence of the European Commission delegation in Chisinau since 2005), economically (through the European Neighbourhood Policy, ENP, and the Eastern Partnership, EaP), and in terms of security (European Union Border Assistance Mission to Moldova and Ukraine, EUBAM, since 2005). According to Volovoj (2017), the European Union pursues the strategy of the "circles of influence", i.e. the EU is a core area, there is a close neighbourhood area and a far zone of interest. The main purpose of the EU is to have stable, democratic and prosperous partners, which live in accordance with European standards and can buy European products. "We want to build stronger relations with our partners and to give you [Moldova and Ukraine] the support you need to come closer to us", said Benita Ferrero-Waldner, then the EU External Relations Commissioner (*Financial Times*, 2005). The ENP is the EU's tool for promoting peace and stability through establishing cooperative relations with the countries important for European security order. The EaP further strengthens (mainly economic) relations. Moldova is not currently included in the pre-accession membership negotiations in either the EU or NATO (Moldova joined the North Atlantic Cooperation Council in 1992 [Euro-Atlantic Partnership Council since 1997] and the Partnership for Peace (PfP) programme in 1994). However, the EU has been developing ties with Moldova through the ENP since it was launched in 2003 and through the EaP since 2009. The recent most important landmarks in the Moldova-EU relations are (1) the 2008 Mobility Partnership which allows Moldovan citizens to travel to the EU without visa since April 2014, and (2) the Association Agreement (AA) with the EU signed in 2013 and ratified in 2014.

Energy and trade: a balancing act between the EU and Russia

In Chisinau, the Communist Party has "realized that one can't ensure sustainable economic development of the country if one only relies on Russia. Thus, they started to seek for other partnerships, including EU and other developed countries" (Interview with a think tank analyst, Chisinau, 2019). Political elite of Moldova at first seemed to be Moscow-oriented. However, in 2003 the president of Moldova, Vladimir Voronin, refused to sign the so-called "Kozak plan" prepared by Russia and meant to reintegrate Transnistria, and changed directions for aligning Moldova with Europe (he eventually lost his power in 2009 to the Alliance for European Integration). As a response, Russia imposed an embargo on Moldovan wines and other agricultural products (Interview with a think tank analyst and a representative of the political NGO, Chisinau, 2019).[1]

In 2015, a corruption scandal discredited the pro-European course and led to massive social protests. A compromise was eventually found: to organise direct presidential elections. These were won in 2016 by a pro-Russian leader, Igor Dodon, for whom "the EU is a project with a past, but without future" (in Volovoj 2017, 52). His first actions were: to remove the EU flag from his office; to go to Moscow for his first official presidential visit where he announced that Moldova's association agreement with the EU may be reviewed and that Moldova will cooperate with the Eurasian Economic Union; to fire the Defense Minister, Anatolie Salaru, because allegedly he was flirting with NATO and was advocating the unification with Romania; to cancel the agreement on establishing a NATO Liaison Office in Chisinau (Volovoj 2017, 52–54). During his visit to Brussels he proposed a trilateral EU-Russia-Moldova trade discussions.

According to Montesano, van der Togt and Zweeres (2016, 21),

> the Kremlin has successfully deployed both obstructive and constructive strategies to preserve or gain influence in Moldova, often through its relations in the Moldovan political and economic elites. Trade embargoes, public campaigns, and by using its de facto monopolist position as a gas supplier as leverage, as well as Moscow's weight in Transnistria, have proved to be successful tools in pressuring Moldova to refrain from more substantial EU-oriented reforms. The remaining strong ties between Russia and Moldova have thus obviously affected the development of Moldova's relations with the EU.

With such "policies of managed stability and managed instability" (Tolstrup 2009, 940), "the Kremlin uses the destructive power of separatism, and the corruption and crime that accompanies it, to obstruct reform" (Orttung and Walker 2015). Russia's goals are incompatible with those of the West and counterbalance the EU/NATO influence in the region (Tolstrup 2009). Together with disputed local symbolic boundaries, tracing Europe-Russia relations in Moldova clearly shows a dynamic where little cooperation exists, and the likelihood of conflict is great and ever present. We mention here just a few examples of this Moldovan disputed playground.

While Euro-Russian relations over Kaliningrad improve in the mid-2000s with new agreements signed and an increase in trade and in FDI, they worsen in the case of Moldova. In the context of the Orange Revolution and more EU involvement with Moldova, in late 2005 Russia announced a change to its energy policy toward its "near abroad". Gazprom insisted on doubling the price of gaz exported to Moldova. Unable to reach consensus, on 1 January 2006, all gas supplies to Moldova (and to Ukraine) ceased. Chisinau appealed for EU help arguing that "it is a difficult situation for a small country like Moldova to negotiate with such a huge neighbour as Russia" (*Financial Times*, January, 17, 2006). Moldova eventually reached a provisional agreement with Gazprom but a new "contest" started a few weeks later. In March 2006, as a result of EU pressures, Ukraine imposed new customs regulations on its border with Transnistria (Popescu 2009, 462). Moldovan customs stamps were now required for Transnistrian exports, which forced Transnistrian companies to register in Chisinau increasing thus their dependence on the Moldovan government and the EU. The reaction was immediate: Transnistria withdrew from the 5+2 negotiations format (*Ria Novosti*, March 7, 2006). The EU reiterated its support for the Moldovan European aspirations, called to resume negotiations and, on Russia, to discontinue its support for the Transnistrian regime, to withdraw its troops and heavy weaponry and ammunition ("European Parliament resolution on human rights in Moldova, and in Transnistria in particular", March 16, 2006). In response, Russia imposed a ban on Moldovan wines and other agricultural products (*New York Times*, April 6, 2006; Interviews in Moldova, 2019). With such sanctions deeply affecting the Moldovan ecomomy, Russia had an adavantage. 2007 negociations resulted in a new deal: in exchange for cheaper gas and the resumption of Moldovan wine and agricultural products exports to the Russian market, Russia took control of the Moldovan transit gas pipeline to Europe (Gazprom possesses 50% of the shares of Moldova-Gaz plus one vote; Interview with a think tank analyst, Chisinau, 2019).

The symbolic boundary being disputed, the dependence of Moldova on Russian gas and markets and the pro-Russian orientation of some actors do not preclude Chisinau to pursue a European course. In that context, the Euro-Russian contest over Moldova continues. In response to the 2013 Vilnius Summit that lead to signing of the Association Agreement in 2014, Moscow imposed another embargo on Moldovan wine (followed by farm products later on), threatened to cut off gas, and carried military exercises in Transnistria (Haukkala 2015). In the meantime, Europe introduced visa-free regime for Moldova and established a fruit import concession to compensate Moldovan producers for their losses due to the Russian ban (European Parliament, December 17, 2014; Interview with a think tank analyst, Chisinau, 2019).

The disputed nature of symbolic boundary in Moldova results in its "geopolitical hesitation" between the European and the Eurasian projects. It is thus arguably a fertile ground for Euro-Russian conflict, even when cooperation exists in other zones of contact.

Conclusion

Departing from IR theories, this article argued that cooperation and conflict are not tightly coupled with the geopolitical level but also shaped by the local dynamics of symbolic boundary making. The case studies show that conflict and cooperation between the EU and Russia may coexist in time and space given that their local patterns are partly autonomous from the geostrategic level. There is no one Euro-Russia relation but rather plural simultaneous relations that together account for the overall cooperative/conflictual pattern over time.

The article established a correlation between the type of locally constructed boundaries and the degree of conflict and cooperation between Europe and Russia. In Estonia, it has been argued, the symbolic boundary is solid as Russia is continuously viewed as the "other". There is very little cooperation between Europe and Russia and, although conflict happens, it is rare and rather contained. In Kaliningrad, the locally constructed symbolic boundary is fluid. Local actors initiate cooperation on trade and cultural issues despite an overall macro-level conflict over military issues. In Moldova, the symbolic boundary is disputed. Cooperation between Europe and Russia over and in Moldova is very difficult, and conflict is recurrent.

Our study does not deny the macro-level IR hypothesis, whether realist, liberal or constructivist. Our approach and findings are complementary. Without desavowing patterns at the geostrategic level, we point to the importance of taking into account local actors and contexts. Geopolitical strategic relations are refracted on the ground and the "local" accounts for variation of Europe-Russia relations over time and space. As argued in the Introduction to this Special Issue, conflict and cooperation coexist and this simultaneity can at least partially be explained by the "local". Instead of focusing on states and international organisations, this research targets this exactly. Local interests and representations matter and should be further taken into account in IR studies. Given our small sample of cases and given that these vary both on boundary and on degree of conflict/cooperation, the research agenda is opened for comparing additional cases that would allow for any generalisation.

The contribution of this article is both academic and political. Scientifically, the local perspective we propose rejects essentialism that would make Russia and Europe as fixed and homogenous entities. Whereas one can trace the formation of symbolic boundaries at the macro-level (see Neumann 2016), our bottom-up approach helps to explain a gap in the literature, namely the coexistence of militarised conflict and of some forms of close cooperation, which varies in time and space. Politically, this study deconstructs the binary opposition between two analytical positions that contain strong normative proposals, namely antagonising Russia, on the one hand, and the abandonment of former Soviet countries to the Russian domination, on the other hand.

Note

1. Throughout the studied period, Russia never imposed embargo on wines from Transnistria and Gagauzia in contrast to numerous restrictions towards the imports of Moldovan agricultural products and wines to Russia (Interview with a think tank analyst, Chisinau, 2019).

Disclosure statement

No potential conflict of interest was reported by the author(s).

Funding

This research is funded by the Social Sciences and Humanities Research Council of Canada.

ORCID

Anastasiya Shtaltovna ⓘ http://orcid.org/0000-0001-8817-028X

References

Archer, Clive, and Tobias Etzold. 2010. "The European Union and Kaliningrad: Taking the Low Road." *Geopolitics* 15 (2): 329–344.

Beyrle, John R. 1996. *Case Study: The Withdrawal of Russian Military Forces from the Baltic States (No. NDU/NWC-ASE-96-10)*. Washington, DC: National War Coll.

Bourdieu, Pierre. 1994. *Raisons pratiques : sur la théorie de l'actio*. Paris: Seuil.

Brubaker, Rogers. 2002. "Ethnicity Without Groups." *European Journal of Sociology* 43 (2): 163–189.

Calus, Kamil. 2014. "Gagauzia: Growing Separatism in Moldova?" *Centre for Eastern Studies* (OSW. Commentary) 129.

Cameron, Fraser. 2007. "The Nord Stream Gas Pipeline Project and its Strategic Implications." *Directorate-General for Internal Policies, European Parliament*.

Chillaud, Matthieu, and Frank Tetart. 2007. "The Demilitarization of Kaliningrad: A 'Sisyphean Task'?" *Baltic Security & Defence Review* 9: 171–186.

Cooper, Anthony, and Chris Perkins. 2012. "Borders and Status-Functions: An Institutional Approach to the Study of Borders." *European Journal of Social Theory* 15 (1): 55–71.

Dembinska, Magdalena. 2012. *Vivre ensemble dans la diversité. Europe Central et orientale après 1989. Les Presses Universitaires de Rennes*.

Dembinska, Magdalena. 2019. "Carving out the Nation with the Enemy's kin: Double Strategy of Boundary-Making in Transnistria and Abkhazia." *Nations and Nationalism* 25 (1): 298–317.

Dembinska, Magdalena, and Frédéric Mérand. 2019. "The Role of International Brokers in Frozen Conflicts: The Case of Transnistria." *Asia Europe Journal* 17 (1): 15–30.

Diener, Alexander, and Joshua Hagen. 2011. "Geopolitics of the Kaliningrad Exclave and Enclave: Russian and EU Perspectives." *Eurasian Geography and Economics* 52 (4): 567–592.

Domaniewski, Stanislaw, and Dominika Studzińska. 2016. "The Small Border Traffic Zone Between Poland and Kaliningrad Region (Russia): The Impact of a Local Visa-Free Border Regime." *Geopolitics* 21 (3): 538–555.

Fairlie, L. D. 1996. "Kaliningrad: NATO and EU Enlargement Issues Focus new Attention on Russia's Border with Central Europe." *Boundary and Security Bulletin* 4: 61–69.

Fedorov, G., M. Gorodkov, and I. Zhukovsky. 2011. "The Role of the Kaliningrad Region in the Development of Russian-German Relations." *Baltic Region* 4 (10): 33–39.

Galbreth, David, and Lasas Ainius. 2011. "The Baltic Factor in EU-Russia Relations: in Search of Coherence and Cooperation in an Era of Complexity." *Journal of Contemporary European Studies* 19 (2): 261–272.

Grigas, Agnia. 2014. "Russia-Baltic Relations after Crimea's Annexation: Reasons For Concern." *Cicero Foundation Great Debate Paper* 14 (05): 1–15.

Haukkala, Hiski. 2015. "From Cooperative to Contested Europe? The Conflict in Ukraine as a Culmination of a Long-Term Crisis in EU–Russia Relations." *Journal of Contemporary European Studies* 23 (1): 25–40.

Herzog, Stephen. 2011. "Revisiting the Estonian Cyber Attacks: Digital Threats and Multinational Responses." *Journal of Strategic Security* 4 (2): 49–60.

Hoff, Magdalene, and Heinz Timmermann. 1993. "Kaliningrad (Königsberg): eine russische Exklave in der baltische Region: Stand und Perspektiven aus europäischer Sicht." *Bundesinstitut für ostwissenschaftliche und internationale Studien* 17.

Horris, James. 2014. "Kaliningrad and Its Effect on EU-Russian Relations." *Towson Journal of International Affairs* 46 (1): 25–44.

Hurt, Martin. 2015. "Are all Russian Speakers in the Baltics Russia's Friends?" *International Centre for Defence and Security Estonia*, April 21.

Ivanova, Valentina, Andrey Gorokhov, Dmitriy Gorokhov, Aleksey Ignatiev, Vitaliy Smirnov, and Anatoliy Tuchinskiy. 2015. "Special Economic Zone in Kaliningrad Region: An Imperfect Legal Framework." *Economics Studies* 6 (127): 90–97. (Originally in Russian). http://ecsn.ru/files/pdf/201506/201506_90.pdf.

Jauhiainen, Jussi. 1997. "Militarisation, Demilitarisation and Re-use of Military Areas: The Case of Estonia." *Geography: Journal of the Geographical Association* 82 (2): 118–126.

Kallas, Kristina. 2016. "Claiming the Diaspora: Russia's Compatriot Policy and its Reception by Estonian-Russian Population." *Journal of Ethnopolitics and Minority Issues in Europe* 15 (3): 1–25.

Kaufman, Stuart J., and Stephen R. Bowers. 1998. "Transnational Dimensions of the Transnistrian Conflict." *Nationalities Papers* 26 (1): 129–146.

Kauppila, Laura. 1999. "The Baltic Puzzle: Russia's Policy towards Estonia and Latvia." *Helsinki: University of Helsinki.* http://ethesis.helsinki.fi/julkaisut/val/yhtei/pg/kauppila/thebalti.pdf.

King, Charles. 2001. "The Benefits of Ethnic War: Understanding Eurasia's Unrecognised States." *World Politics* 53 (4): 524–552.

Kirch, Marika, and Aksel Kirch. 1995. "Ethnic Relations: Estonians and non-Estonians." *The Journal of Nationalism and Ethnicity* 23 (1): 43–59.

Kolossov, Vladimir. 2005. "Border Studies: Changing Perspectives and Theoretical Approaches." *Geopolitics* 10 (4): 606–632.

Kolstø, Pål, and Andrei Edemsky. 1995. *Russians in the Former Soviet Republics.* Bloomington: Indiana University Press.

Korosteleva, Elena. 2011. "Change or Continuity" *International Relations* 25: 243–262.

Krickus, Richard J. 1998. "US Foreign Policy and the Kaliningrad Question." *Kopenhagen: DUPI*, Working Papers No. 18.

Lamont, Michèle, and Virag Molnar. 2002. "The Study of Boundaries in the Social Sciences." *Annual Review of Sociology* 28: 167–195.

Larsson, Robert L. 2007. "Nord Stream, Sweden and Baltic Sea Security." *Swedish Defence Research Agency* (FOI) No. FOI-R-2251.

Laurinavicius, Ceslovas. 2002. "The Euro-Atlantic Integration and the Future of Kaliningrad Oblast." NATO-Euro-Atlantic Parthnership Council. https://www.nato.int/acad/fellow/99-01/laurinacius.pdf.

Liik, Kadri. 2007. "The 'Bronze Year' of Estonia-Russia Relations." *Estonian Ministry of Foreign Affairs Yearbook*, 71–76.

Lungu, Karina. 2016. "Transnistria: From Entropy to Exodus." *European Council on Foreign Relations*, 1–5.

Lynch, Allen. 2001. "The Realism of Russia's Foreign Policy." *Europe-Asia Studies* 53 (1): 7–31.

Malling, Jens. 2015. "The Value of a Frozen Conflict." *Le Monde Diplomatique.*

Mann, Michael. 1984. "The Autonomous Power of the State: its Origins, Mechanisms, and Results." *European Journal of Sociology* 25: 185–213.

Mälksoo, Maria. 2009. "Liminality and Contested Europeanness: Conflicting Memory Politics in the Baltic Space." In *Identity and Foreign Policy: Baltic-Russian Relations in the Context of European Integration*, edited by T. E. Berg and P. Ehin, 65–83. Aldershot: Ashgate.

Melvin, Neil J. 2000. "Post-Imperial Ethnocracy and the Russophone Minorities of Estonia and Latvia." In *The Politics of National Minorities Participation in Post-Communist Europe. State-Building, Democracy and Ethnic Mobilization*, edited by Jonathan P. Stein, 129–166. Armonk, NY: East-West Institute M. E. Sharpe.

Montesano, Francesco S., Tony van der Togt, and Wouter Zweers. 2016. "The Europeanisation of Moldova: Is the EU on the Right Track?" Clingendael Report. Netherlands Institute of International Repations.

Munuera, Gabriel. 1994. "Preventing Armed Conflict in Europe: Lessons from Recent Experience." Institute for Security Studies, Western European Union.

Neumann, Iver B. 2016. *Russia and the Idea of Europe*. 2nd ed. London: Routledge.

Newman, David. 2003. "On Borders and Power: A Theoretical Framework." *Journal of Borderlands Studies* 18 (1): 13–25.

Nitoiu, Cristian. 2017. "Still Entrenched in the Conflict/Cooperation Dichotomy? EU–Russia Relations and the Ukraine Crisis." *European Politics and Society* 18 (2): 148–165.

Oldberg, Ingmar. 2009. "The Changing Military Importance of the Kaliningrad Region." *Journal of Slavic Military Studies* 22 (3): 352–366.

O'Loughlin, John, Gerard Toal, and Vladimir Kolosov. 2016. "Who Identifies with the 'Russian World'? Geopolitical Attitudes in Southeastern Ukraine, Crimea, Abkhazia, South Ossetia, and Transnistria." *Eurasian Geography and Economics* 57 (6): 745–778.

Onken, Eva Clarita. 2007. "The Baltic States and Moscow's 9 May Commemoration: Analysing Memory Politics in Europe." *Europe-Asia Studies* 59 (1): 23–46.

Orttung, Robert, and Christopher Walker. 2015. "Putin's Frozen Conflicts." *Foreign Policy*.

Paasi, Anssi. 1996. "Inclusion, Exclusion and Territorial Identities: the Meanings of Boundaries in the Globalizing Geopolitical Landscape." *Nordisk Samhallsgeografisk Tidskrift* 23 (3): 3–17.

Palmowski, Tadeusz. 2010. "Problems of Cross-Border Cooperation Between Poland and the Kaliningrad Oblast of the Russian Federation." *Quaestiones Geographicae* 29 (4): 75–82.

Parker, Noël and Nick Vaughan-Williams. 2009. "Lines in the Sand? Towards an Agenda for Critical Border Studies." *Geopolitics* 14 (3): 582–587.

Popescu, Nicu. 2009. "EU and the Eastern Neighbourhood: Reluctant Involvement in Conflict Resolution." *European Foreign Affairs Review* 14 (4): 457–477.

Quinlan, Paul D. 2008. "Foot in Both Camps: Moldova and the Transnistrian Conundrum From the Kozak Memorandum." *East European Quarterly* 42 (2): 129–160.

Roth, Mathias. 2009. "Bilateral Disputes between EU Member States and Russia." *CEPS Working Document* 319.

Ruus, Kertu. 2008. "Cyber war I: Estonia Attacked From Russia." *European Affairs* 9 (1-2): 1–4.

Skala, Michal, and Julia Miklasova. 2015. "Transnistria: Russia's Bargaining Chip in the EU Periphery." *Central European Policy Institute*. http://www.cepolicy.org/publications/transnistriarussiasbargain ingchipeuperiphery.

Smith, Karen. 2005. "The Outsiders: the European Neighborhood Policy." *International Affairs* 81 (4): 757–773.

Stratfor. 2012. "Estonia: Split Opinions about Nord Stream." *Stratfor Global Intelligence*, 25 octobre. https://www.stratfor.com/analysis/estonia-split-opinions-about-nord-stream.

Sukhankin, Sergey. 2016. "Kaliningrad in the 'Mirror World': From Soviet 'Bastion' to Russian 'Fortress'". *Barcelona Centre for International Affairs (CIDOB)*. http://www.cidob.org/publicaciones/serie_de_publicacion/notes_internacionals/n1_151/kaliningrad_in_the_mirror_world_from_soviet_bastion_to_russian_fortress.

Toal, Gerard. 2017. *Near Abroad. Putin, The West and The Contest Over Ukraine and the Caucasus*. New York: Oxford University Press.

Tolstrup, Jakob. 2009. "Studying a Negative External Actor: Russia's Management of Stability and Instability in the 'Near Abroad." *Democratization* 16 (5): 922–944.

Topaloglou, Lefteris, Dimitris Kallioras, Panos Manetos, and George Petrakos. 2005. "A Border Regions Typology in the Enlarged European Union." *Journal of Borderlands Studies* 20 (2): 67–89.
Varu, V. 1995. *Unpublished Statistics About Military Bases*. Tallinn: Estonian Ministry of Defence.
Vihalemm, Triin, and Anu Masso. 2007. "(Re) Construction of Collective Identities After the Dissolution of the Soviet Union: The Case of Estonia." *Nationalities Papers* 35 (1): 71–91.
Vitunic, Brian. 2003. "Enclave to Exclave: Kaliningrad Between Russia and the European Union." *Intermarium* 6 (1): 1–28.
Volovoj, Vadim. 2017. "How The West Lost Moldova To Russia." *Ante Portas–Studia nad Bezpieczeństwem* 1: 47–59.
Whist, Bendik Solum. 2008. "Nord Stream: Not Just a Pipeline." *age* 30 (4): 1–77.
Winnerstig, Mike. 2014. "Tools of Destabilization: Russian Soft Power and Non-Military Influence in the Baltic States." *Totalförsvarets Forskningsinstitut (FOI)* 13: 1–146.
Worden, Elizabether Anderson. 2011. "The 'Mock Reform' of History Education in Moldova: Actors Versus the Script." *Comperative Education Review* 55 (2): 231–251.

Appendices

Appendix 1

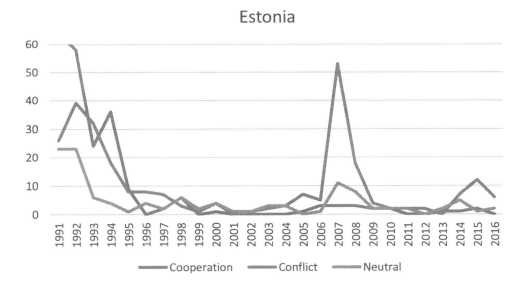

Appendix 2

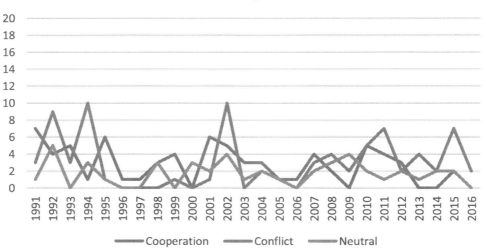

Appendix 3

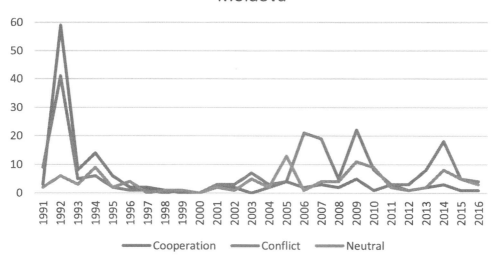

Hybrid geopolitics in EU-Russia relations: understanding the persistence of conflict and cooperation

Cristian Nitoiu and Florin Pasatoiu

ABSTRACT
The article analyses the way the rise of geopolitics has affected the conflict and cooperation dichotomy in EU-Russia relations. It contends, that the role of geopolitics in the security architecture of the European continent is characterised by continuity, as its pervasive effects have constrained the agency and autonomy of both Russia and the EU.

Introduction

In recent years, developments in Ukraine, but also more broadly on the European continent, have emphasised that competition (and even conflict) has almost completely overshadowed cooperation between the European Union (EU) and Russia. However, this seems to mark a departure from the conflict and cooperation dichotomy that characterised EU-Russia relations following the end of the Cold War. According to the literature, the conflict and cooperation dichotomy involves complementarity between overlapping processes of collaboration and competition (Samokhvalov 2018; Nitoiu 2017; Rak 2017; Diesen 2017). Mainstream analyses of EU-Russia relations have proliferated on an impressive scale since 2014, these with an emphasis on the perceived rise of geopolitics as a key driving factor on the European continent (Barkanov 2015; Bekus 2017; Laruelle 2015; Youngs 2017). Besides the Ukraine crisis, symptoms of the emerging role of geopolitics centre around the wide range of crises that the EU has experienced during the last decade: e.g. the Eurozone crisis, the Arab, or the migrant crisis. Studies here highlight the way in which geopolitics constrain EU actions towards Russia and its eastern neighbourhood. Geopolitics are generally understood to hinder meaningful cooperation among states and lead to conflict (Raik 2016; Raik and Dinesen 2015; Casier 2016).[1]

Against this backdrop, this article analyses the way the rise of geopolitics has affected the conflict and cooperation dichotomy in EU-Russia relations. It contends that the role of geopolitics in the security architecture of the European continent is characterised by continuity, as its pervasive effects have constrained the agency and autonomy of both Russia and the EU. Moreover, the growing number of studies on EU-Russia relations tend to employ a classical or traditional understanding of geopolitics.[2] From this perspective, states are prone to experience security dilemmas as they engage in the self-interested promotion of power beyond their borders (Cadier 2014; Grygiel 2015). By contrast, this article contends that both Russia and the EU have developed distinct and hybrid geopolitical approaches. These approaches are shaped by their unsettled and hybrid identities, as well as by shifting perceptions of the self and other, and by the role played by geographical space (Oskanian 2018; Zielonka 2008). This contention resembles the concept of fluid symbolic boundaries developed in the introduction to this special issue. Hybrid geopolitics thus shape the way the EU and Russia seek to gain autonomy and agency, and also shapes their bid to achieve administrative influence or even hegemony in their shared neighbourhood.

The main claim of the article is that the apparent increasing role of geopolitics in EU-Russia relations can be best understood by focusing on the concept of hybrid geopolitics. It should be noted, however, that the article does not aim to present a well-defined framework for analysing the conflict and cooperation dichotomy or the notion of hybrid geopolitics. Consequently, it should be read as an initial attempt to understand the conflict and cooperation dichotomy through the lens of hybrid geopolitics, with future research aiming to analyse the relationship across a range of relevant and timely case studies. The article begins with an exploration of the way in which geopolitics characterised the development of the conflict and cooperation dichotomy during the post-Cold War period. The section that follows discusses the perception of the rise of classical forms of geopolitics and argues that continuity in developing distinct hybrid approaches to geopolitics represents the main driver of symptoms of traditional geopolitics. The last sections reflect on EU and Russia's approaches to hybrid geopolitics and their impact on the conflict and cooperation dichotomy.

The conflict and cooperation dichotomy

The evolution of EU-Russia relations following the end of the Cold War has been at best convoluted and marked by often contradictory and simultaneously overlapping processes. Better known as the conflict and cooperation dichotomy, the concept describes the constant state of limbo that underpins interactions between Russia and the EU (Averre 2016; Nitoiu 2014; Haukkala 2015). Cooperation tends to coexist with competition and conflict, often overlapping and creating a complex dynamic, which, in turn, hinders the development of genuine cooperative patterns. The persistence of the conflict and cooperation dichotomy allows both Moscow and Brussels to avoid a full breakdown in their relationship. A series of key studies attempts to explicitly analyse the evolution of the dichotomy (Nitoiu 2011; Chebakova et al. 2017; Casier 2017; Korosteleva 2016; Ademmer, Delcour, and Wolczuk 2016). However, most of the literature on EU-Russia relations only indirectly tackles the constant overlapping of conflict and cooperation. The Ukraine crisis has led to a period of intense geopolitical conflict and competition, and with it a proliferation of studies on EU-Russia relations. Nevertheless, even in the face of seemingly antagonistic and conflictual modes of interactions, cooperation is still present: e.g. trade and investment (European Parliament 2017), business links (Wigell and Vihma 2016), tailor-made Russian counter-sanctions (that do not target Russia-friendly EU member states), or sanctions busting through countries like Turkey or Kazakhstan (Hedberg 2018). Much of the dynamic of the conflict and cooperation dichotomy has its roots in the dissolution of the Soviet Union and the subsequent evolution of a new

European security architecture. The end of the Cold War led to the emergence of a series of expectations in Russia and the West regarding the scope of their future relationship. On the Russian side, post-Soviet leaders shared the belief that embracing the liberal world order and aiming to adapt to Western rules and values would see Moscow accepted as an equal. Having willingly given up the clout of its empire, and (from its perspective) single handedly ending the Cold War, post-Soviet Russia would deserve acknowledgement, respect, and support from the West (Tsygankov 2013). This was the heyday of Westernisers and Europeanisers, who promoted the need for Russia to embrace Western values and modes of governance in order to modernise. To that extent, The West (as well as the EU) was perceived as a beacon, which would guide Russia during its transition to democracy while allowing the latter to set the agenda of international relations (Baranovsky 2000). On the other hand, in the US and the EU, the end of the Cold War was framed as the defeat of the Soviet Union, and proof that history had entered a new stage where capitalism and liberal democracy would be the only viable options. In this interventionist mode, the West engaged in a "civilising" mission, to spread liberal democracy around the world. Even though it was influenced by a collaborative agenda, the promotion of liberal democracy tended to apply a one- size-fits-all approach, disregarding the views of other states. Hence, relations between the West (and the EU) and post-Soviet Russia were framed by a willingness to cooperate on both sides, but also developed out of contrasting views (and expectations) of the other. In this context, both the EU and Russia have not been ready and willing to come together and discuss the nature and role of power on the European continent.

The end of the Cold War thus created a series of lingering contradictions in relations between the EU and Russia, which neither had the willingness nor the ability resolve. These salient and unresolved contradictions have an impact on issues such as: the European security architecture, regional integration, spheres of influence, or the role of norms and values. First, the development of the post-Cold War security architecture has followed a rather one-sided and monistic approach (Sakwa 2018). This view is primarily influenced by an EU and transatlantic- centred mindset, which has not engaged with the more pluralistic image outlined in the Common European Home project, presented by Gorbachev during the 1980s (Malcolm 1989). During the honeymoon period of the 1990s and early 2000s, both the EU and Russia chose to gloss over the nature of the security architecture of the European continent in order to achieve greater cooperation.

Second, the dissolution of the Soviet Union left a vacuum of power in the post-Soviet space, which Russia was unable to fill for much of the post-Cold War period. Nevertheless, throughout this period Russian policymakers did not give up on the ideal of persevering or reinstating the old sphere of influence in the post-Soviet space, even though they rarely articulated it up until the middle of the 2000s (Baranovsky 2000). Third, in spite of a willingness during the first part of the post-Cold War period to engage on a cooperative path, neither the EU nor Moscow made headway in expanding European integration towards Russia. At the same time, following the wave of enlargement towards Central and Eastern Europe (CEE), the EU started to push its integration project in the post-Soviet space, coming into collision with the integration efforts spearheaded by Russia. With the creation of the Eurasian Economic Union (EEU), tensions and contradictions between EU and Russian models of integration were exacerbated and left the post-Soviet states in the stark position of having to choose between two mutually exclusive alternatives. Fourth, both the EU and Russia have developed contrasting approaches to the promotion of norms and values in international relations, as well as what constitutes normal behaviour in world politics. For example, while the EU frames its promotion of universal norms and values beyond its borders as a legitimate endeavour (Smith 2016), Russia puts national sovereignty at the centre of its worldview and perceives the external promotion of norms and values as a security threat (Lavrov 2016).

Besides these four contradictions, the persistence of the conflict and cooperation dichotomy has also been driven by the deeply inward approaches to foreign policy developed by Russia and the EU. In both cases, foreign policy has been used primarily for internal purposes. For the EU, foreign policy has been epiphenomenal to European integration, providing its model of governance impetus during periods of discontent or crisis (Bickerton 2011). On the other hand, the Kremlin is increasingly using foreign policy in order to safeguard the regime against domestic risks and disorder (Cadier and Light 2015). Hence, their approaches towards each other in the post-Soviet space have been rather insular and not sensitive to the needs, interests, and views of the other. This paints the picture of a dialogue of the deaf, where partners engage in monological interactions with a limited willingness to meaningfully engage with the other. What is even more surprising is the fact that the EU has framed its approach towards Russia as beneficial for Moscow, aimed as it is at helping the country develop and democratise (Prodi 2004). Conversely, the Kremlin has argued that it has made impressive efforts and concessions in an altruistic manner in order to meet the EU's requirements for cooperation without receiving anything in return (Putin 2013a). Starting in the latter half of the 2000s, the literature narrates a Russia and an EU that have stopped paying attention to the views and interest of the other (Forsberg 2019). This range of insular approaches to foreign policy is also part of the larger identity crises that the EU and Russia have been experiencing since the end of the Cold War. At the root of these identity crises are key questions regarding the civilisational models that the two actors promote in world politics, which, as the next section shows, have increasingly collided and led to the perception of the emergence of classical forms of geopolitics.

The rise of geopolitics

Recent years have marked the rise of geopolitics in the discourse of both academics and policymakers in the EU and on the European continent (Smith and Youngs 2018; Youngs 2017; Nitoiu 2017). This is in sharp contrast with much of the development of the EU, where geopolitics had been framed as a deeply negative remnant of the past which led to the two world wars (Grygiel 2015). Consequently, the perception of the return of geopolitics on the European continent is underpinned by the range of crises that the EU has recently experienced: e.g. the Ukraine crisis, the migrant crisis, the Eurozone crisis, or the Arab spring. Advocates of the (re-)emergence of geopolitics stress the EU's inadequate response to these crises. Nevertheless, following the Ukraine crisis, EU policymakers have been forced to come to terms with the role of geopolitics, and with the need to embark on a process of renewal and revision in foreign policy. In strategy documents such as the 2015 revision of the ENP (European Commission 2015) or the 2016 Global Strategy (European External Action Service 2016), the EU emphasises the need to reassess the role of geopolitics in the world order, with the goal to increase resilience in the face of structural geopolitical pressures. For the last two decades, scholars have argued for the EU's need to develop a strategic approach that would accommodate the role of geopolitics (Gehring, Urbanski, and Oberthür 2017; Smith 2016; Howorth 2016; Hyde-Price 2006). While becoming more aware of the salience of geopolitical constraints, and as such needing to revise its foreign policy strategy, the EU seems to have downsized its ambitions and has been more reluctant of late to exercise international actorness (Youngs 2017). The Ukraine crisis, the Arab spring or the migrant crisis have circumscribed the limits of EU actorness and have raised awareness of the perils of the Union overextending its reach.[3] In practice, the EU has been engulfed by a deep identity crisis whereby it tries to cling to its former ambitions of promoting norms and principled behaviour-infused actorness, while seeking to accommodate its own failures in the context of acknowledging the salience of traditional forms of geopolitics (Pänke 2019). The same range of crises has also affected Russia, but unlike the case of the EU, these events reconfirm the salience of geopolitics, as the concept has been central to the country's foreign policy for the last three decades (Tsygankov 2013).

The perception of the rise of geopolitics is predicated on a traditional or classical understanding of the concept, which emphasises the preeminence of material power and the promotion of interests over principled behaviour in world politics. Classical geopolitics is very often equated with realist approaches in international relations theory that stress the need for states to enhance their security and material power (Kelly 2016; Cohen 2014). When states, responding to geopolitical constraints, seek to enhance their power by encroaching upon the interests and even borders of other states, anarchy ensues. Structure trumps agency, as great powers with limited autonomy must constantly adapt to geopolitical constraints, further curtailing the autonomy of small states (Larson and Shevchenko 2010). A world order dominated by classical geopolitics underlines the need for states to secure their borders and project their power and influence onto various geographical spaces. The only way states can achieve resilience is by understanding geopolitical constraints and engaging with them. For states seeking to play a more important role in the international arena, mastering geopolitics (from a traditional perspective) would imply securing influence over specific geographic spaces, especially within their respective neighbourhoods. This leads to the creation of spheres of influence, which are recognised by smaller neighbours, together with important actors in the international arena. The emergence of competing claims of influence binds states in a zero-sum logic, which has the potential to break out into all-out conflict. In the post-Soviet space, the persistence of the conflict and cooperation dichotomy has been increasingly characterised by this zero-sum logic, one of the key reasons that leads analysts to point to the rise of traditional forms of geopolitics (Cadier 2019; Auer 2015).

The proliferation of studies on Russia's foreign policy and its relations with the EU is converging with the perception that geopolitics has come to shape the European continent and the international arena (Romanova 2018). Competing integration projects, the increasing importance of material power, the use of military capabilities by Russia in eastern Ukraine or Crimea, or the EU's shift towards principled pragmatism, can all be interpreted as key symptoms that geopolitics is the main driver in relations between Brussels and Moscow. There has been a qualitative change, where geopolitics seems to have shifted the balance decisively towards cooperation and conflict. However, these analyses overlook two key aspects: geopolitical concerns have continuously influenced the evolution of EU-Russia relations during the post-Cold War period; and, following this article's main claim, both the EU and Russia have developed a distinct brand of hybrid geopolitics.

The salience of geopolitics in the post-Cold War evolution of EU-Russia relations is underscored by the role of geography and the willingness and ability [of both entities?] to project power beyond their borders. First, geography plays a key role in the identities of both the EU and Russia and the way they perceive and interact with each other. The EU employs a rather exclusionary approach, whereby it sets out to clear spatial boundaries that limit its nature and composition. Even though universal values are placed discursively at the core of the EU's existence and development, it engages in a practice of clear difference (Ganzle 2007; Hardacre and Smith 2009). Due to the multiple ethnic minorities living in various spaces on its territory, Russia has applied a looser and rather more inclusionary approach. Engaging with these individuals as equal representatives of Russianness has thus implied a more inclusionary approach to geography, where intention and willing allegiance trump space in defining difference with the outside world (Feklyunina 2015; Laruelle 2015). The two distinct approaches collide in the post-Soviet space, where the EU is keen to shape while excluding, and Russia to include. Both approaches can be understood as efforts to create spheres of influence in the the post-Soviet geography. In reality though, neither have engaged in practices that would lead to the creation of an effective sphere of influence according to classical geopolitics. Rather, each has merely focused on achieving specific influence: e.g. the EU has aimed to promote half-heartedly liberal norms, while Russia has been primarily interested in influencing the security architecture of the area.[4]

Secondly, both the EU and Russia have aimed to project their power in various geographic spaces in order to claim actorness and higher status in the international arena. In their shared neighbourhood, EU and Russian power projection efforts have often collided and even overlapped during the post-Cold War period. The evolution of post-Soviet regimes, colour revolutions, the Georgian-Russian war of 2008, the creation of the Eastern Partnership or the EEU and the development of the Ukraine crisis, are all results of power projection strategies used by the EU and Russia in their shared neighbourhood. For the EU, effectively projecting power in the neighbourhood is a prerequisite for developing greater presence in the international arena, while for the Kremlin the space allows Russia to prove that it has not lost (or it has the ability to recover) the former status of the Soviet Union. As a key aspect of the persistence of geopolitical concerns in EU-Russia relations, it is worth pointing out that the two actors have in various instances worked together in projecting power in various parts of the world. Some examples here would include dealing with terrorism and brokering the Iran nuclear deal.

It is the very absence of meaningful discussion over the nature of power on the European continent that, in turn, exacerbated growing post-Cold War contrasts and contradictions between the EU and Russia, and precluded the two actors from engaging on these issues. Together with an emphasis on power, the gradual and convoluted overlapping between conflict and cooperation also touched upon interpretations of space. Nevertheless, questions of power or space have tended not be on the forefront of EU-Russia relations, even though they create and reproduce key contradictions. Against this backdrop, the article contends that hybrid geopolitics (discussed in the following sections), with its emphasis on space, power, and unsettled identities, can shed light on the presence of conflict and cooperation.

Traditional vs. hybrid geopolitics

Traditional geopolitics emphasises the salience of material power and geographical spaces. It tends to act as a fixed structural constraint on the behaviour of states. In this interpretation, international actors must learn how to master the constraints posed by traditional geopolitics in order to survive and thrive in the international system. However, as Cohen (2014) points out, successfully acting in a geopolitical manner presupposes a coherent set of sources of material power, as well as settled interpretations of geographical space. Classical forms of geopolitics centre on the need of states to safeguard their geographical territory and focus on expansion (Flint 2012). Developing effective strategies that merge territorial defense, expansion, and power acquisition is a key aspect of traditional geopolitics. Norms, values, or identities are rather absent or silent in this traditional interpretation. Geography creates a range of material constraints that shape the behaviour of states in world politics (Kelly 2016). To that extent, classical geopolitics, much like realist theories of international relations, emphasises objectivity and tends to represent a one-size-fits-all approach that states need to accommodate and master in order to survive and thrive in world politics. There is a linear causal relationship between geographical space and the dynamics of power in world politics, where the latter has the potential to augment states' power and status. More critical perspectives on geopolitics highlight the fact that geographical space is socially constructed through the practice, interactions, and interpretations of states (Omelicheva 2016). The assumption that space and power are bound in a causal relationship is challenged as identities, norms, and values are seen as intervening variables that can affect the way states perceive and construct both notions of power and space (Foxall 2019). Moreover, these approaches emphasise the link between statecraft and geopolitics, namely the way international actors employ geopolitics as a way of legitimising behaviour in world politics and particular views of the world order (Cohen 2014).

This article contends that states develop their own approaches to geopolitics, which is based both on objective calculations regarding the relationship between power and space, as well as their own identities and the norms or values that underpin them (or that prevail in the international system). The more these two objective and intersubjective aspects become intertwined in the construction of states' approaches to geopolitics, the more states steer towards hybridity. Hybrid geopolitics as an approach to statecraft is primarily influenced by states' hybrid and unsettled identities. As was highlighted earlier, the scholarship points to the fact that relatively stable identities equate to an effective management of geopolitical constraints (Cohen 2014). In turn, states that present identity crises and deep uncertainty regarding their place in the world order (or the civilisational model they seek to promote externally) are bound to experience difficulties in managing the structural constraints imposed by traditional geopolitics.

Identity crises refer to the sense of anxiety, trauma, and uncertainty caused by the presence of multiple alternatives for the way states perceive themselves and seek to develop actorness in the world order (Crossley 2000; Hutchison 2010). This may also be caused by a mismatch between the aspirations or expectations of states and their capabilities. In order to deal with identity crises, states require a certain degree of creativity and innovation, as hybridity implies the development of new ways of behaving in international relations. These can take the form of the promotion of a series of norms, values, and ideologies, or the development of alternative views regarding the workings of the world order. However, theses aspects ultimately serve as a proxy for states to manage what they perceive to be the risks and challenges pertaining to traditional geopolitics.

Space plays a key role in the construction of state identities. However, the concept of space is rather flexible for states suffering from identity crises (Nordin and Smith 2019). Relations with the other are, in the same way, more fluid and tend to be underpinned by constantly evolving notions of borders and spatiality. Accommodating the perceived geography of the self and the other thus becomes less clear and fixed than classical geopolitics would prescribe. In this context, the article claims that throughout the post-Cold War period, Russia and the EU have been rather ill-suited to engaging in traditional geopolitics. Both have been experiencing deep identity crises, which have shaped their perceptions of the self and other. Moreover, in the current American-led liberal world order they have found it difficult, if not impossible, to act (as equals of the US) in traditional geopolitical terms. Hybridity has thus occurred both as a reflection of the self and an adaptation to structural geopolitical constraints.

The EU and Russia's approach to hybrid geopolitics

Hybrid geopolitics has evolved in the case of the EU and Russia as a result of their hybrid identities, which, as such, do not allow them to adequately address constraints generated by classical forms of geopolitics. Both international actors are distinct forms of empires, each bent on constructing and promoting hybrid exceptionalism. Russia embodies a type of empire that is fraught with contradictions. Morozov (2015) posits that the country is a subaltern empire, which in terms of the world economy is placed at the periphery of the world order, while its military power and natural resources position it towards the centre of the system. Consequently, although the Kremlin might possess the material capabilities to act in a classical geopolitical manner, it does not have the economic potential to sustain this approach in the long term. Moreover, Russia's own perception of its limitations as an empire point to the need to develop hybridity rather than play by traditional geopolitical rules observed by the US and more recently China (Lavrov 2016). Nevertheless, the Kremlin does argue that other empires and would-be empires are increasingly engaging in classical geopolitics and threatening Russia's very survival (Putin 2013b). On the other hand, the EU sees itself as a rather positive and postmodern form of empire that transcends the constraints imposed by traditional understandings of power and borders (Smith 2003; Morgherini 2017). This perception, in turn, provides legitimacy to the EU's efforts to promote power beyond its borders and seek to shape the behaviour of those actors regarded as being stuck in an outdated world dominated by traditional geopolitics (De Zutter 2010).

The EU and Russia share contradictory views regarding their own and each other's behaviour in world politics. On the one hand, the EU imagines itself to be an altruistic actor, promoting universal values around the world. Russia, as well as a wide range of actors in the international arena, view the EU's conduct as pedagogical [in theory] and patronising [in effect], which strips away the agency of those states under tuition as it were and disregards their particular values and interests (Chaban, Elgström, and Gulyaeva 2017; Chaban et al. 2013). On the other hand, Russia holds to the notion of civilising others while also being civilised by the West. It is simultaneously an agent of and is subject to processes of orientalisation (Neumann 2016). Most narratives developed by the EU orientalise Russia and frame it as uncivilised international actor.

Throughout the post-Cold War period, Russia and the EU have experienced deep identity crises guided by the need to define the civilisational model they embody and promote in the international arena. The dissolution of the Soviet Union gave way to a Russia without great power and status. This led to a state of confusion regarding the role that Russia would play and what its place might be in the Western-led world order. Even during the 1990s, Russia aspired to maintain or recapture the Soviet Union's influence in the post-Soviet space. One of the driving factors in Russia's foreign policy was the need to develop a new type of civilisational model that could replace the promotion of Communism in the world order. Nevertheless, due to the multiple domestic issues that post-Soviet Russia faced during the first decade of the post-Cold War period, limited attention was given to solving the identity crisis. Putin's two-decade long leadership has brought a new and ample layer of complexity to the identity crisis. Disaffection with the EU and the West has pushed the Kremlin to go back to more traditional debates about Russia's purpose and nature in world politics: i.e. the debate between Western or liberal views versus more conservative, Eurasian approaches. The latter set of views can be seen to currently hold sway over the official policy of the Kremlin, with some analysts arguing that Russia's identity has moved away from Europe (Romanova 2018; Braghiroli and Makarychev 2016; Holslag 2016). Russia's hybrid identity in international relations has its origins in the imperial period of the eighteenth century (Neumann 2016; Tsygankov 2014). Proponents of liberal approaches still maintain key positions in the Kremlin even if the official narrative seems to have embraced Eurasianism, Putin's attempt to articulate a new civilisational model (and legacy).

Even before the end of the Cold War, the EU had been grappling with the need to develop and promote an innovative civilisational model in world politics. Debates throughout the 1970s and 1980s centred on the idea that the EU is ill-suited to act in a classical geopolitical manner (similarly to the US or the Soviet Union). This was primarily influenced by its ontology and a lack of capabilities or institutional structures (Bull 1982; Duchene 1972; 1973). The dissolution of the Soviet Union left a vacuum in CEE, which the EU was keen to fill – but was also constrained by the demands of the countries in the region. Hence, there was a growing expectation that the EU would attain a strong presence in the international arena, with the first step of the process entailing the successful "return to Europe" of the former Communist states from CEE (Allen and Smith 1990). A stronger EU in international affairs prompted questions regarding the ontology of the EU as an international actor (Risse-Kappen 1996). At this point, the identity crisis meant having to figure out the EU's international actorness in relation to nation states. The latter have resources and institutional structures that allow them to build coherent foreign policies and strategies and engage in traditional geopolitics. Lacking these aspects, the EU's answer to its identity crisis was to emulate nation states in creating coherent foreign policy institutions and capabilities: most importantly, a diplomatic system (i.e. the future European External Action Service) and a potential European army.

The buildup to the enlargement towards CEE and its relative success added an additional layer to the identity crisis, shifting the debate to the EU's innovative behaviour guided by principled action rather than narrow self-interest. Indeed, during the 2000s the response to its identity crisis took the form of a narrative of a *sui generis*, a hybrid and principled actor that had the potential to transcend the constraints of nation states and those imposed by traditional geopolitics. Normative, ethical, or principled behaviour became the backbone of the EU's identity and the model of governance it sought to promote in the international arena (Manners 2008). With the range of crises that have plagued the EU during the last decade, hybridity has further evolved. A developing consciousness of the role of geopolitics following the Ukraine crisis or the migrant crisis, principled pragmatism, and a sheer obsession with enhancing resilience have magnified the EU's identity crisis (Juncos 2017). More than ever, the EU needs to accommodate a hybrid identity that contains deeply contradictory elements: being sui generis but striving to mimic nation states, while promoting self-interest and claiming normative, principled, and altruistic behaviour in world politics. As with Russia, hybridity shapes the EU's approach to geopolitics, which precludes it from engaging in more classical forms.

In practice, hybridity implies that both Russia and the EU have developed their approach to geopolitics as a way of dealing with their identity crises, but also as a result of their perceptions of the self and other. The recognition of the fact that they lack the necessary characteristics to fully engage in traditional geopolitics has pushed both actors to use their hybrid approaches to geopolitics in order to gain increased autonomy and agency. The relationship between domestic and foreign policy is central to the post-Cold War development of Russia and the EU. In the case of the former, the literature tends to converge around the idea that foreign policy developments should be primarily interpreted as a way of proofing the regime and deflecting attention away from domestic challenges (Cadier and Light 2015). Conversely, up until recently due to high levels of public support for stronger EU international actorness, foreign policy has been epiphenomenal to furthering European integration (Bickerton 2011). Hence, domestic issues have been mediated through the use of success in the international arena. In the same vein, structural pressures pertaining to traditional geopolitics are seen as key risks that affect the deepening and expansion of European integration, or the survival of the regime in the Kremlin or of Russia itself. The two actors' hybrid approaches to geopolitics are thus a manifestation of their efforts to secure their existence and deal with domestic and structural pressures, the same constraints that underlie their respective identity crises. Moreover, these hybrid approaches privilege solving the identity crises of the two actors through adaptation to structural pressures based on their ontologies – rather than the mere promotion of power and interests beyond borders (as traditional geopolitics would have it). Internal coherence is coupled with the need to display authenticity in the international arena, which results in a rather non-linear pattern of power projection. Ultimately, hybridity as a proxy to ensuring agency and autonomy allows the EU and Russia to have the option of choosing to act in a traditional geopolitical manner or framing their behaviour as authentic – in line with their hybrid identities.

Very often the EU and Russia have framed their power projection and subsequent policies as increasing autonomy for both the self and the other. While, traditional geopolitics underlies the zero-sum situations created by structural constraints, the EU and Russia's hybrid approaches have aimed to construct what are perceived as win-win situations.

In their shared neighbourhood, both Russia and the EU's power projection efforts have been characterised by oscillating levels of interests, commitment, and willingness. However, they have been framed by two different rationales, which stand in contrast to the key tenet of classical geopolitics that emphasises the promotion of material power for the sake of power and influence. For the EU, expanding European integration in the eastern neighbourhood is a proxy for achieving a sense of administrative control or even hegemony over the political and economic systems of the states in the region. By conditioning benefits on the adoption of various reforms aimed at long term transformations, the EU sets the boundaries of governmentality in the region (Ademmer, Delcour, and Wolczuk 2016). Similarly, Russia also aims to shape notions of governmentality, but in a looser, short term and obvious manner (Korosteleva 2016). It demands an abstract form of allegiance from the post-Soviet states, the terms of which seem to be ever shifting. The two forms of administrative hegemony, either loose or more precise in form, can be seen as a result of the Russia and the EU's hybrid identities, coupled with the need to deal with structural constraints pertaining to traditional geopolitics.

Conclusions: hybridity and the conflict cooperation dichotomy

In contrast to hybrid geopolitics, classical forms are accompanied by rather fixed identities and structural constraints. To that extent, the preeminence of traditional geopolitics would indeed imply tilting the conflict and cooperation dichotomy decisively towards competition (and conflict). Moreover, the current perception of the rise of more traditional forms of geopolitics has also been fuelled by the intentionality of two international actors. As a strategy for enhancing autonomy, support for the perception of the rise of traditional geopolitics acts as a self-fulfilling prophecy. On the one hand, classical geopolitics allows Russia and the EU to frame each other as existential threats and deflect attention from internal issues. For the Kremlin, this has informed the "besieged fortresses" narrative, whereby Russia is subject to a multitude of hostile forces primarily influenced by structural constraints pertaining to traditional geopolitics. The Putin regime has employed this narrative in order to portray itself as the only one capable of ensuring Russia's survival and agency (Tsygankov 2012). Conversely, the EU has had to come to terms with the fact that the neighbourhood and the international arena is not as conducive to its leadership as it imagined in the 15-year buildup to EU enlargement. The perception of the rise of classical geopolitics, in this case, has allowed the EU to enter a process of revision and renewal, which focuses on principled pragmatism and the need to enhance resilience. On the other hand, the focus on this perception prescribes the inability of the EU and Russia to address geopolitical tensions. This range of perceptions – even though, as the article showed, do not capturing the complexity of hybrid geopolitical evolutions –, prompts policy responses to the structural constraints that underlie traditional geopolitics. The perception of the rise of traditional forms of geopolitics is further magnified, which seems to decisively tilt the dichotomy towards conflict over cooperation.

The perception of the emerging role of classical geopolitics is also predicated on the way the hybrid identities of the EU and Russia have been constructed. This indeed seems to have tilted the dichotomy towards conflict, but the focus on classical geopolitics should be seen as a process of othering on the part of the EU and Russia, as well as a strategy focused on gaining autonomy. Mutual exclusiveness is thus a strategy for the EU and for Russia to address their identity crises that both inform and are informed by their hybridity. Each actors perceives the other as embodying [and implementing] classical geopolitics and each with the menacing manner that accompanies these ideological functions. If we were to take these processes of othering at face value, structural constraints pertaining to traditional geopolitics would point to fixed identities, irreconcilable and politicised misunderstandings, and power imbalances. On the contrary, hybrid approaches to geopolitics entail greater flexibility (as well as the concept of fluid symbolic boundaries developed in the introduction to the special issue), due to the unsettled nature of Russia and the EU's identities in world politics. In their shared neighbourhood, hybrid geopolitics takes the form of the strategies employed by the two actors to project power in order to achieve administrative authority or hegemony and enhance their autonomy. These strategies may, in turn, help them avoid the medium- to long-term zero-sum situations that would allow the conflict cooperation dichotomy to persist. It also paves the way for future studies to explore the ways in which hybrid geopolitics can lead to less mutually exclusive identities and approaches in their shared neighbourhood.

Notes

1. While there are diverging views among the member states regarding Russia, during the last five years the EU has shown a significant degree of unity (among the member states) in relation to policy towards Moscow (Forsberg and Haukkala 2016). The article focuses on the approach taken up by EU's institutions, as supported by the member states. In the midst of the cacophony of views among member states regarding Russia, the scholarship points to the fact that a coherent EU approach towards Moscow can be identified (Rieker and Gjerde 2016).
2. In this article, traditional and classical geopolitics are used interchangeably. In a similar fashion, the term state is used to address the approaches to geopolitics of both countries and international actors (such as the EU).
3. The 2008 Georgian-Russia war can indeed be also be seen as a crisis that highlighted the role of geopolitics in relations between Russia and the EU, but at that time the Union was still bent on exercising ambitious actorness in the neighbourhood and around the world, and in this process ignored the structural geopolitical causes and effects of the war (Nitoiu 2011) – even though some of the new member states like Poland were sounding alarm bells (Baun and Marek 2013).
4. What is noteworthy here is the fact that Russia and the EU have recognised their distinct approaches to neighbourhood, and official documents often include the shared neighbourhood as a key geographical space where their values and interests should intersect and be made manifest (Putin 2009; 2013a; 2013b; European External Action Service 2011; Füle 2014; EU High Representative for Foreign Affairs and Security Policy 2011). Thus, the post-Soviet space is subject to three distinct region-building strategies from the EU and Russia, all of which place geography at the core: i.e., the EU's eastern neighbourhood that is inclined to pursue European integration, the post-Soviet space which forms [or should form?] the backbone of Russia's Eurasian integration aspirations, or the so-called shared neighbourhood where the EU and Russia achieve complementarity.

Disclosure statement

No potential conflict of interest was reported by the author(s).

References

Ademmer, Esther, Laure Delcour, and Kataryna Wolczuk. 2016. "Beyond Geopolitics: Exploring the Impact of the EU and Russia in the 'Contested Neighborhood." *Eurasian Geography and Economics* 57 (1): 1–18.

Allen, David, and Michael Smith. 1990. "Western Europe's Presence in the Contemporary International Arena." *Review of International Studies* 16 (1): 19–37.

Averre, Derek. 2016. "The Ukraine Conflict: Russia's Challenge to European Security Governance." *Europe-Asia Studies* 68 (4): 699–725.

Baranovsky, Vladimir. 2000. "Russia: A Part of Europe or Apart from Europe?" *International Affairs* 76 (3): 443–458.

Barkanov, Boris. 2015. "Crisis in Ukraine: Clash of Civilizations or Geopolitics?" In *Power, Politics and Confrontation in Eurasia: Foreign Policy in a Contested Region*, edited by Roger E. Kanet, and Matthew Sussex, 210–239. Basingstoke: Palgrave Macmillan.

Baun, Michael, and Dan Marek, eds. 2013. *The New Member States and the European Union: Foreign Policy and Europeanization*. New York: Routledge.

Bekus, Nelly. 2017. "Constructed 'Otherness'? Poland and the Geopolitics of Contested Belarusian Identity." *Europe-Asia Studies* 69 (2): 242–261.

Bickerton, Chris J. 2011. *European Union Foreign Policy: From Effectiveness to Functionality*. Basingstoke: Palgrave Macmillan.

Braghiroli, Stefano, and Andrey Makarychev. 2016. "Russia and Its Supporters in Europe: Trans-Ideology à La Carte?" *Southeast European and Black Sea Studies* 0 (0): 1–21.

Bull, Hedley. 1982. "Civilian Power Europe: A Contradiction in Terms?" *JCMS: Journal of Common Market Studies* 21 (2): 149–170.

Cadier, David, ed. 2014. *The Geopolitics of Eurasian Economic Integration*. London: LSE IDEAS. Accessed 15 May. http://www.lse.ac.uk/IDEAS/publications/reports/SR019.aspx.

Cadier, David. 2019. "The Geopoliticisation of the EU's Eastern Partnership." *Geopolitics* 24 (1): 71–99.

Cadier, David, and Margot Light, eds. 2015. *Russia's Foreign Policy: Ideas, Domestic Politics and External Relations*. New York, NY: Palgrave Macmillan.

Casier, Tom. 2016. "Great Game or Great Confusion: The Geopolitical Understanding of EU-Russia Energy Relations." *Geopolitics* 21 (4): 763–778.

Casier, Tom. 2017. "The Different Faces of Power in European Union–Russia Relations." *Cooperation and Conflict* 53 (1): 101–117.

Chaban, Natalia, Ole Elgström, and Olga Gulyaeva. 2017. "Russian Images of the European Union: Before and After Maidan." *Foreign Policy Analysis* 13 (2): 480–499.

Chaban, Natalia, Ole Elgström, Serena Kelly, and Lai Suet Yi. 2013. "Images of the EU Beyond Its Borders: Issue-Specific and Regional Perceptions of European Union Power and Leadership." *JCMS: Journal of Common Market Studies* 51 (3): 433–451.

Chebakova, Anastasia, Olga Gulyaeva, Tatsiana Shaban, and Amy Verdun. 2017. "Russia and EU Cooperation in Energy Policy – Sending and Receiving Messages?" *Comparative European Politics* 15 (1): 45–63.

Cohen, Saul Bernard. 2014. *Geopolitics: The Geography of International Relations*. Lanham, MD: Rowman & Littlefield.

Crossley, Michele L. 2000. "Narrative Psychology, Trauma and the Study of Self/Identity." *Theory & Psychology* 10 (4): 527–546.

De Zutter, Elisabeth. 2010. "Normative Power Spotting: An Ontological and Methodological Appraisal." *Journal of European Public Policy* 17 (8): 1106–1127.

Diesen, Glenn. 2017. "The EU, Russia and the Manichean Trap." *Cambridge Review of International Affairs* 30 (2–3): 177–194. doi:10.1080/09557571.2017.1410099.

Duchene, Francois. 1972. "Europe's Role in World Peace." In *Europe Tomorrow: Sixteen Europeans Look Ahead*, edited by Richard J Mayne, 32–47. London: Fontana.

Duchene, Francois. 1973. "The European Community and the Uncertainties of Interdependence." In *A Nation Writ Large?: Foreign-Policy Problems before the European Community*, edited by Max Kohnstamm, 1–21. London: Wiley.

EU High Representative for Foreign Affairs and Security Policy. 2011. "Speech of High Representative Catherine Ashton on the EU-Russia Summit." A 513/11.

European Commission. 2015. "Review of the European Neighbourhood Policy." Accessed 15 May. http://eeas.europa.eu/enp/documents/2015/151118_joint-communication_review-of-the-enp_en.pdf.

European External Action Service. 2011. "EU-Russia Common Spaces: Progress Report 2010." Accessed 15 May.

European External Action Service. 2016. "Shared Vision, Common Action: A Stronger Europe." Accessed 15 May. https://eeas.europa.eu/top_stories/pdf/eugs_review_web.pdf.

European Parliament. 2017. "Russia's and the EU's Sanctions: Economic and Trade Effects, Compliance and the Way Forward." Accessed 15 May. http://www.europarl.europa.eu/RegData/etudes/STUD/2017/603847/EXPO_STU(2017)603847_EN.pdf.

Feklyunina, Valentina. 2015. "Soft Power and Identity: Russia, Ukraine and the 'Russian World(s)." *European Journal of International Relations* 22 (4): 773–796.

Flint, Colin. 2012. *Introduction to Geopolitics*. Abingdon: Routledge.

Forsberg, Tuomas. 2019. "Explaining Russian Foreign Policy towards the EU through Contrasts." *International Politics* 56 (6): 762–777.

Forsberg, Tuomas, and Hiski Haukkala. 2016. *The European Union and Russia*. Basingstoke: Palgrave Macmillan.

Foxall, Andrew. 2019. "From Evropa to Gayropa: A Critical Geopolitics of the European Union as Seen from Russia." *Geopolitics* 24 (1): 174–193.

Füle, Štefan. 2014. "Russian Pressure on Eastern Partnership Countries, Destabilisation of Eastern Ukraine." http://europa.eu/rapid/press-release_SPEECH-10-706_en.htm?locale=en.

Ganzle, Stefan. 2007. "The EU's Policy toward Russia: Extending Governance Beyond Borders?" In *The Boundaries of EU Enlargement: Finding a Place for Neighbours*, edited by Joan DeBardeleben, 53–69. New York: Palgrave Macmillan.

Gehring, Thomas, Kevin Urbanski, and Sebastian Oberthür. 2017. "The European Union as an Inadvertent Great Power: EU Actorness and the Ukraine Crisis." *JCMS: Journal of Common Market Studies* 55 (4): 727–743.

Grygiel, Jakub. 2015. "The Geopolitics of Europe: Europe's Illusions and Delusions." *Orbis* 59 (4): 505–517.

Hardacre, Alan, and Michael Smith. 2009. "The EU and the Diplomacy of Complex Interregionalism." *The Hague Journal of Diplomacy* 4 (2): 167–188.

Haukkala, Hiski. 2015. "From Cooperative to Contested Europe? The Conflict in Ukraine as a Culmination of a Long-Term Crisis in EU–Russia Relations." *Journal of Contemporary European Studies* 0 (0): 1–16.

Hedberg, Masha. 2018. "The Target Strikes Back: Explaining Countersanctions and Russia's Strategy of Differentiated Retaliatifelkay on." *Post-Soviet Affairs* 34 (1): 35–54.

Holslag, Jonathan. 2016. "Hedging the Hard Way: Russia's Response to World Disorder." *Global Affairs* 2 (2): 165–176.

Howorth, Jolyon. 2016. "EU Global Strategy in a Changing World: Brussels' Approach to the Emerging Powers." *Contemporary Security Policy* 37 (3): 389–401.

Hutchison, Emma. 2010. "Trauma and the Politics of Emotions: Constituting Identity, Security and Community after the Bali Bombing." *International Relations* 24 (1): 65–86.

Hyde-Price, Adrian. 2006. "'Normative' Power Europe: A Realist Critique." *Journal of European Public Policy* 13 (2): 217–234.

Juncos, Ana E. 2017. "Resilience as the New EU Foreign Policy Paradigm: A Pragmatist Turn?" *European Security* 26 (1): 1–18.

Kelly, Phil. 2016. *Classical Geopolitics: A New Analytical Model.* Stanford, CA: Stanford University Press.

Korosteleva, Elena A. 2016. "The European Union, Russia and the Eastern Region: The Analytics of Government for Sustainable Cohabitation." *Cooperation and Conflict* 51 (3): 365–383.

Larson, Deborah Welch, and Alexei Shevchenko. 2010. "Status Seekers: Chinese and Russian Responses to U.S. Primacy." *International Security* 34 (4): 63–95.

Laruelle, Marlene. 2015. *The 'Russian World' Russia's Soft: Power and Geopolitical Imagination.* Washington, D.C.: The Center on Global Interests (CGI).

Lavrov, Sergey. 2016. "Russia's Foreign Policy: Historical Background." *Russia in Global Affairs*, March. Accessed 15 May. http://www.mid.ru/en/foreign_policy/news/-/asset_publisher/cKNonkJE02Bw/content/id/2124391.

Malcolm, Neil. 1989. "The 'Common European Home' and Soviet European Policy." *International Affairs* 65 (4): 659–676.

Manners, Ian. 2008. "The Normative Power of the EU in a Globalized World." In *EU Foreign Policy in a Globalized World: Normative Power and Social Preferences*, edited by Zaki Laïdi, 23–37. London: Routledge.

Morgherini, Federica. 2017. "Speech by Federica Mogherini at the Munich Security Conference." Accessed 15 May. https://eeas.europa.eu/headquarters/headquarters-homepage_en/20832/Speech%20by%20Federica%20Mogherini%20at%20the%20Munich%20Security%20Conference.

Morozov, Viachestlav. 2015. *Russia's Postcolonial Identity - A Subaltern Empire in a Eurocentric World.* London: Palgrave Macmillan.

Neumann, Iver B. 2016. "Russia's Europe, 1991–2016: Inferiority to Superiority." *International Affairs* 92 (6): 1381–1399.

Nitoiu, Cristian. 2011. "Reconceptualizing 'Cooperation' in EU-Russia Relations." *Perspectives on European Politics and Society* 12 (4): 462–476.

Nitoiu, Cristian. 2014. "EU–Russia Relations: Between Conflict and Cooperation." *International Politics* 51 (2): 234–253.

Nitoiu, Cristian. 2017. "European and Eurasian Integration: Competition and Cooperation in the Post-Soviet Space." *Journal of European Integration* 39 (4): 469–475.

Nordin, Astrid H. M., and Graham M. Smith. 2019. "Relating Self and Other in Chinese and Western Thought." *Cambridge Review of International Affairs* 32 (5): 636–653.

Omelicheva, Mariya Y. 2016. "Critical Geopolitics on Russian Foreign Policy: Uncovering the Imagery of Moscow's International Relations." *International Politics* 53 (6): 708–726.

Oskanian, Kevork K. 2018. "A Very Ambiguous Empire: Russia's Hybrid Exceptionalism." *Europe-Asia Studies* 70 (1): 26–52.

Pänke, Julian. 2019. "Liberal Empire, Geopolitics and EU Strategy: Norms and Interests in European Foreign Policy Making." *Geopolitics* 24 (1): 100–123.

Prodi, Romano. 2004. "Russia and the European Union: Enduring Ties, Widening Horizons." Accessed 15 May. http://europa.eu/rapid/press-release_SPEECH-04-198_en.htm.

Putin, Vladimir. 2009. "The Draft of the European Security Treaty." Accessed 15 May. http://en.kremlin.ru/events/president/news/6152.

Putin, Vladimir. 2013a. "Meeting of the Valdai International Discussion Club." Accessed 15 May. http://russialist.org/transcript-putin-at-meeting-of-the-valdai-international-discussion-club-partial-transcript/.

Putin, Vladimir. 2013b. "The Foreign Policy Concept of the Russian Federation." Accessed 15 May. http://www.mid.ru/en/foreign_policy/official_documents/-/asset_publisher/CptICkB6BZ29/content/id/122186.

Raik, Kristi. 2016. "Liberalism and Geopolitics in EU–Russia Relations: Rereading the 'Baltic Factor." *European Security* 25 (2): 237–255.

Raik, Kristi, and Ruxandra Lupu Dinesen. 2015. "The European Union and Upheavals in Its Neighborhood: A Force for Stability?" *International Journal of Public Administration* 38 (12): 902–914.

Rak, Joanna. 2017. "Russia, 'Near Abroad', and the West: Struggling with the Research Field of Geopolitical Cultures." *Geopolitics* 22 (4): 984–990.

Rieker, Pernille, and Kristian Lundby Gjerde. 2016. "The EU, Russia and the Potential for Dialogue – Different Readings of the Crisis in Ukraine." *European Security* 25 (3): 304–325.

Risse-Kappen, Thomas. 1996. "Exploring the Nature of the Beast: International Relations Theory and Comparative Policy Analysis Meet the European Union." *JCMS: Journal of Common Market Studies* 34 (1): 53–80.

Romanova, Tatiana. 2018. "Russia's Neorevisionist Challenge to the Liberal International Order." *The International Spectator* 53 (1): 76–91.

Sakwa, Richard. 2018. "One Europe or None? Monism, Involution and Relations with Russia." *Europe-Asia Studies* 70 (10): 1656–1667.

Samokhvalov, Vsevolod. 2018. "Russia and Its Shared Neighbourhoods: A Comparative Analysis of Russia-EU and Russia-China Relations in the EU's Eastern Neighbourhood and Central Asia." *Contemporary Politics* 24 (1): 30–45.

Smith, Michael. 2003. "The Framing of European Foreign and Security Policy: Towards a Post-Modern Policy Framework?" *Journal of European Public Policy* 10 (4): 556–575.

Smith, Michael E. 2016. "Implementing the Global Strategy Where It Matters Most: The EU's Credibility Deficit and the European Neighbourhood." *Contemporary Security Policy* 37 (3): 446–460.

Smith, Michael H., and Richard Youngs. 2018. "The EU and the Global Order: Contingent Liberalism." *The International Spectator* 53 (1): 45–56.

Tsygankov, Andrei P. 2012. *Russia and the West from Alexander to Putin: Honor in International Relations*. Cambridge: Cambridge University Press.

Tsygankov, Andrei P. 2013. *Russia's Foreign Policy: Change and Continuity in National Identity*. 3rd ed. Lanham, Maryland: Rowman & Littlefield Publishers.

Tsygankov, Andrei P. 2014. "The Frustrating Partnership: Honor, Status, and Emotions in Russia's Discourses of the West." *Communist and Post-Communist Studies* 47 (3–4): 345–354.

Wigell, Mikael, and Antto Vihma. 2016. "Geopolitics Versus Geoeconomics: The Case of Russia's Geostrategy and Its Effects on the EU." *International Affairs* 92 (3): 605–627.

Youngs, Richard. 2017. *Europe's Eastern Crisis: The Geopolitics of Asymmetry*. Cambridge: Cambridge University Press.

Zielonka, Jan. 2008. "Europe as a Global Actor: Empire by Example?" *International Affairs* 84 (3): 471–484.

Kaliningrad: a dual shift in cooperation and conflict

Anna-Sophie Maass

ABSTRACT
Poland's accession to NATO in 1999 undermined Russian-NATO relations. A similar contestation occurred before the EU's eastern enlargement when the transit of Russians to and from Kaliningrad was a contentious topic in EU-Russian diplomacy. Currently Russia's deployment of missiles in Kaliningrad has become a security concern. This article argues that NATO's security concerns replaced EU-Russian contestation about visa liberalisation as the main source of conflict in their relationship. It demonstrates that the case of Kaliningrad reflects a dual shift from a contested to a *fluid* boundary in EU-Russian relations, and from a contested to a *solid* boundary in NATO-Russian relations.

Introduction

With the double eastern enlargement Kaliningrad became a contentious topic in both EU-Russian and NATO-Russian relations. Poland's accession to NATO in 1999 followed by Lithuania's in 2004 which coincided with their accession to the EU, resulted in the Russian exclave's encirclement by EU and NATO territory. At the time the military security situation was known to be problematic, as NATO was starting to be the object of strategic contestation by Russia. Regarding human transit, the inclusion of Poland and Lithuania in the Schengen area had a tangible impact for citizens travelling between Russia and Kaliningrad. Seeking to regulate transit the European Commission introduced facilitated transit documents which members of the Russian political elite condemned as infringements of the right of the free movement of persons (Maass 2017).

More than a decade after this denunciation, Kaliningrad is not a contentious issue in EU-Russian relations anymore. However, Russia's deployment of nuclear missiles in the exclave has intensified already existing security concerns for the US, NATO and the Baltic States. Russia's stationing of missiles and its suspension from its membership in the Consultative Group of the Treaty of Conventional Armed Forces in Europe signed in 1990 aimed at limiting weaponry (Tass 2015) are recent examples of lacking "checks and balances" in the European security system. According to Richard Sakwa, there was a "failure to create a mutually acceptable European security system" since the end of the Cold War (Kempster and Murphy 1994 in Sakwa 2015). This lacking post-Cold War security architecture was compounded by "systemic tensions" between Russia's and the West's political systems, "values issues, incompatible identities, struggles for hegemony, institutional inertia and differing visions of the future […]" (Sakwa 2015). The Ukraine crisis, the deployment of missiles in Kaliningrad and the open Ukrainian-Russian confrontation in the Sea of Azov in November 2018 fanned fears in Europe regarding the possibility of war.

This article examines Kaliningrad as a border-zone of contact where cooperation and conflict fluctuated between the EU, Russia and NATO in order to elucidate both the emergence and implications of the latest security threats stemming from the oblast. So far Kaliningrad as a border region resulting in shifts from EU-Russian to NATO-Russian contestation has not been assessed in academic literature. Anke Schmidt-Felzmann examined how Kaliningrad became sidelined on the agenda of EU-Russian relations after their initial cooperation in seeking to "prevent soft security threats stemming from the exclave of gaining an upper hand" (Schmidt-Felzmann 2018). In this vein, her article touches upon the EU-Russian diplomacy regarding Kaliningrad and is complemented by Grønbjerg's (2018) assessment of EU-Russian contestation over visa-free travel to and from the exclave. Therefore, Schmidt-Felzmann's and Grønbjerg's work complement the analysis of EU-Russian diplomacy over Kaliningrad addressed in the first section of this article. However, their work does not intend to explain the shift from EU-Russian tensions to NATO-Russian contested engagement over the exclave, which is at the core of this article. Other scholarly accounts on Kaliningrad assessed visa-free transit, such as Baxendale's assessment of the progress regarding EU-Russian discourse on Kaliningrad in 2001, Aalto's examination of EU-Russian cooperation "creating order to the Kaliningrad region" and Holtom's analysis of the transit of people between 2002 and 2004 (Holtom 2005, 45; Aalto 2002; Baxendale 2001). Domaniewski's and Studzińska's assessment of the Polish-Russian visa free agreement regarding Kaliningrad is complementary to Holtom's account (2016). By contrast, Vinokurov assesses "political and economic vulnerabilities" stemming from Kaliningrad's unique geographic location (2005). In a similar vein, Diener and Hagen contend that Kaliningrad faces several problems in the economy and in inter-state relations (2011).

This article exceeds the scope of the above-mentioned examinations. It analyses whether and how cooperation and conflict co-exist in Europe-Russian relations over Kaliningrad. It argues that EU-Russian contention over human transit in Kaliningrad in 2002 was replaced as the main flashpoint for conflict by NATO-Russian contestation over the stationing of Iskander missiles in the oblast. In seeking to examine the coexistence of cooperation and conflict and their divergent effects on EU-Russian and NATO-Russian relations in the border zone of Kaliningrad, this article adopts the same approach as the special issue by focusing on symbolic boundaries. The latter are understood as "principles of vision and division" (Bourdieu 1989) that distinguish the self from the other, the neighbour from the alien, and the allied from the enemy (Mérand and Dembinska, Introduction to this Special Issue).

The conceptual purpose of this article is to demonstrate that symbolic boundaries between Europe and Russia around Kaliningrad have evolved over the past two decades. Initially the symbolic boundaries that emerged from Kaliningrad's double encirclement in 2004 when the Baltic States joined the EU and NATO could be characterised as contested. Fifteen years later the symbolic boundary between the EU and Russia has become more fluid, implying that a distinction between the "self" and the "other" is in flux implying a transformation of this symbolic boundary. According to Domaniewski and Studzińska, "not all borders conform to a traditional or rationally coherent set of norms" or a "set of fixed policies applied to them", as was the case with Kaliningrad due to Russia's, the EU's and NATO's divergent political and military approaches in their engagement with the oblast (2016, 638). It is in light of these actors' engagement with Kaliningrad that the article argues that a dual shift regarding this boundary occurred, namely from a fluid boundary which manifested itself in an EU-Russian dialogue over visa-free travel to a solid boundary in NATO-Russian engagement. As a consequence no direct interaction took place between Russia and NATO but their interests over the oblast remained divergent. For Russia, Kaliningrad remained a prime location for certain military operations but for NATO the stationing of Russian nuclear missiles embodied a potential security threat.

The shift from Kaliningrad as a fluid boundary between the EU and Russia to a solid boundary between Russia and NATO was shaped by two factors. First, the end of the Cold War resulted in a new constellation of actors with varying political, economic and military clouts shaping their roles in contemporary international politics. Second, the EU's security policy had only recently been institutionalised by the launch of the post of the High Representative for the Common Foreign and Security Policy in 1999 (Maass 2017). As a result, the EU was not yet prepared to assume responsibilities due to its lacking capacities in security and defence policies. In order to address this shortcoming, the EU's enhanced cooperation with NATO was required to deal with increasing security concerns stemming from Kaliningrad as this paper will demonstrate. It assesses the actors' approaches towards these changing symbolic boundaries on the one hand and examines the resulting effect on Russia's engagement with the EU and NATO over Kaliningrad on the other hand.

The article begins with setting the conceptual framework before describing the EU-Russian dilemma over Kaliningrad. It continues with assessing the rationale underpinning Russia's deployment of missiles in Kaliningrad and the EU's and NATO's approaches on this issue. Foreign policy analysis with process tracing was chosen as a methodology to allow for an analysis exceeding domestic boundaries (Hill 2003) in light of the multiple actors whilst accounting for shifts over both issue areas and time. The analysis begins with the EU-Russian contestation over visa-free travel in 2004 before addressing the increasing confrontation between NATO and Russia in 2018.

The fluidity of evolving borders in the case of Kaliningrad

Prior to NATO's and the EU's eastward expansion, Kaliningrad was a contested boundary which was marked not only by strategic rivalry with NATO but also by the absence of an EU-Russian mutual agreement over transit regulations to and from the exclave. The result was a lengthy dispute over the issue which will be discussed in the following section. For the EU, this contested boundary evolved into a fluid boundary marked by temporary cooperation regarding transit regulations to and from Kaliningrad. But for NATO, there was a shift to a solid boundary characterised by the concern to maintain security in the aftermath of the stationing of Iskander missiles in Kaliningrad. A dialogue with Russia on the deployment of nuclear missiles remains highly contentious and is marked by polar-opposite views. However, the result of this lacking dialogue is not a direct but rather a frozen conflict which could boil to the surface as was exemplified by the open Ukrainian-Russian confrontation in the Sea of Azov in November 2018 (Maass 2019). Only time will tell whether cooperation or conflict will gain the upper hand in the fluid boundary in Kaliningrad in the medium to long-term. This assessment on the evolution of boundaries in the case of Kaliningrad shows that while some boundaries may become fluid and ease cooperation, this process can go alongside a hardening of other boundaries that leads to conflict as the following section on EU-Russian contestation over visa free travel in Kaliningrad will demonstrate.

The EU-Russian diplomacy on Kaliningrad

For almost two decades, Kaliningrad was on the agenda of EU-Russian relations to varying extents. At the EU-Russia summit in autumn 1999 Prime Minister Vladimir Putin reiterated that Kaliningrad shall become a "pilot project" of EU-Russian cooperation, withstanding that an agreement safeguarding Kaliningrad's interests as part of the Russian Federation in light of the EU's eastern enlargement was to be concluded (Karabeshkin and Wellmann 2004, 25). However, such an agreement has not been adopted and is one of the main reasons why the idea of the pilot project did not materialise.

From a political point of view, the status of Kaliningrad as a pilot project could have resulted in a "reciprocal and open strategic partnership" between the EU and Russia. From an economic point of view, Kaliningrad's modernisation entails the application of "institutional, technical and social standards which are new for Russia but routine for the EU" (Karabeshkin and Wellmann 2004, 58). Karabeshkin and Wellmann denounce the idea of the pilot region as a "public relations activity, due to the lack of a concept supporting this idea accompanied by President Yeltsin's weakened support: The [idea of the pilot project reflected] […] Russia'[s] [willingness] for cooperation with the EU" whilst agreeing to add issues on their joint agenda which were previously considered as Russian "domestic affairs" (Karabeshkin and Wellmann 2004, 59).

About a year after the deliberations on this pilot region, a lengthy debate over Kaliningrad marked EU-Russian relations after Poland's and Lithuania's accession to the EU resulted in Kaliningrad's enclosure within EU territory. As a consequence residents wishing to travel between Kaliningrad and Russia had to cross EU territory. Poland's and Lithuania's accession to the Schengen zone required Russian citizens travelling to and from Kaliningrad to obtain visas given that they crossed an EU border. In an attempt to regulate this transit of people the European Commission introduced a facilitated transit document (FTD), which was comparable to a visa. Members of the Russian political elite directed vociferous condemnations against the EU claiming that this introduction of the FTDs was an infringement of the right of the free movement of persons (Maass 2017).

According to Forsberg and Haukkala, Russia sought to facilitate visa liberalisation with the EU. At the EU-Russia summit in St Petersburg in May 2003 visa liberalisation was mentioned as a "long-term perspective" (Forsberg and Haukkala 2016, 139). Despite European Commission President Romano Prodi's promise that this liberalisation could be implemented within five years no concrete date was set (Forsberg and Haukkala 2016). Five years later after the idea of the visa liberalisation was uttered, Russian Foreign Minister Sergei Lavrov expressed Russia's readiness for visa liberalisation, but the EU considered this to be an objective, which had to be met by a concrete schedule and a series of reforms by Russia. Several measures aimed at facilitating visa policies were implemented, such as the EU-Russian Visa Facilitation Agreement which entered into force in June 2007. This agreement also introduced "privileged categories" of citizens who could obtain visas by providing less documents supporting their application. The Visa Free Dialogue aimed at paving the way to visa-free short-term travel without implying an "automatic right for visa free travels" (Forsberg and Haukkala 2016, 141).

During the preparations for the Olympic winter games in Sochi in February 2014, Russia undertook a renewed attempt to achieve visa freedom. Lavrov stated that from a practical point of view the EU and Russia would be ready to implement visa liberalisation but regretted that the failure to introduce it was "symbolic, exemplify[ing] all the differences between the EU and Russia" (Forsberg and Haukkala 2016, 144). The EU's imposition of freezing of the visa free regime in March 2014 was among the first series of sanctions implemented against Russia after its annexation of Crimea. It was the nail in the coffin of the dialogue on visa liberalisation (Forsberg and Haukkala 2016, 145).

Meanwhile the contentious issue of EU-Russian visa-free travel moved to cooperation on a bilateral level involving Poland and Russia. A "simplified border crossing procedure", which entered into force in July 2012 was a testing ground for visa-abolition between Russia and the EU (Tass 2012a). According to the Polish Foreign Minister Radoslaw Sikorski this agreement "will facilitate the speediest introduction of visa-free travel between Russia and the EU" (Tass 2012a). He reiterated his wish by stating that it was in Poland's "interest [...] that the Kaliningrad region [...] become[s] a gateway to Russia for the EU and a trade gateway to stronger ties with the [EU] for Russia" (Tass 2012a). About a month after the agreement's establishment about 2000 Polish citizens submitted applications for visa-free travel to Russia's exclave (Tass 2012b). Once a permission is granted, the applicant can stay in Kaliningrad up to ten days (Tass 2012b). Initially people living at the Polish-Russian border can travel freely for two years, a period which can be extended to five years for 20€ (Domaniewski and Studzińska 2016, 544). Even though border crossings quadrupled in 2012 as compared to 2009 (Domaniewski and Studzińska 2016, 545), Sikorski's aspirations were not fulfilled. On the contrary, in July 2016 the Polish government temporarily annulled this agreement, due to security issues linked to the NATO summit taking place in Warsaw and the Pope's stay in Krakow (European Parliament 2016).

The evolution of the Ukraine crisis and the related worsening of EU-Russia relations compounded this agreement's abolition (Domaniewski and Studzińska 2016, 543). When asked about the Polish government's intention to abrogate the agreement, an official working at the Russia division of the European External Action Service (EEAS) stated that the Service cannot comment on bilateral agreements with third states. This official explained that the opportunity for the agreement was created by the EU Local Border Traffic Regulation, an adapted regulation regarding external border crossings of Schengen states (European Commission 2019; Interview with official working at the Head of the Russia unit, European External Action Service (EEAS). Interview conducted via email, July 31, 2018). Despite this temporary suspension of the Polish-Russian border agreement, transit across this border continued; thus indicating that the deferral did not have wide-ranging negative repercussions (Zęgota 2018).

This assessment on visa-free travel demonstrated that the contentious EU-Russian dialogue was replaced by brief Polish-Russian cooperation on the matter. Thus, concerning the issue of transit, Kaliningrad was a contested boundary in EU-Russian relations yet a fluid boundary in the Polish-Russian visa-free dialogue. The emergence of the Ukraine conflict rendered the border of Kaliningrad rigid, bringing about security risks which are examined in the following section. It can be stated that from a geopolitical perspective, the EU-Russian boundary was rigid but that at the local level cooperation between Russia and Poland took place regarding visa free travel which reflects cooperation as a characteristic of a fluid boundary. The following section addresses Kaliningrad as a border shifting from a contested to a solid boundary in NATO-Russia relations.

The shifting discourse on Kaliningrad: from transit to security

The year 2015 witnessed a shift from EU-Russian contestation over transit regulations regarding Kaliningrad to security concerns in NATO-Russian relations. This shift was shaped by Russia's deployment of missiles in Kaliningrad. As a consequence, NATO as well as Lithuania which shares a border with Kaliningrad became increasingly concerned about security threats stemming from the exclave. This section examines the evolution of these concerns.

Kaliningrad had military importance for Russia as the base for the Russian Navy's Baltic Fleet. The militarisation of the region was perceived as an obstacle to foreign direct investment (Karabeshkin and Wellmann 2004, 75). In a different vein, Vladimir Yegorov, former Commander in Chief of the Baltic Fleet supported Kaliningrad's militarisation of the Russian enclave. Kaliningrad, he argued, "plays an important role in ensuring Russian national interest in the Baltic and in Europe, as well as in constituting an element of European security. The NATO enlargement to the East further strengthens this role" (Karabeshkin and Wellmann 2004).

In contrast with Yegorov, Chris Donnelly, former special adviser for Central and Eastern European Affairs at NATO dismissed security concerns of Kaliningrad. He stated that Kaliningrad

> no longer features as a classic security concern […]. The fundamental change in East–West relations may not have resulted in perfectly harmonious relations between the West and Russia but it has completely removed any fear in the West of military confrontations with Russia. Russia is no longer seen as a threat. […] [T]his has changed the perception of Kaliningrad. (Donnelly in Baxendale, Dewar, and Gowan 2000, 215)

In light of the demilitarisation of Kaliningrad by reducing "serving officers" stationed in the Russian exclave, Donnelly stated in 2000 that there "is no sense at all of the military establishment now being a threat, either to neighbouring states or to the existing social order in Kaliningrad" (Baxendale, Dewar, and Gowan 2000, 217). Donnelly's assessment of the reduced security risks stemming from Kaliningrad was legitimate at the time. However, over a decade and a half after his assessment there was a threat perception originating from Kaliningrad due to two reasons.

First, the large-scale military exercises Russia increasingly carried out in its exclave since 2013 became a security concern for the EU and NATO. It was estimated that 9000 soldiers, 55 navy ships and all military aircrafts were deployed in a military drill in 2015 (The Economist 2015). The Alliance's Secretary General Stoltenberg acknowledged that NATO has been enhancing its "intelligence and better situational awareness" over the past years (NATO 2018a) and asserted that NATO will "defend all allies against any threat" (NATO 2018b).

Second, the deployment of missile Iskander M in Kaliningrad in October 2016 increased fears about security threats stemming from this Russian oblast. This missile has the capacity of reaching up to 500 km, thus being able to target European capitals such as

Riga, Vilnius, Tallinn, Stockholm, Berlin or Warsaw (Sukhankin 2017). These ten Iskander missiles and the most extensive military exercises Russia carried out with Kaliningrad and Belarus since the end of the Cold War poses a direct threat to NATO and the EU. These drills involved about 100.000 personnel and contributed to an increased threat perception for Lithuania (MacAskill 2017). About two weeks after Ukraine's abstention from signing an Association Agreement (AA) with the EU in November 2013, Lithuania's President Dalia Grybauskaite stated that "Russia for us is a neighbour that continues to exploit its influence: through its energy policy, through cyber-attacks, by corrupting our political system and exerting influence on our media" (BBC Monitoring Europe 2013). In April 2015 at an annual security conference taking place in Tallinn, NATO officials and heads of states of the Baltic States discussed the potential threats emanating from Russia, which manifested itself in inter alia flights of military planes in the Baltic airspace. Representatives at the conference were blunt about the Baltic States being on the "front line" since the emergence of the Ukraine crisis, the lacking post-Cold War security architecture whilst acknowledging that Russia posed the biggest threat to security since the end of the Second World War (Rashid 2015).

After the deployment of Iskander missiles in Kaliningrad in October 2016 the threat perceived by heads of states and government of the Baltic States increased. Grybauskaite stated that "the neighbour is starting to be aggressive and threatening in the geopolitical sense […] It is now […] important to speak about deescalating the situation so that it does not lead to very serious military conflicts" (Baltic News Service 2016). Lithuania's Foreign Minister Linas Linkevicus denounced the deployment of missiles of being in breach of international law due to the capacity of their range (Sims 2016). Russian Major General Igor Konashenkov dismissed these concerns and explained that this deployment was merely part of a "military exercise (Sims 2016) [which] is mobile [and] part of the plan of combat training [;] missile troops are engaged in training on a year-round basis covering great distances of the Russian territory in various ways: by air, by sea and under their own power" (Sims 2016).

The rationale for the deployment of missiles in the Russian oblast dates back to Dmitrii Medvedev's presidency. In his State of the Nation Address in November 2008 he explained that the stationing of Iskander was being primarily a response to NATO's deployment of warships in the Black Sea. Medvedev claimed that the increasing tensions in the Caucasus stemming from "the Georgian army's attack on Russian peace-keepers" which became widely known as the Russian-Georgian war in August 2008, was used as a "pretext" to undertake this deployment of warships and bring American anti-missile systems to Europe (Medvedev 2008). These developments "forces Russia to take measures in response" (Medvedev 2008). At the same time, he warned that they "destabilised the foundations of the world order" (Medvedev 2008). In this context Medvedev refers to measures Russia will undertake to counter "persistent and consistent attempts of the current American administration to install new elements of a global missile defence system in Europe" (Medvedev 2008). Medvedev stated that in order to "neutralise the missile defence system Iskander missiles will be deployed in Kaliningrad" (Medvedev 2008). One of the reasons underpinning this US-Russian contention over missiles was the US' decision in 2001 to abrogate the Anti-Ballistic Missile Treaty. The rationale of this Treaty signed with the Soviet Union in 1972 was to restrict the US and Soviet Union's missile defence to two to protect the capital and the intercontinental ballistic missile launch area (US Department of State).

Medvedev's explanation regarding the motivation for the deployment of Iskander missiles remained a narrative of Putin's third term as president. Dimitry Peskov, a spokesman for Putin, warned that Iskander could be deployed in response to the US positioning of its nuclear weapons in Germany. In this vein, he alluded to a US-German agreement regarding the eventual launch of US nuclear missiles in the event of an attack by Russia on Europe (The Wall Street Journal 2019). This US-German agreement developed in the context of the US' decision to withdraw from the Intermediate-Range Nuclear Forces Treaty (INF) signed between the US and Russia in 1987. This treaty abolished missiles on land in Europe travelling between 500 and 5500 km. According to Peskov, these US plans were a "serious [step] towards escalation of tensions on the European continent. [...] Hence, Russia will naturally have to take countermoves [and] countermeasures for restoring this strategic balance and parity" (The Times 2015). These developments exemplify the scope of US-Russian tensions on the issue of nuclear disarmament.

Russia's and the US' mutual accusations about breaching the INF Treaty do not indicate potential for the development of an emerging cooperative dialogue but instead reflect a contested boundary. On 24 October 2018 President Putin stated that Russia would respond to the stationing of such American missiles with counter-measures (Zeit Online 2018). The development of missile 9M729, which exceeds the limit of the accepted range is considered to be in breach of the treaty (Zeit Online 2018). President Putin, however, stated that the US had no evidence to proof this contractual violation. In what can be considered a way to distract from accusations against Russia, he accused the US government of having established missile defense systems in Poland and Romania as well as the use of drones which fall under obligations of the treaty (Zeit Online 2018).

In addition to the US-Russian tension over the INF, signs of confrontation between Russia and NATO emerged in February 2015. A Russian fighter jet buzzed an US military jet over the Baltic Sea "veering off after coming within twenty feet of causing a mid-air collision" (Rashid 2015). The actual collision could have resulted in NATO's military response. Since the emergence of the Ukraine crisis, the frequency of encounters between Russian and US military jets has increased mainly over the Baltic Sea; thus, increasing risks of military confrontation between Russia and NATO. The presence of Russian fighter jets in Kaliningrad enables a rapid take-off, not allowing the Baltic States sufficient time to prepare for an eventual retaliation. At a time of lingering EU-Russian confrontation over Ukraine, people in the Baltic States are not "frightened" by a "war by design but by accident"; the likelihood of this is being increased by the fact that the electronic transponders which are able to track planes in Russian military jets are usually turned off (Rashid 2015).

The lack of trust in Russian-NATO relations is also reflected in the latest revision of Russia's former Military Doctrine published in July 2015. It refers to NATO's "danger" to Russia (Oliker 2015). The "build-up of the power potential of NATO and vesting the alliance with global functions carried out in violation of the rules of international law, bringing the military infrastructure of NATO member countries near the borders of [Russia], including further expansion of the alliance" is listed under "main external military risks" [confronting] Russia (Military Doctrine of the Russian Federation 2015). In contrast to NATO, the EU is mentioned only once in this military doctrine. In the section referring to Russia's strategies of preventing military conflict, the doctrine states that "equitable dialogue on European security issues with the European Union and NATO" should be maintained (Military Doctrine of the Russian Federation 2015). However, in practice a dialogue between NATO, Russia and the EU on European security has been difficult due to Russia's and the US' conflicting approaches as exemplified by Russia's stance towards the INF.

The level of hostility in Russian-NATO relations had been previously expressed by Russian Foreign Minister Lavrov. In 2014 in an interview with France 24 he was asked whether Russia intended to suspend ties with NATO, Lavrov asserted that "[w]e don't need to do this because NATO did it for us. [...] They have cut practically all ties between the Alliance and Russia" (Tass 2014). This denunciation of Russian-NATO relations is illustrative of the intensity of the crisis in their relationship. Lavrov's assessment is a reminder of the statement of his predecessor Igor Ivanov, who declared in 1999, whilst NATO was bombing Russia's ally Serbia that "at present Russia's relations with NATO are suspended, but those with the EU continue with an intensive dialogue" (Shevtsov 1999). In 1999 Russian policy makers perceived NATO as an aggressor, whilst the EU was perceived as a benign actor (Maass 2017). This change of perception is indicative of the shift of the zones of confrontation between the EU and Russia on the one hand and Russia and NATO on the other hand.

The prevalence of conflict over cooperation in NATO-Russian relations is shaped by the actors' perceived security threats stemming from Kaliningrad. The shift of EU-Russian contestation over transit regulations to NATO's security concerns in the case of Kaliningrad demonstrates a transformation of symbolic boundaries. The symbolic boundary in EU-Russian relations moved from a contested boundary over transit regulations to a fluid boundary where cooperation over this regulation can take place as exemplified by the Polish-Russian agreement. The symbolic boundary in NATO-Russian relations shifted from a contested to a solid boundary which was marked by lacking cooperation over security related aspects stemming from Kaliningrad. However, this lack of cooperation did not imply a perpetual open conflict between NATO and Russia but merely underlying tensions in the relationship. According to the Foreign Policy Concept of the Russian Federation of November 2016, there are more "systemic problems in the Euro-Atlantic region" which "accumulated over the last quarter of the century" (Russian Foreign Policy Concept 2016, 18). These problems are reflected in both NATO's and the EU's expansion in addition "with their refusal to begin implementation of political statements regarding the creation of a common European security and cooperation framework result[ing] in a serious crisis in the relations between Russia and the Western States" (Russian Foreign Policy Concept 2016).

A fragment of the mistrust at the core of Russia's relations with NATO was inherited by the impreciseness of the guidelines of cooperation as stated in the NATO-Russia Founding Act of 27 May 1997. This Act launched the Russian-NATO Permanent Joint Council guiding cooperation in peacekeeping, nuclear safety, air traffic control or missile defence, among others (Hill 2003, 136). According to William H. Hill, the Founding Act is a "political commitment, not a formal treaty obligation" (Hill 2003, 137). As a consequence there remains a certain flexibility when it comes to adhering to the Act's guidelines of mutual cooperation. This is also implied by the reference that deployments on the territory of new NATO members was dependent upon the "current and foreseeable security environment" (Hill 2003), a clause which had been implemented despite US Secretary of State Christopher's assurance at the North Atlantic Council meeting in December 1996 that the Alliance had "no need, no plans and no intentions of extending nuclear deployments in Europe" (Hill

2003). In addition to NATO's lacking commitment of this promise, its eastward expansion in 1999 was an additional aspect shaping the increasing level of mistrust in NATO-Russian relations before Russia's stationing of nuclear weapons in Kaliningrad further deteriorated the relationship.

Russia's deployment of missiles in Kaliningrad, continuous tensions in Russia's relations with NATO in the wake of the current deadlock in EU-Russian relations pose security risks for Europe in light of a lacking post-Cold War security architecture. According to Sakwa, "between 1989 and 2014 none of the fundamental issues of European security [...] were resolved, provoking the breakdown of 2014", a reference to the Ukraine crisis, the latest example of a security threat stemming from the EU's eastern neighbourhood (2017). Sakwa likens the Ukraine crisis to the "gravest challenge to world peace of our age" (2017). The lacking substitute for such a security architecture creates a vacuum which does not enable Russia, the EU, NATO and the US to create checks and balances at a time of increasing mistrust and enhanced threat perceptions in their relations. In light of Russia's increasingly confrontational relations with the Baltic States on the one hand and the US on the other hand, the responsibility for NATO in seeking to guarantee peace has increased since the deployment of Iskander missiles.

The EU's awareness of the urgency to maintain peace in light of the manifold security risks including the Ukraine crisis is reflected in its Global Strategy for the Common Foreign and Security Policy published in July 2016. In its section on European Security order, the strategy holds Russia accountable for the current threats to European security. According to the Strategy, "Russia's violation of international law and the destabilisation of Ukraine, on top of protracted conflicts in the wider Black Sea region have challenged the European Security order at its core" (EEAS 2016). Surprisingly, the Strategy does not refer to potential threats to security in the Baltic States and in countries within reach of the Iskander missiles. This could presumably be indicative of the fact that the EEAS does consider the presence of the missiles as a primary concern for NATO instead of for the EU due to the latter's inadequate security and defense capabilities.

The deployment of Iskander missiles reflects an ideological confrontation between Russia and NATO. The European Commission's White Paper on the Future of Europe published in March 2017 mentions the prospect of launching a European Defense Union by 2025, achieved through close cooperation with NATO (European Commission 2017). This intended collaboration cannot be merely traced back to the threats perceived from Kaliningrad but can be considered as a reflection of multiple security concerns the EU faces also in the context of the migration crisis, the struggle against sources of terrorism, continuing conflicts in neighbouring states to its East and its South as well as increasing tensions in Russian-NATO relations.

A further evidence of Russian-NATO tensions is the fact that meetings of the NATO-Russia Council had not been taking place anymore for two years since Russia's annexation of Crimea. Upon its first re-convention on October 31 2018, NATO's Secretary General Jens Stoltenberg stated that NATO

> need[ed] to manage a difficult relationship with Russia, meaning that with more military presence [and] exercises, higher tensions, we need to make sure that we prevent incidents, accidents, misunderstanding, miscalculations and if they happen make sure that they don't get out of control. (NATO 2018a)

His assessment implies the possibility of an intensified conflict between NATO and Russia in the future, which is compounded by the US' and Russia's clash over the INF Treaty. On 2 February 2019 the US informed Russia that it will withdraw from the treaty within six months (US Department of State 2019). Russia retaliated by withdrawing from the treaty as well (New York Times 2019). According to Stoltenberg, the problem was that the deployment of "more and more new Russian missiles, missiles capable of carrying nuclear warheads [...] [had] put the INF treaty to jeopardy" (New York Times 2019). For decades the US' policies towards Russia have been shaped by numerous and vociferous pleas for compliance with this treaty and international law. Russia does respond with its own assessment of the situation, which was for instance reflected in the referendum in Crimea or its deployment of missiles in Kaliningrad. For the time being, a more reciprocal development in the form of dialogues on contentious issues in Russia's relations with the EU, the US and NATO is not in sight. As a consequence, there is no guarantee for the perseverance of cooperation over conflict in the short to medium-term which implies that further shifts in symbolic boundaries could take place.

Conclusion

On an empirical level, this article demonstrated that Kaliningrad has proven to be a case of several boundaries which shaped cooperation and conflict between the EU and Russia as well as between NATO and Russia between 2004 and now. EU-Russian diplomatic relations were tainted by a dispute over transit regulations of Russians to and from Kaliningrad since the exclave's inclusion into the EU's territory epitomised by Poland's and Lithuania's EU accession. This contestation was replaced by enhanced cooperation between Russia and the EU over the visa free regulation exemplified by the Polish-Russian transit agreement about a decade after the initial dispute over transit to and from the exclave. NATO-Russian relations, which had been strained by the alliance's eastward expansion in the 1990s, became more conflict-prone since the gradual increase of Russia's deployment of Iskander missiles in the exclave since 2013.

On a conceptual level, this article demonstrated that Kaliningrad mirrors a shift from a contested to a *fluid* boundary in EU-Russian relations. Simultaneously it also portrays the shift from a contested to a *solid* boundary in NATO-Russian relations. As a consequence of this shift, the relationship is more prone to conflict given the lack of a security architecture able to guarantee the prevalence of peace in light of the deployment of the Iskander missiles. This lacking security architecture is compounded with the increasing level of mistrust in Russian-NATO relations which became strained since both the Alliance's enlargement in the 1990s and its bombing of Kosovo in 1999. This prevalent conflict between NATO and Russia results in tensions at a time when EU-Russia relations already face an extensive crisis since the emergence of the Ukraine conflict.

The examination of the afore-mentioned divergent types of symbolic boundaries in the case of Kaliningrad demonstrates a fluctuation between fluid boundaries easing cooperation and the hardening of boundaries, which could facilitate conflict. The risk of the eruption of such a conflict is enhanced by a lacking post-Cold War security architecture apt at tackling the manifold security challenges at the core of EU-Russia and Russia-NATO relations. The result is a current frozen conflict in Russia's relations with the US, the EU and

NATO enhanced by Russia's demonstration of its military capacities in Kaliningrad. The exclave as a playing field where Russia, NATO and EU Member States come together is likely to be shaped by fluctuations between conflict and cooperation in the short to medium-term.

This article did not provide an exhaustive analysis of Kaliningrad as a border zone of cooperation and conflict between the EU, Russia and NATO. This multiplicity of actors reflects the "level of analysis" problem of foreign policy analysis requiring the need to transcend analytic shortcomings by exceeding domestic boundaries as a result of an overlap between the domestic and the international level (Hill 2003). The engagement of multiple actors in Kaliningrad makes this analysis very complex. Thus, future research needs to further examine the evolution of underlying tensions of NATO-Russian relations which were not extensively covered in this article due to evolving contentions of this relationship over issue areas and time. A wider understanding about divergent interests of actors in moments of cooperation or conflict with Kaliningrad would also need to include China's engagement in Kaliningrad, which is exemplified by Russian-Chinese military drills taking place since 2012 (Higgins 2017). The assessment of the rationale of these operations and its implications for potentially sustained Russian-Chinese cooperation lies beyond the scope of this article. However, potential implications of this cooperation on EU-Russian, US-Russian relations as well as on NATO-Russian relations will need to be assessed in the near future.

Disclosure statement

No potential conflict of interest was reported by the author(s).

References

Aalto, P. 2002. "A European Geopolitical Subject in the Making? EU, Russia and the Kaliningrad Question." *Geopolitics* 7 (3): 142–174. https://www.tandfonline.com/doi/abs/10.1080/714000977.
Baltic News Service. 2016. "Russia Demonstrates Aggression, Situation Shouldn't be Escalated – Lithuanian President." October 20.
Baxendale, J. 2001. "EU-Russia Relations: Is 2001 a Turning Point for Kaliningrad." *European Foreign Affairs Review* 6 (4): 437–464.
Baxendale, J., S. Dewar, and D. Gowan, eds. 2000. *The EU and Kaliningrad: Kaliningrad and the Impact of EU Enlargement*. London: Federal Trust for Education and Research.
BBC Monitoring Europe. 2013. "Political. Supplied by BBC Worldwide Monitoring. 'Lithuanian President Says Not Surprised by Russian Pressure on Ukraine'." December 3.
Bourdieu, P. 1989. "Social Space and Symbolic Power." *Sociological Theory* 79 (1): 14–25.
Diener, A., and J. Hagen. 2011. "Geopolitics of the Kaliningrad Exclave and Enclave: Russian and EU Perspectives." *Geopolitics* 52 (4): 567–592.
Domaniewski, S., and D. Studzińska. 2016. "The Small Border Traffic Zone Between Poland and Kaliningrad Region (Russia): The Impact of a Local Visa-Free Border Regime." *Geopolitics* 21 (3): 538–555. https://www.tandfonline.com/doi/abs/10.1080/14650045.2016.1176916.

European Commission. 2017. *White Paper on the Future of Europe – European Commission*. Accessed July 31, 2018. https://ec.europa.eu/commission/sites/betapolitical/files/white_paper_on_the_future_of_europe_en.pdf.

European Commission. 2019. *Migration and Home Affairs. Local border traffic regime*. https://ec.europa.eu/home-affairs/content/local-border-traffic-regime_en.

European External Action Service. 2016. *Shared Vision, Common Action, A Stronger Europe: Global Strategy for the European Union's Common Foreign and Security Policy*. Accessed February 22, 2018. https://europa.eu/globalstrategy/en/global-strategy-promote-citizens-interests.

European Parliament. 2016. *At a Glance. EU-Russia People-to-People Contacts*. Accessed May 14, 2019. http://www.europarl.europa.eu/RegData/etudes/ATAG/2016/595843/EPRS_ATA (2016)595843_EN.pdf.

Forsberg, T., and H. Haukkala. 2016. *The European Union and Russia*. The European Union Series. London: Palgrave Macmillan.

Grønbjerg, L. 2018. "Kaliningrad – a Danger Zone for EU-Russia Relations." In *Marketplace or Military Bastion? Kaliningrad Between Brussels and Moscow*. UI Paper. No. 3, edited by I. Oldberg. Published by the Swedish Institute for International Affairs. https://www.ui.se/globalassets/ui.se-eng/publications/ui-publications/2018/ui-paper-no.-3-2018.pdf.

Higgins, A. 2017. "China Holds Naval Drill in Baltic Sea with Russia." *The New York Times*, July 26.

Hill, C. 2003. *The Changing Politics of Foreign Policy*. New York: Palgrave Macmillan.

Holtom, P. 2005. "The Kaliningrad Test in EU-Russia Relations." *Perspectives on European Politics and Society* 6 (1): 31–54.

Karabeshkin, L., and C. Wellmann. 2004. *The Russian Domestic Debate on Kaliningrad. Integrity, Identity and Economy*. Kieler Schriften zur Friedenswissenschaft. Band 11. New Brunswick: Transaction Publishers.

Kempster, N., and D. E. Murphy. 1994. "Broader NATO May Bring "Cold Peace", Yeltsin Warns: Europe: Russian President accuses U.S. of Being Power Hungry. Speech Comes as Nations Finalize Nuclear Treaty." *Los Angeles Times*, December 6. Accessed April 5, 2015. http://articles.latimes.com/1994-12-06/news/mn-5629_1_cold-war.

Maass, A.-S. 2017. *EU-Russia Relations, 1999–2015. From Courtship to Confrontation*. London: Routledge.

Maass, A.-S. 2019. "From Vilnius to the Kerch Strait: Wide-Ranging Security Implications from the Ukraine Crisis." *European Politics and Society* 20 (5): 609–623. https://www.tandfonline.com/doi/full/10.1080/23745118.2019.1570667.

MacAskill, E. 2017. "Russia Readies for Huge Military Exercises as Tensions with West Simmer." *The Guardian*, August 24.

Military Doctrine of the Russian Federation. 2015. "The Embassy of the Russian Federation of the United Kingdom of Great Britain and Northern Ireland." Press Releases. Accessed July 25, 2018. https://rusemb.org.uk/press/2029.

NATO. 2018a. "Press Conference by NATO Secretary General Jens Stoltenberg Following the Morning Meeting of the North Atlantic Council (NAC) in Foreign Ministers' Session." April 27. Accessed July 30, 2018. https://www.nato.int/cps/en/natohq/opinions_154092.htm.

NATO. 2018b. "Press Conference by the NATO Secretary General Jens Stoltenberg at the Launch of His Annual Report for 2017." March 15. Accessed July 30, 2018. https://www.nato.int/cps/en/natohq/opinions_152678.htm.

New York Times. 2019. "Russia Pulls Out of I.N.F. Treaty in 'Symmetrical' Response to U.S. Move." Accessed May 14, 2019. https://www.nytimes.com/2019/02/02/world/europe/russia-inf-treaty.html.

Oliker, O. 2015. "Russia's Military Doctrine: Same as the Old Doctrine, Mostly." *Rand Corporation*. Accessed November 8, 2017. https://www.rand.org/blog/2015/01/russias-new-military-doctrine-same-as-the-old-doctrine.html.

Rashid, A. 2015. "Russia: Twenty Feet from War." *The New York Review of Books*, May 14. Accessed November 7, 2017. http://www.nybooks.com/daily/2015/05/14/russia-nato-twenty-feet-from-war/.

Sakwa, R. 2015. "Death of Europe? Continental Fates After Ukraine." *International Affairs* 91 (3): 553–579.

Sakwa, R. 2017. "The Ukraine Syndrome & Europe: Between Norms & Space." *The Soviet and Post-Soviet Review* 44 (1): 9–31.

Schmidt-Felzmann, A. 2018. "Kaliningrad in EU-Russia Relations – the Neglected Enclave by the Baltic Sea." In *Marketplace or Military Bastion? Kaliningrad Between Brussels and Moscow.* UI Paper. No. 3. 2018, edited by I. Oldberg. Published by the Swedish Institute for International Affairs. https://www.ui.se/globalassets/ui.se-eng/publications/ui-publications/2018/ui-paper-no.-3-2018.pdf.

Shevtsov, N. 1999. "Vokrug konflikta. Evrosoyiuz – Eto ne NATO. Pul's planety. Trud." May 9.

Sims, A. 2016. "Poland 'Highly Concerned' After Russia Moves Nuclear-Capable Missiles into Kaliningrad; Estonia and Lithuania Who Have Ports on the Baltic Sea Have Also Protested the Move." *The Independent*, October 8.

State of the Nation Address by Russian President Dmitry Medvedev. 2008. November 5. Accessed May 13, 2019. https://www.c-span.org/video/?282252-1/russian-state-nation-address.

Sukhankin, S. 2017. *Kaliningrad: From Boom-Town to Battle Station.* European Council on Foreign Relations. Accessed May 12, 2019. http://www.ecfr.eu/article/commentary_kaliningrad_from_boomtown_to_battle_station_7256.

Tass. Russian News Agency. 2012a. "Poland to Resume Accepting Applications for Visa-Free Border Crossing with RF." August 23.

Tass. Russian News Agency. 2012b. "Over 1000 Poles Get Permits for Visa-Free Access to Kaliningrad Region." August 27.

Tass. Russian News Agency. 2014. "Russia has Never Called NATO and Enemy – Lavrov/Updates." December 16.

Tass. Russian News Agency. 2015. "NATO Disappointed with Russia's Decision to Suspend Participation in CFE Consultative Group – Stoltenberg." March 11.

The Economist. 2015. "What Russia Wants. From Cold War to Hot War." February 12. Accessed November 7, 2017. https://www.economist.com/news/briefing/21643220-russias-aggression-ukraine-part-broader-and-more-dangerous-confrontation.

The Foreign Policy Concept of the Russian Federation. 2016. *Approved by the President of the Russian Federation Vladimir Putin on November 30, 2016.* Accessed May 13, 2019. https://www.rusemb.org.uk/rp_insight/.

The Wall Street Journal. 2019. "In Germany, a Cold War Deal to Host U.S. Nuclear Weapons Is Now in Question." Accessed February 4, 2012. https://www.wsj.com/articles/in-germany-anger-at-trump-throws-cold-war-nuclear-pact-into-question-11549976449.

US Department of State. "Treaty Between the United States of America and The Union of Soviet Socialist Republics on The Limitation of Anti-Ballistic Missile Systems (ABM Treaty)." Accessed July 31, 2018. https://www.state.gov/t/avc/trty/101888.htm.

US Department of State. 2019. "U.S. Intent to Withdraw from the INF Treaty." February 2. Accessed May 14, 2019. https://www.state.gov/secretary/remarks/2019/02/288722.htm.

Vinokurov, E. Y. 2005. "The Enclave Specific Vulnerability of Kaliningrad." In *Kaliningrad 2020. Its Future Competitiveness and Role in the Baltic Sea Economic Region,* edited by K. Liuhto. University of Turku. Accessed July 27, 2018. http://www.utu.fi/fi/yksikot/tse/yksikot/PEI/raportit-ja-tietopaketit/Documents/Liuhto_72005.pdf#page=58.

Zęgota, K. 2018. "The Kaliningrad Oblast: An Area of Cooperation or Conflict of Interests Between the Russian Federation and the West." In *Marketplace or Military Bastion? Kaliningrad Between Brussels and Moscow.* UI Paper. No. 3. 2018, edited by I. Oldberg. Published by the Swedish Institute for International Affairs. https://www.ui.se/globalassets/ui.se-eng/publications/ui-publications/2018/ui-paper-no.-3-2018.pdf.

Zeit Online. 2018. "Putin warnt vor neuem Wettrüsten." Accessed May 14, 2019. https://www.zeit.de/politik/ausland/2018-10/abruestungsvertrag-russland-wladimir-putin-inf-europa-wettruesten.

Not on speaking terms, but business as usual: the ambiguous coexistence of conflict and cooperation in EU-Russia relations

Tom Casier

ABSTRACT
Since the crisis over Ukraine erupted, relations between Russia and the EU have been characterised by the coexistence of competition and cooperation. How can we explain this ambiguity? First, a distinction is made between the multi-actor structure of low politics versus polarised discursive positions in high politics. Construal-Level Theory is invoked to explain how low politics is characterised by concrete images, while high politics is characterised by abstract, ideologised images. Second, the article considers the interaction between both levels and argues that the contagion from more cooperative low level practices to the defrosting of EU-Russia relations is unlikely.

Introduction

Since the Ukraine crisis erupted in late 2013, early 2014, the EU and Russia have found themselves in the deepest crisis since the end of the Cold War. Their Strategic Partnership was suspended. Sanctions and counter-sanctions get renewed on a regular basis. Rhetoric on both sides is often sharp. Yet, in different specific policy fields, business seems to continue as usual. Trade has largely recovered. The import of natural gas has peaked. Educational exchanges still reach high levels. How can this ambivalence be explained? Why does business continue as usual, while Moscow and Brussels are not on speaking terms, at least not within an institutionalised setting like the Strategic Partnership?

To answer these questions, this article draws on the distinction between low and high politics. In low politics, relations are based on multi-actor structures with diffuse interests. High politics, on the other hand, are characterised by a limited number of actors and strong paradigmatic positioning. Construal-Level Theory is used to explain the latter: greater psychological distance at the level of high politics leads to more abstract, essentialised ideological mental representations of the other, its behaviour and intentions.

Though taking a different, social psychological, theoretical approach, this article engages with the same questions underlying the conceptual framework of "symbolic boundaries" presented in the introduction to this special issue (Mérand and Dembinska). It acknowledges that patterns of cooperation and conflict in specific "geopolitical fields" of EU–Russia relations are partly autonomous and have their own dynamics. On this basis the question is raised why the patterns of cooperation and conflict are so fundamentally different in the (constructed) categories of low and high politics, or in terms of this issue's conceptual framework why there is a gap between practices of conflict and cooperation between local geopolitical fields and the geostrategic macro-level. After that, the article deals with the vertical dimension. It investigates why bottom-up contagion from low to high politics has not occurred, as Liberal theories would expect. The other way around, it also considers the possibility of "reverse contagion", top-down, from high to low politics. Related to this, it highlights attempts to reframe predominantly cooperative domains of low politics into issues of high politics, characterised by conflictual practices. The analysis draws in particular on the domain of EU–Russia energy relations to illustrate these processes.

The article argues that a contagion from the more cooperative levels of low politics to high politics is unlikely. Equally, turning issues of low into high politics is far from evident. Therefore, the awkward combination of confrontation with diverse forms of pragmatic and selective cooperation may be the new normal in EU–Russia relations for a while to come. The staring contest which has characterised their relations over the last years may not come to an end soon.

The paradox of EU–Russia relations

When the EU and Russia embarked on a Strategic Partnership in 2003, this was accompanied by great optimism. The two parties agreed to cooperate in four common spaces: the common economic space; the common space of freedom, security and justice; the common space of research, education and culture; and the common space of external security.[1] They put in place a highly institutionalised framework for their relations: with no other country was the EU meeting more frequently at the highest level than with Russia. Trade volumes increased sharply until the 2008 financial crisis. Yet, despite this growth and despite a continued pragmatic cooperation, tensions accumulated already well before the eruption of the Ukraine crisis (Haukkala 2015) and trust dwindled, resulting in a "logic of competition" (Casier 2016a). Little progress was made, except for the largely symbolic Partnership for Modernisation of 2010. Brussels and Moscow did not manage to conclude a new agreement, as a follow-up for the 2004 Partnership and Cooperation Agreement (PCA), which was supposed to last until 2007 and since then is extended on an annual basis. Increasing competition and distrust spiralled out of control over Ukraine in late 2013, early 2014. The developments over the Euromaidan protests, the regime change in Kyiv, the Russian annexation of Crimea and its involvement in the war in Eastern Ukraine led to a suspension of the Strategic Partnership. The EU imposed sanctions, both economic and individual, and has renewed them every half year since then. The EU's unity on maintaining sanctions against Russia has surprised many. Before the Ukraine crisis, the Union was traditionally highly divided on Russia. Moscow retaliated with counter-sanctions, targeting agricultural and food products mainly.

For over six years, since the escalation of the Ukraine crisis, EU–Russia relations are in their most profound crisis since the end of the Cold War. Despite this deep crisis, there are some interesting ambiguities in current EU–Russia relations. One of them is in the field of trade. In 2015, the EU's import of Russian goods dropped with – 25.2% and its exports to Russia with – 28.6%.[2] In 2017, however, Russia recovered from its recession and problems in the financial sector and trade largely restored with +22.0% for imports and +18.8% for exports (DG Trade 2018). As a result, trade is now more or less back at the level it was before the Ukraine crisis, despite years of economic sanctions. The EU is still the first trading partner for Russia; Russia is the third trading partner for the EU. When looking at Foreign Direct Investments (FDI), 75% of FDI stocks in Russia come from the EU (Haukkala 2018, 54), though this includes Russian money kept in European banks and reinvested in the Russian economy.

In the field of energy the import of Russian natural gas in the EU reached a new peak in 2016. Not less than 39.9% of imported gas was of Russian origin, in comparison to figures fluctuating around one third before the Ukraine crisis. For crude oil, this was 31.6% (DG Energy 2018, 26). Energy relations remain of key importance to both parties. The potential volume for the transmission of natural gas is further increased by the planned Nord Stream 2 pipeline.

In the field of education, cooperation remains strong, in particular in the field of mobility. From 2015 to 2017, the EU has increased the budget for Erasmus+ cooperation with Russia to almost 80 million EUR. No country scores higher than Russia when it comes to short term student exchanges. From 2015 to 2017, nearly 11,000 Russian and EU students participated in Erasmus+ exchanges. Over the same period, 90 Jean Monnet projects were awarded to Russian institutions (European External Action Service 2017).

The stalemate in EU–Russia relations has also not stopped frequent bilateral contacts between Russia and individual EU member states. There are hardly any heads of government or state from EU countries who have not made an official visit to Moscow. The other way around, President Putin has paid numerous visits to EU capitals and made a mediatised private visit to the wedding of Austrian Foreign Minister Kneissl. During official bilateral meetings, commercial relations often top the agenda. This suggests a certain division of tasks, whereby issues of political relations and security are left to the EU. Also at that level, EU–Russia, we have seen an increase of bilateral visits at higher level over the last years, usually at foreign minister level or below.

In 2016, the EU formulated its five guiding principles for relations with Russia. They consist of the full implementation of the Minsk agreements; strengthening relations with Eastern partners, including in Central Asia; strengthening internal EU resilience (in particular energy security, hybrid threats, strategic communication); selective engagement with Russia; support for Russian civil society and people-to-people contacts. In particular, selective engagement is worth noting. It implies that the EU and Russia continue to work together in areas where they have common interests and consider collaboration useful. This includes issues such as the Joint Comprehensive Plan of Action (JCPOA), also known as the Iran nuclear deal, in particular after the American withdrawal in 2018. It is also the case for counter-terrorism. This principle has introduced a stretchable pragmatic element into the EU's policy. Despite the deep crisis and sanctions, Brussels cooperates "as usual" in selected fields. For other issues, such as the war in Eastern Ukraine, the EU has resorted to alternative channels, such as the Normandy format. It was within this setting that Germany, France, Ukraine and Russia negotiated and concluded the Minsk agreements, which were meant to put an end to the war in Eastern Ukraine. Richard Youngs argues that the EU seeks a balance between "bounded containment" of Russia and trying to take into account its interests where possible (Youngs 2017, 220).

The overall impression is that, five years after the Ukraine crisis erupted, EU–Russia relations are a mixed bag. There are substantive and lasting sanctions, profound distrust, harsh rhetoric. At the same time, there is selective engagement, extended bilateral relations and business as usual in areas like trade and energy. To understand this paradox, the next section will situate the issues of conflict and cooperation along the dichotomy of low versus high politics. It will be clarified how EU–Russia relations are fundamentally different at these levels and which implications this entails. In doing so, this article takes a predominantly theoretical approach, which will be illustrated through the case of energy relations.

Low versus high politics

The distinction between high and low politics in International Relations is an ill-defined one. High politics usually refers to issues of security or survival of the state, but also to conventional state-to-state diplomacy. By extension it refers to all issues of geopolitical or strategic importance. Low politics, on the other hand, refers to relations in geostrategically less sensitive areas, such as commercial relations, cooperation on environmental matters, etc. In Realist literature, the distinction assumes two things. First, that both spheres are distinct and have their own autonomy (Barnett 1990). Second, as the terms themselves indicate, a hierarchy is assumed whereby high politics are seen as what fundamentally matters, while low politics are of secondary importance. This has led to critique the distinction between low and high politics as a "false dichotomy" (Ripsman 2005).

In this article the terms are used in a different way from this Realist understanding, as a subjective categorisation in political discourse itself. What matters here is how policy makers or political leaders themselves categorise certain areas as of key strategic importance for the survival and core national interests of the state (high politics) or not (low politics). Also the supremacy of high over low politics is approached as a subjective category. Moreover, in line with the conceptual framework outlined in the introduction of this special issue, not only do the spheres of high and low politics have a relative autonomy. Also individual domains of low politics ("geopolitical fields" in terms of the special issue's conceptual framework) have relative autonomy vis-à-vis each other, implying that they display varying patterns of cooperation and conflict (Mérand and Dembinska).

Notwithstanding the difference in theoretical approach, some findings of conventional literature on high and low politics and on "issue politics" are relevant to our analysis. In the "issue politics paradigm", the issue position of key actors and decision-makers becomes itself the main dependent variable (Vasquez 1998, 378). Milner and Tingley even refer to the "shaping of high and low politics" (2015, 13) and how this is affected by domestic politics.[3] This adds an element of construction of high and low politics to the issue areas literature, though it is not really developed theoretically by the authors. What is of interest to our analysis is thus how issues move *discursively* between the categories of low and high politics. Energy relations are a good case in point and will also serve as a case in this article. While conventionally seen as an issue of low politics, it can be elevated to high politics when it becomes seen as an issue of vital importance for the security of a state. This was the case with the OPEC oil embargo in 1973–1974. It was also the case with the gas spats of 2006 and 2009 when several EU member states were cut off from Russian gas. Inside the EU this item was widely read as a security threat, requiring a strategic response. As a result, it moved to the "high politics" agenda.

Today EU–Russia energy relations are predominantly a low politics issue again, whereby most decisions taken have limited national strategic implications, are often of a rather technical nature and taken on the basis of routine. The interaction in the field of energy is between numerous actors, economic and non-economic, producers and consumers, in function of their own interests or preferences (Aalto et al. 2014). In other words, the daily practices of energy relations are constituted by millions of acts and decisions by a huge number of public and private actors. As a result, the interests are highly diffuse and driven by dispersed commercial interests rather than "high" political national interests. In this area, states often act as brokers and mediators for commercial contracts. Exactly this has remained unchanged in areas not affected by EU–Russia mutual sanctions.[4] In other words, the daily practices of trade, energy relations, academic exchange, etc. take place within a complex multi-actor structure, characterised by direct interaction. The interests of this wide array of actors are diffuse.

A different image emerges when we look at high politics. Positions are taken by a limited number of actors, political leaders in the first place. They are governed by dominant, in this case diametrically opposed, discourses. EU leaders frame Russia – to different degrees – in terms of threat and as a state which has deviated from the EU's guiding model. Russian leaders accuse the EU and the West to follow a policy of neo-containment (Putin 2014a) and to impose its "unilateral Diktat" (Putin 2014b) on other countries. The EU is seen as part of "an elite club" using the extension of the liberal world order as an instrument of "domination over everyone else" (Lavrov 2017).

What stands out in this process is the paradigmatic positioning of both actors. As Joan DeBardeleben has argued, the EU–Russia paradigm for interaction has shifted from a "greater/common Europe" paradigm to one of "competing regionalisms" (DeBardeleben 2018). Moscow puts itself on an anti-hegemonic position. It openly challenges the EU's imposition of its political and economic model and claims its right to make its own "sovereign" choices. Brussels traditionally identifies with the position of "normative" power, a non-geopolitical actor driven primordially by norms and values, rather than interests. The diverging narratives on both sides went through a process of escalation whereby positions got more entrenched and reactions more assertive.

The contrast between direct relations in complex, multi-actor structures with frequent, routinised interaction and the polarised paradigmatic positioning of political leaders in foreign policy discourses does not feature in most International Relations theories. As a result, many theories struggle to explain the discrepancy between more cooperative relations at the level of low politics and more acrimonious relations in high politics. Realism assumes there is a strict hierarchy of issues whereby security and survival of the state dominate. Liberal approaches, on the other hand, expect close cooperation in areas of low politics to produce common interests and ultimately a more cooperative context for high politics, something that has clearly not happened in the realm of EU–Russia relations (Forsberg 2019). Here an alternative theory is presented which grasps this contrast better: Construal-Level Theory (CLT) (Trope and Liberman 2010). This theory offers a solid ground for explaining the difference between diffuse and often common interests at the level of low politics and strongly polarised discursive positions and disagreement at the level of high politics. CLT is a theory from Social Psychology. It starts from the idea that in order to think about something, we need to transcend the self and the immediate. We do this through the creation of mental representations or "construals". It argues that the "construals" we create of objects, events or others become more abstract ("higher") as the psychological distance from our direct experience grows. This distance may take different forms: social, spatial, temporal or hypothetical. The greater the distance along one of these dimensions, the more abstract the construal becomes: it is ruled by essentialised images, whereby the event or other is reduced to a few simple characteristics. The smaller the distance, the more concrete, specific ("lower") the construal is. In other words,

> CLT contends that people use increasingly higher levels of construal to represent an object as the psychological distance from the object increases. This is because high-level construals are more likely than low-level construals to remain unchanged as one gets closer to an object or farther away from it. (Trope and Liberman 2010, 441)

When determining one's attitude towards something that is psychologically distant, it will be detached from the specific, local context or from the incidental attitudes or behaviour of others. Instead, it will be determined by abstract construals such as ideologies. These ideologies are abstracted from the reality of our direct experience and become the lens through which this behaviour is understood. It will be argued below that while interaction in domains of low politics implies small psychological distances and is therefore determined by the specific context and the direct experience of interaction with others, the level of high politics implies higher psychological distance and is ruled by abstract, ideological images, which may, in case of tensions, develop into enemy images.

The daily "low politics" practices in trade, energy, academic mobility, interregional cooperation are driven by a multitude of actors who interact on a regular basis in a direct, very specific way, i.e. in terms of CLT, with small psychological distances. For example, in the field of energy, they interact as negotiators of commercial contracts, as technicians, as sales managers, etc. They have very specific interests or preferences (concluding a contract, solving a technical problem, selling a product) and are aware of those of the others (see Aalto et al. 2014). They see the other in a fairly concrete way, not in abstract images. As a result, their daily interaction will be less affected by abstract political images.[5] High politics, on the other hand, happens exactly at the level of abstracted images of national interests. The behaviour of the other is judged in the first place on the basis of discursive representations and abstract images one has formed of the intentions of the counterpart. In a context of tensions, whereby distance grows further, abstract negative images easily get radicalised (Trope and Liberman 2010). This makes political leaders more prone to stereotypical paradigmatic positioning and even enemy thinking.

Again, this finding displays a parallel with the more conventional approaches to issue areas. On the basis of empirical research and refining Rosenau's "issue area typology", Vasquez has argued that "as issues become more tangible they will become more cooperative, and as issues become more intangible they become more conflict-prone" (1983, 188). This relation becomes more outspoken when certain variables are present. Intangible aspects of an issue, for example, will generate more conflict if there is "frequent contention over the issue" and "it is not linked to other issues" (Vasquez 1983, 189). The other way around, "issues with tangible ends and means ... tend to be cooperative, especially when there is a high number of actors" (Vasquez 1983, 189). The logical question that emerges from this is whether contagion is possible. Can concrete images from domains of low politics spill over into high politics and affect more abstract construals? And may more cooperative patterns in certain local domains of low politics in this away change more conflictual patterns in high politics? The other way around, do abstract construals at the level of high politics trickle down to domains of low politics and negatively affect patterns of conflict and cooperation? These questions will be dealt with in the next two sections.

Contagion: a spillover of cooperative practices from low to high politics?

Is a contagion of more cooperative practices from certain domains of low politics to high politics likely? Have the pragmatic interaction and links that exist at bilateral level the potential to produce a normalisation of relations? These questions deal with the vertical hypothesis presented in the introduction to this special issue (Mérand and Dembinska), more specifically a bottom-up change of conflictual patterns at the geostrategic level through contagion by more cooperative practices in specific domains of low politics.

Drawing on the theoretical perspective given above, Construal-Level Theory, a bottom-up contagion is unlikely because concrete low-distance images do not simply spill over into abstract high-distance images. As explained above, there is a strongly polarised discourse at the level of high politics, in which Russia puts itself in an anti-hegemonic position, while the EU legitimises its position on the basis of the threat posed by Russia.

The very idea that intense economic cooperation and interdependence generate common interests and form the basis for interstate cooperation is a liberal proposition. It was one of the core theoretical narratives about EU–Russia relations throughout the 1990s and early 2000s. Developments have proven this interpretation wrong (Forsberg 2019).[6] Strongly interwoven economic interests at low politics level were unable to produce stable political relations between Russia and the EU. Romanova has analysed how transgovernmental and transnational energy institutions were unable "to cushion the crisis" (Romanova 2018, 73). Krickovic has even argued that interdependence in the energy sector has generated a security dilemma, rather than fostered cooperation. Both parties have tried to reduce respectively their demand and supply dependence, but this has triggered concerns on the other side of asymmetrical interdependence and insecurity (Krickovic 2015).

As explained in the conceptual section above, this analysis sees the domains of high and low politics as constructed domains. This implies that issues get discursively defined by political actors as high politics or not. Whether an issue gets defined as belonging to the realm of high or low politics ultimately depends on the criterion against which domains of EU–Russia interaction are defined as vital or not to the interests of the Russian state or of the European Union.[7] It is in these areas that Russia and the EU get entangled in a "logic of competitive influence seeking": "the Kremlin vies with the West for influence, considering any loss of such influence ultimately as a threat to its role as a regional hegemon and its aspirations for global major-power status" (Malyarenko and Wolff 2018, 193). Areas where a loss of influence is not seen by the actors as a threat to vital interests are understood as low politics.

In the Constructivist tradition, these vital interests are not exogenously given, but a social construction. Extending this to our social psychological CLT approach, the definition of an issue as vital interest is a function of the degree to which the construals of the other or the situation are abstract or concrete. In other words, the images held and the level of abstraction determine how they define the situation (when is rivalling influence threatening?), how they interpret the behaviour of their counterparts and attribute certain intentions to them. The latter is of particular importance. Intentions of the other are in interstate relations a classic uncertainty,[8] thus not based on concrete, direct experience. As a result, images about intentions are almost per definition "high distance" and thus abstract. Related social psychological theories of attribution have argued that, in particular in a context of escalating tensions and high psychological distance, the actions of the other party are not understood in the first place on the basis of their actual behaviour, but on the basis of the intentions attributed to them according to of the abstract images formed (see, e.g. Kowert 1998). In the field of Russia's relations with the West, where there is a disproportionate emphasis on intentions (in particular speculation about Russia's long-term geostrategic intentions), this is of utmost importance.

In sum, with uncertainty about intentions abounding in EU–Russia relations, negative abstract images at the level of high politics are unlikely to be affected by more positive concrete images in certain fields of, for example, economic interaction. Moreover, this polarisation has been entrenched through the dualistic structures which have taken form in Europe. This dualism refers to the two-pronged institutions and structures of governance which have been created around the Euro-Atlantic Community, on the one hand, and around Russia, on the other. It is clearly visible in the security field (NATO versus the Collective Security Treaty Organisation, CSTO), as well as in the field of economic cooperation (Eastern Partnership versus Eurasian Economic Union). This type of dualistic structures tends to stimulate highly abstract images of the adversary and his intentions rather than mitigating them. Besides, dualistic structures imply the absence of a shared normative framework of agreed principles that underpins multilateralism (Ruggie 1982, 1992). What we have witnessed is the gradual erosion of the shared post-Cold War framework, formulated in the "Charter of Paris for a New Europe" of 1990 (CSCE 1990) and translated into various agreements and institutions afterwards. This thinning out of shared principles in relations between Russia and the West in general and the EU more specifically risks to foster polarisation at the level of high politics, where abstracted paradigmatic positions dominate.

Reverse contagion: the trickling down of conflictual dynamics from high to low politics?

If bottom-up contagion (from low to high politics) is unlikely, as argued in the previous section, how about top-down contagion? Can specific domains of low politics be negatively affected by the conflictual patterns at the level of high politics? In other words, may the logic of competition at geostrategic level trickle down to specific, local geopolitical fields?

A distinction needs to be made between deliberate political decisions introducing conflictual practices into domains of low politics versus spontaneous trickle down effects. The former is best illustrated through sanction regimes.[9] Hereby political actors decide to introduce sanctions in specific fields of low politics, thus imposing a conflictual logic on these domains. The EU has progressively introduced sanctions since the Russian annexation of Crimea and has renewed them every half year since then. In the economic field, the restrictive measures concern inter alia Russian access to capital markets, to certain sensitive technologies in the field of oil exploitation and the implementation of certain cooperation programmes (Council 2019). Russian counter-sanctions targeted the import of agricultural products from EU countries. These forms of extension of conflictual dynamics to local domains of low politics can be seen as extension by force. Interestingly, they have not triggered a conflictual dynamic in other fields of low politics. Conflict over the Russia embargo against EU agricultural products, for example, has not spilled over to other fields of trade. As illustrated above, the total volume of EU–Russia trade has recovered and is back at the level before the Ukraine crisis. The effects of the sanctions are thus divergent and have not led to a spillover of conflictual dynamics into other areas of low politics.

On the other side of the spectrum is spontaneous top-down contagion: the trickling down of conflict dynamics from high politics into domains of low politics. Looking again at the area of EU–Russia energy relations, little can be discerned in case of trickling down effects. In contrast to the widespread speculation on the eve of the Ukraine crisis that Russia would cut off gas supplies in case of a conflict, energy relations between Russia and the EU have continued as normal since the Ukraine crisis (Stulberg 2015) and have clearly been approached predominantly as domain of low politics.[10] As indicated above, the import of Russian gas into the EU even broke a new record in 2016, hitting almost 40% (DG Energy 2018, 26). This absence of conflict stands in sharp contrast with the gas conflicts of 2006 and 2009. Twice Russia shut down gas supplies over debt issues with Ukraine, disrupting the supplies of natural gas to several EU member states. This caused a shock effect in the EU and led to calls for emergency measures and reinforced energy security. The events of 2006 and 2009 did not repeat themselves after the last gas spat due to the signing of an Early Warning Mechanism between Russia and the EU. The mechanism was invoked on several occasions and prevented further escalation. Also the agreement on the Nord Stream 2 pipeline in June 2015, a good year after the eruption of the Ukraine crisis, indicates that conflictual dynamics did not trickle down to the energy sector. Though controversial within the EU, Nord Stream 2 is a project based on cooperation between Gazprom and partners from different EU member states: Uniper and Wintershall from Germany, Engie from France, OMV from Austria and British-Dutch Shell.

As explained, energy relations are characterised by their multi-actor nature, whereby a multitude of actors with their own interests and preferences interact and produce a high variety of particular intentions rather than clear collective intention (Aalto et al. 2014). A trickledown effect would imply that the multitude of individual intentions and practices are brought in line with a collective, consensus-based strategic goal. Given the many particularistic interests in the energy sector, commercial ones in the first place, this alignment would be extremely difficult. On top of that, there was a shared, pragmatic understanding in both Brussels and Moscow that the disruption of highly important energy relations would inevitably damage economies severely. While the EU is strongly dependent on the supply of Russian natural gas, Russia is strongly dependent on demand from the EU (Casier 2016b).

However, there is a third possibility whereby the dynamics of high politics are not simply trickling down or imposed, but whereby a domain of low politics is discursively reframed as touching vital interests and thus relabelled as field of high politics. Again, this can be illustrated in the field of energy, this time on the basis of an external attempt to convert energy into an issue of high politics. More specifically, there has been tremendous American pressure on the EU to reduce supply dependence on Russian natural gas by buying US Liquefied Natural Gas (LNG). The pressure is not new; it existed already under the Obama administration. But under the Trump administration it has taken unprecedented forms and is more "bullish and vocal" (Mitrova and Boersma 2018, 35). US Secretary of Energy Rick Perry, stated:

> The United States is not just exporting energy, we're exporting freedom. … We're exporting to our allies in Europe the opportunity to truly have a choice of where do you buy your energy from. That's freedom. And that kind of freedom is priceless. (Perry quoted in Cama 2018)

The American ambassador to Germany, Richard Grenell, threatened in a letter to German energy companies with sanctions against companies supporting the building of the Nord Stream 2 pipeline, for they are "actively undermining Ukraine's and European security" (Grenell 2019). In a reaction to the American mounting pressure, Russian Foreign Minister Lavrov spoke of "a big battle":

> the United States wants to use the current situation in order to separate Europe from Russia economy-wise and bargain for the most favourable conditions for themselves in the context of the ongoing negotiations on the creation of a transatlantic trade and investment partnership. (Lavrov quoted in Mitrova and Boersma 2018, 36)

In December 2019 the National Defence Authorization Act was approved in the United States, providing for sanctions on the companies involved in the construction of Nordstream 2. This led main contractor Allseas to withdraw from the project and provoked sharp reactions from Moscow, Brussels and Berlin.

Behind the American framing of the European choice as one between Russian natural gas or American LNG is a changing energy reality. The US evolves from a net importer to net exporter of energy. In 2019, it became the world's third LNG player (EIA 2018; Stratfor 2018). In January–April 2019, 35% of American LNG export went to the EU and considerable increases are projected (European Commission 2019). American LNG imports have been increasing in Europe with 14% in 2019, but companies are confronted with an oversupply on the European market. This puts them in direct competition with Russia and explains the drastic efforts of Washington to "break into" the European gas market, in which Russia is the biggest player.[11]

Self-evidently this is open for discussion, but there are strong indications that the main motive of the Trump administration is commercial rather than geopolitical: "It does seem like the current [Trump] administration is pushing European countries to wean themselves off Russian gas and switch to American gas in a move that would benefit American companies" (Mitrova and Boersma 2018, 35). In this case, geopolitical and security arguments are only a pretext to increase the American share of the gas market.[12]

Whether American attempts are effective to turn the predominantly commercial issue of energy into a high politics issue on the basis of simple, abstract images of security and freedom is a different question. As things look now, the US approach mainly seems to work in EU member states that have already made it a priority to drastically reduce their dependence on Russian gas. Poland, for example, increased its imports of American LNG considerably as part of its ongoing strategy to reduce dependence on Russian gas. It signed major deals with American LNG companies in 2018, amounting to the equivalent of almost 40% percent of Polish gas consumption (Crooks 2018). Along the same lines, some actors within the EU continuously attempt to reframe energy relations with Russia in security terms and make it an issue of high politics. So far, at least until the American imposition of sanctions, they have been little successful. This stands in sharp contrast with the crisis atmosphere surrounding the Russia–EU gas conflicts in 2006 and 2009, when energy was framed as a high politics issue.

To sum up, attempts are definitely undertaken to extend the conflictual dynamics of high politics to specific domains of low politics by reframing them as affecting vital interests. Yet, these attempts are not necessarily driven by geostrategic motives, but they may follow from particularistic motives, such as commercial interests. That success of these actions has so far been limited seems to confirm the relative autonomy of different local domains of low politics. Reverse contagion, from high to low politics, does not occur easily in the absence of a political decision, for example to impose sanctions in these areas.

Conclusion

Relations between the EU and Russia display a major ambiguity. On the one hand, relations are at their worst since the collapse of the Soviet Union. The EU–Russia Strategic Partnership has been suspended. Sanctions and counter-sanctions are in place. Trust is at an all-time low and there are very few signs that the current staring contest may come to an end. On the other hand, bilateral diplomatic activity between Moscow and EU member states seems to flourish. Trade has recovered from the dip after the start of the Ukraine crisis. This is even more the case for energy. In 2016, a new record was hit for Russia's share in EU natural gas imports.

This confirms that even today, in a context of crisis, a simple paradigm of conflict still does not suffice to grasp the essence of EU–Russia relations.[13] What needs to be explained is the ambivalence: the deep conflict between the EU and Russia going hand in hand with business as usual in some areas. This article explained this awkward combination on the basis of the distinction between low and high politics, understood here as subjective categories. The continued cooperation in fields labelled as low politics, like trade and energy, mainly results from the interaction between a multitude of actors (private and public) in a multi-actor structure. On the basis of Construal-Level Theory, this interaction was understood as relations of low psychological distance, i.e. dominated by rather concrete mental representations of the attitudes and behaviour of the other, based on direct experience. For example, in the conclusion of an energy contract, the images the parties hold of each other are specific and immediate. In high politics, on the other hand, the mental representations of the attitudes and behaviour of the counterpart are characterised by high psychological distance. They are abstract, essentialised images of the intentions of the other. They are more disconnected from the daily "reality" of interaction and governed by ideologised images and more prone to enemy thinking. The two parties thus tend to position themselves discursively in a strongly antagonistic way in areas which are framed as affecting vital interests.

On the basis of the above, the article studied the possibility of contagion effects between domains of low and high politics against the background of Construal-Level Theory. Bottom-up contagion effects imply that (more) cooperative practices would spill over from domains of low politics into high politics. Reversely top-down contagion effects imply that (more) conflictual practices would trickle down from high politics to domains of low politics. Drawing on the case of EU–Russia energy relations since the start of the Ukraine crisis, little support was found either for bottom-up or top-down contagion.

In others words, there is little chance that continued cooperation in fields like trade and energy will lead to a shift in the foreign policy positions of Russia and the EU and defrost relations. This is the case because concrete low-distance images do not easily contaminate abstract, high distance polarised images. The dualistic structures which exist in wider Europe help to maintain high psychological distance and entrench polarisation. On the contrary, we continue to face active attempts to turn issues of low politics into conflictual high politics issues. A case in point are the attempts of the Trump administration to frame the EU's choice between Russian natural gas and American LNG not as a commercial one, but as a vital choice over security and freedom.

In conclusion, the pragmatism that has survived in some specific areas is unlikely to provide the basis for a U-turn in EU–Russia relations. Changing the polarised discursive positions of both actors and the abstract, high distance representations they have formed of each other will be an inevitable step. It is clear that this cannot happen over-night, but will require a long and winding road of trust building and normalisation.

Notes

1. The cooperation in these four common spaces was translated into Roadmaps, agreed in Moscow in 2005 (Roadmaps 2005).
2. Russia's global trade in goods dropped in 2015 by 19.7% (DG Trade 2018).
3. Some authors have argued that domestic politics matter considerably for the issue position of leaders (Putnam 1988), a factor which is often related to the distribution of costs and benefits over domestic actors (Milner and Tingley 2015, 14).
4. The same holds for student mobility and collaborative research projects: they result from a multitude of decisions by individual students and academics and, as such, do not imply high political decisions.
5. For a more extended argumentation about low psychological distance in energy relations between Russia and the EU, see Casier (2016b).
6. Despite this negative evaluation, Forsberg notes that interdependence "can be regarded as a factor that has prevented the parties from further escalating their confrontation" (Forsberg 2019).
7. Scholars themselves differ over what exactly Moscow defines as its vital interests and analysts have variously emphasised geopolitical control, power distribution, status or regime survival (see among many others: Götz 2015; Mearsheimer 2014; Forsberg 2014; White 2018).
8. Rathbun argues that uncertainty is central to all traditions in International Relations theory, but is understood differently across them (Rathbun 2007).
9. On sanctions between the EU and Russia, see inter alia Romanova (2016).
10. Note that this also contrasts with the gas spats of 2006 and 2009 when the disruption of Russian gas supplies to some member states sent shock waves through the EU and became seen as an issue of high politics.
11. In terms of the effects of an increased presence of US LNG on the EU energy market, it has been argued that the increasing American share is unlikely to outcompete Russia, but

rather to make the European gas market more competitive and flexible (Mitrova and Boersma 2018).

12. Geopolitical motives need to be distinguished from the geopolitical "wrapping", i.e. the use of geopolitical and security arguments to gain commercial benefit, as described in this article. As to the former, it has been argued that Russia has the geopolitical objective with Nord Stream 2 to bypass Ukraine. In the case of Southern routes, both the EU (with the Southern Gas Corridor) and Russia (with Turkstream) had geopolitical objectives (Siddi 2019).

13. A similar statement was made before the Ukraine crisis in Casier (2012).

Disclosure statement

No potential conflict of interest was reported by the author(s).

References

Aalto, P., D. Dusseault, M. Kennedy, and M. Kivinen. 2014. "Russia's Energy Relations in Europe and the Far East: Towards a Social Structurationist Approach to Energy Policy Formation." *Journal of International Relations and Development* 17 (1): 1–29.

Barnett, M. 1990. "High Politics Is Low Politics: The Domestic and Systemic Sources of Israeli Security Policy, 1967–1977." *World Politics* 42 (4): 529–562.

Cama, T. 2018. "Perry: US 'Not Just Exporting Energy, We're Exporting Freedom.'" *The Hill*, January 24. https://thehill.com/policy/energy-environment/370468-perry-us-is-not-just-exporting-energy-were-exporting-freedom.

Casier, T. 2012. "Are the Policies of Russia and the EU in Their Shared Neighbourhood Doomed to Clash?" In *Competing for Influence. The EU and Russia in Post-Soviet Eurasia*, edited by R. Kanet and M. R. Freire, 31–53. Dordrecht: Republic of Letters.

Casier, T. 2016a. "From Logic of Competition to Conflict: Understanding the Dynamics of EU-Russia Relations." *Contemporary Politics* 22 (3): 376–394.

Casier, T. 2016b. "Great Game or Great Confusion? The Geopolitical Understanding of EU-Russia Energy Relations." *Geopolitics* 21 (4): 763–778.

Council of the EU. 2019. "Timeline – EU Restrictive Measures in Response to the Crisis in Ukraine." Accessed December 11, 2019. https://www.consilium.europa.eu/en/policies/sanctions/ukraine-crisis/history-ukraine-crisis/.

Crooks, E. 2018. "Poland Adds to US Natural Gas Imports with Sempra Deal." *Financial Times*, December 19. https://www.ft.com/content/6790a1dc-038c-11e9-99df-6183d3002ee1.

CSCE. 1990. *Charter of Paris for a New Europe*, November 19–21. https://www.osce.org/mc/39516?download=true.

DeBardeleben, J. 2018. "Alternative Paradigms for EU-Russian Neighbourhood Relations." In *EU-Russia Relations in Crisis. Understanding Diverging Perceptions*, edited by T. Casier and J. DeBardeleben, 115–136. London: Routledge.

DG Energy. 2018. *EU Energy in Figures. Statistical Pocketbook 2018*. Luxembourg: Publications Office of the EU. https://publications.europa.eu/en/publication-detail/-/publication/99fc30eb-c06d-11e8-9893-01aa75ed71a1/language-en.

DG Trade. 2018. *European Union, Trade in Goods with Russia*. https://webgate.ec.europa.eu/isdb_results/factsheets/country/details_russia_en.pdf.

EIA. 2018. "US Liquefied Natural Gas Export Capacity to More Than Double by the End of 2019." https://www.eia.gov/todayinenergy/detail.php?id=37732#.

European Commission. 2019. *EU-US LNG Trade*. https://ec.europa.eu/energy/sites/ener/files/eu-us_lng_trade_folder.pdf.

European External Action Service. 2017. *Erasmus+ 2017 Selection Results for Russia Have Hit Record Highs*, October 13. https://eeas.europa.eu/headquarters/headquarters-homepage/33862/erasmus-2017-selection-results-russia-have-hit-record-highs_en.

Forsberg, T. 2014. "Status Conflicts Between Russia and the West: Perceptions and Emotional Biases." *Communist and Post-Communist Studies* 47 (3–4): 323–331.

Forsberg, T. 2019. "Explaining Russian Foreign Policy Towards the EU Through Contrasts." *International Politics* 56 (6): 762–777.

Götz, E. 2015. "It's Geopolitics, Stupid: Explaining Russia's Ukraine Policy." *Global Affairs* 1 (1): 3–10.

Grenell, R. 2019. "US Ambassador Richard Grenell's Letter in Full." *Handelsblatt*, January 14. https://www.handelsblatt.com/today/politics/threatening-sanctions-us-ambassador-richard-grenells-letter-in-full/23863160.html.

Haukkala, H. 2015. "From Cooperative to Contested Europe? The Conflict in Ukraine as a Culmination of a Long-Term Crisis in EU-Russia Relations." *Journal of Contemporary European Studies* 23 (1): 25–40.

Haukkala, H. 2018. "Negative Mutual Interdependence? The Clashing Perceptions of EU-Russia Economic Relations." In *EU-Russia Relations in Crisis. Understanding Diverging Perceptions*, edited by T. Casier and J. DeBardeleben, 53–71. London: Routledge.

Kowert, P. 1998. "Agent Versus Structure in the Construction of National Identity." In *International Relations in a Constructed World*, edited by V. Kubalkova, N. Onuf, and P. Kowert, 101–122. New York: M.E. Sharpe.

Krickovic, A. 2015. "When Interdependence Produces Conflict: EU–Russia Energy Relations as a Security Dilemma." *Contemporary Security Policy* 36 (1): 3–26.

Lavrov, S. 2017. "Foreign Minister Lavrov's Address and Answers to Question at the 53rd Munich Security Conference," February 18. www.mid.ru/en/press_service/minister_speeches/-/asset_publisher/7OvQR5KJWVmR/content/id/2648249/pop_up?_101_INSTANCE_7OvQR5KJWVmR_viewMode=print&_101_INSTANCE_7OvQR5KJWVmR_qrIndex=1.

Malyarenko, T., and S. Wolff. 2018. "The Logic of Competitive Influence-Seeking: Russia, Ukraine, and the Conflict in Donbas." *Post-Soviet Affairs* 34 (4): 191–212.

Mearsheimer, J. 2014. "Why the Ukraine Crisis Is the West's Fault. The Liberal Delusions that Provoked Putin." *Foreign Affairs*, September/October.

Mérand, F., and M. Dembinska. "Introduction: Theorizing Cooperation and Conflict in Euro-Russian Relations." [Introduction to this Special Issue].

Milner, H. V., and D. Tingley. 2015. *Sailing the Water's Edge. The Domestic Politics of American Foreign Policy*. Princeton: Princeton University Press.

Mitrova, T., and T. Boersma. 2018. *The Impact of US LNG on Russian Natural gas Export Policy*. New York: Columbia SIPA/Center on Global Energy Policy.

Putin, V. 2014a. "Address by President of the Russian Federation," March 18. http://en.kremlin.ru/events/president/news/20603.

Putin, V. 2014b. "[Speech at the] Meeting of the Valdai International Discussion Club," October 24. http://en.kremlin.ru/events/president/news/46860.

Putnam, R. 1988. "Diplomacy and Domestic Politics: The Logic of Two-Level Games." *International Organization* 42 (3): 427–460.

Rathbun, B. C. 2007. "Uncertain About Uncertainty: Understanding the Multiple Meanings of a Crucial Concept in International Relations Theory." *International Studies Quarterly* 51 (3): 533–557.

Ripsman, N. 2005. "False Dichotomy: Why Economics Has Always Been High Politics." In *Guns and Butter: The Political Economy of International Security*, edited by P. Dombrowski, 15–31. Boulder: Lynne Rienner.

Roadmaps. 2005. *15th EU-Russia Summit, Road Maps*. Moscow, May 10. http://www.consilium.europa.eu/ueDocs/cms_Data/docs/pressdata/en/er/84815.pdf.

Romanova, T. 2016. "Sanctions and the Future of EU–Russian Economic Relations." *Europe-Asia Studies* 68 (4): 774–796.

Romanova, T. 2018. "EU-Russia Energy Relations: do Institutions Stand the Test?" In *EU-Russia Relations in Crisis. Understanding Diverging Perceptions*, edited by T. Casier and J. DeBardeleben, 72–92. London: Routledge.

Ruggie, J. G. 1982. "International Regimes, Transactions and Change: Embedded Liberalism in the Postwar Economic Order." *International Organization* 36 (2): 379–415.

Ruggie, J. G. 1992. "Multilateralism: the Anatomy of an Institution." *International Organization* 46 (3): 561–598.

Siddi, M. 2019. "The EU's Botched Geopolitical Approach to External Energy Policy: The Case of the Southern Gas Corridor." *Geopolitics* 24 (1): 124–144.

Stratfor. 2018. "US LNG Exports Are About to Reshape the Global Market," November 8. https://worldview.stratfor.com/article/us-lng-export-global-qatar-russia-china.

Stulberg, A. N. 2015. "Out of Gas? Russia, Ukraine, Europe, and the Changing Geopolitics of Natural Gas." *Problems of Post-Communism* 62 (2): 112–130.

Trope, Y., and N. Liberman. 2010. "Construal-Level Theory of Psychological Distance." *Psychological Review* 117 (2): 440–463.

Vasquez, J. A. 1983. "The Tangibility of Issues and Global Conflict: A Test of Rosenau's Issue Area Typology." *Journal of Peace Research* 20 (2): 179–192.

Vasquez, J. A. 1998. *The Power of Power Politics. From Classical Realism to Neotraditionalism*. Cambridge: Cambridge University Press.

White, D. 2018. "State Capacity and Regime Resilience in Putin's Russia." *International Political Science Review* 39 (1): 130–143.

Youngs, R. 2017. *Europe's Eastern Crisis. The Geopolitics of Asymmetry*. Cambridge: Cambridge University Press.

Theorising conflict and cooperation in EU-Russia energy relations: ideas, identities and material factors in the Nord Stream 2 debate

Marco Siddi ⓘ

ABSTRACT
Relations between the European Union and Russia have been framed around a conflict/cooperation dichotomy. Following the Ukraine crisis, confrontation has extended to the economic arena, which had previously epitomised the post-Cold War rapprochement between Russia and the EU. Nevertheless, the cooperative side of the dichotomy has not disappeared. The paper argues that ideational factors, notably different conceptualisations of Russia in the national identities of EU member states, are essential to understand the conflict/cooperation dichotomy in the energy sector. The argument is illustrated through an analysis of national leaders' discourses on Nord Stream-2, with a focus on Germany and Poland.

Introduction

Since the end of the Cold War, relations between the European Union and Russia have been framed around a conflict/cooperation dichotomy (Averre 2009; Haukkala 2015; Nitoiu 2017; Webber 2000). While both sides officially agreed to build a comprehensive strategic partnership, practically cooperation developed mostly in a limited number of sectors, particularly in the economic realm. On crucial themes such as European security, the resolution of post-Soviet conflicts and relations with the shared neighbourhood, mutual suspicions, misunderstandings and clashing geopolitical agendas largely prevented genuine and lasting cooperation. In the wake of the Ukraine crisis and the reciprocal imposition of sanctions, the pendulum in the dichotomy has markedly shifted towards conflict. Sanctions have extended the confrontation to economic relations, an area which had previously epitomised the post-Cold War rapprochement between Russia and the West and remained relatively unaffected by political tensions (Aalto and Forsberg 2016).

Nevertheless, the cooperative side of the dichotomy has not disappeared completely. The level of economic interdependence achieved in the previous decades and the inevitable consequences of each side's policies for the security of the other acted as a strong incentive for maintaining dialogue and a certain level of cooperation (David and Romanova 2015; Yafimava 2015). Some scholars have argued that the debate has become more polarised, but cooperative zones of contact have persisted (Nitoiu 2017). This article takes the relevant research a step further by analysing one of these zones, energy trade. It argues that, as previous literature has noted, energy policy remains a relatively cooperative field of EU-Russia relations (Judge, Maltby, and Sharples 2016; Siddi 2018a). However, the escalation of tensions in other policy areas has had repercussions on energy relations too. The conflict/cooperation dichotomy now characterises not only the broader EU-Russia relationship, but also the internal dynamics of energy relations, which had previously been dominated by a pragmatic, economic logic (cf. Hadfield 2016).

In order to highlight the increasingly controversial nature of the energy relationship, the article focuses on the EU debate concerning gas trade with Russia. Departing from the observation of post-2014 trade and market developments (Belyi 2015; Henderson and Sharples 2018), it argues that ideational (rather than material) factors play an essential role in the growing influence of conflictual logic in energy trade. Most notably, political tensions have (re)activated identity narratives and constructions of the Russian Other that also affect discourses and policies in the energy domain (see also Siddi 2017a; Smith 2014). In no other instance does this become clearer than in the debate on the Nord Stream 2 pipeline project (for a full background analysis, see Goldthau 2016), which is thus the case study of the article. Different, identity-based conceptualisations of Russia as an energy actor at the national level contribute to explaining the intra-EU divisions on Nord Stream 2.

While the article does not dismiss the importance of material and strategic factors, it addresses the Nord Stream 2 controversy from a different conceptual and theoretical perspective that focuses on the role of identities, ideas and discursive constructions. Arguably, most scholarly analyses on Nord Stream 2 have neglected ideational aspects so far, and rather investigated the topic from neorealist, geoeconomic or neoliberal perspectives (see for instance Boersma and Goldthau 2017; Vihma and Wigell 2016). Other, policy-oriented studies have focused on the economic and political consequences of the project (Goldthau 2016; Loskot-Strachota 2015), as well as on the extensive legal controversy that it has generated (Fischer 2017; Yafimava 2019).

The analysis starts with the presentation of the conceptual framework. This section outlines the constructions of the Russian Other in national identity discourses in the EU and puts forward a framework that relates these constructions to energy policy. In subsequent sections, the economic and political aspects of the Nord Stream 2 pipeline are discussed briefly in order to provide context and supplement the discursive analysis with considerations concerning material factors and Russian agency. The article then proceeds to the analysis of the case study, which focuses on the investigation of European discourses and stances concerning Nord Stream 2. Here, the main focus is on German and Polish discourses, which epitomise the opposing European approaches to Nord Stream 2. With regard to sources, the empirical analysis is based on official statements made by top officials (heads of governments, foreign ministers and ministers of the economy) between 2015 and 2018 – that is, following the launch of the Nord Stream 2 project. The sources have been retrieved from national governmental websites and the press.[1] This investigation is integrated with recent scholarly analyses of the broader, contemporary national public debate, which helps contextualise official statements.

The main contribution of the article consists in unearthing the ideational reasons for the post-2014 conflict/cooperation dichotomy in EU-Russia energy relations. It argues that an analysis of ideational factors is essential in order to understand the current debates and controversies on EU-Russia gas trade. National discourses on energy relations with Russia illustrate two types of symbolic boundaries between the EU and the Russian Other, across which both cooperation and conflict coexist (for a discussion of symbolic boundaries and different types thereof, see Introduction to the Special Issue). In particular, the article reveals that the EU-Russia energy relationship is more controversial close to the geographical zones of contact of the two blocs, for instance between Russia and Poland. It is argued that this is due to long-standing conflictual interaction at the local/regional level and its repercussions for Eastern European national identities. At this level, conflictual national identities tend to generate a solid boundary in the energy relationship. On the other hand, the EU-Russia energy relationship is more cooperative at the macro level, further away from the geographical EU-Russia border. In large EU member states such as Germany and Italy, the biggest importers of Russian gas, Russian energy supplies are broadly considered reliable and even desirable in order to strengthen the political relationship. Ideational factors play an important role also at the macro level, most notably through the conceptualisation of Russia as an important economic partner and a fundamental interlocutor for European (energy) security. At this level, more positive discourses on Russia generate a fluid boundary, where patterns of cooperation dominate conflict.

The Russian Other and energy policy

Social constructivist research has highlighted the link between national identity and foreign policy (Hopf 2002; Lebow 2008; Samokhvalov 2017; Siddi 2017b; Wendt 1999). National identity is a type of collective identity where the "collective" coincides with a defined nation.[2] It tends to be constructed through emphasis on a common culture, language, history, territory and through differentiation from external collectives – that is, other groups that do not share the same features. Differentiation from external collectives, a process that constructivist scholars call "the construction of the Other", is a particularly important part of national identity formation because it defines the boundaries of the national Self, as well as who is included in it and who is not. National identities are a social construct, and as such they are fluid and subject to changes. However, there can be no national identity without the construction of boundaries and distinction from outer groups (the Others). While boundaries and the emphasis on difference often lead to clashes between the Self and the Other, conflict is not preordained. The differentiation between Self and Other does not necessarily have to be a negative or a conflictual one (Lebow 2008). Summing up, national identity construction is always relational, but not necessarily oppositional (Hopf 2002, 7).

As much scholarship has argued, Russia played an important role as Other (as an external entity in relation to which the Self was built) in the construction of both European identity and of national identities in Europe (see for instance Morozov and Rumelili 2012; Neumann 1998; Siddi 2017b). However, the role that the Russian Other played in identity construction varies greatly from country to country. In many Eastern European states that found themselves under Moscow's coercive control after 1945, and in some cases also during the Tsarist period, Russia was constructed as a central and profoundly negative Other, or even as a security threat. In Poland, for instance, mainstream political discourse has portrayed Russia as an imperialist, aggressive, "Oriental" and corrupt Other that brutalised Poland for most of its modern history (Siddi 2017b, 49–57; Zarycki 2004).

Conversely, the Russian Other has played a more nuanced role in the construction of German identity. In Germany, narratives of Russia as an authoritarian and threatening country co-exist with discourses portraying it as an important economic partner and as a benevolent Other during the political process that led to German reunification in 1990 (Siddi 2018b). *Ostpolitik*, the (West) German policy of diplomatic and economic engagement with (Soviet) Russia that was first initiated in the 1960s, has retained such influence in policy-making circles that it can be seen as an important component of German foreign policy identity. In other European countries, particularly in Western and Southern Europe, the Russian Other was generally less central to national identity construction. In these cases (i.e. France, Italy), identity-based narratives are less pervasive in the domestic debate on Russia, which tends to be influenced more by immediate contingencies and current economic and political considerations (Cadier 2018; Siddi 2018c).

Therefore, following social constructivist theory, it can be argued that both the role and the centrality of the Russian Other in national identity discourses significantly influences the foreign policy debate on Russia. With its vast foreign policy ramifications, external energy policy is an important part of this debate. This is particularly true for European debates concerning Russia, because Russia is the largest external provider of energy to the EU. The relationship between identity constructions of the Russian Other and external energy policy towards Russia can be conceptualised along two continuous axes which describe such constructions as central/marginal to national identity and antagonistic/cooperative. Figure 1 summarises this conceptualisation.

When the Russian Other is central to national identity construction, energy relations with Russia tend to be discussed in a closer relationship with politics and other bilateral issues. The way both energy trade and its political implications are discussed depends on whether Russia is perceived as an antagonistic or a cooperative Other. At the "antagonistic" end of the axis, where for instance the Law and Justice governments of Poland

Figure 1. Identity constructions of the Russian Other and energy policy towards Russia.

(2005–2007 and 2015-present) could be located, Russia is seen as a political and security threat, and energy trade with it is seen as undesirable and as a source of vulnerability for the country. At the "cooperative" end of the axis, where Gerhard Schröder's German governments (1998–2005) could be located[3], energy cooperation with Russia is seen as being both commercially advantageous and politically desirable because it strengthens bilateral relations and leads to a rapprochement in unrelated areas, including people-to-people contacts. Conversely, if the Russian Other does not play a major role in identity construction, energy policy towards Russia focuses more, or exclusively, on technical and commercial aspects. In this case, economics usually trumps politics, regardless of whether Russia tends to be seen more positively (as for instance in Italian domestic debates) or negatively (as arguably in the British domestic debate).

An Addendum to the model: material factors and Russian agency

The theoretical framework presented above focuses on ideational factors (identity and the construction of the Other) in order to show that they also matter in defining energy policy. On the other hand, it does not fully account for other, material determinants of energy policy, such as economic profitability or strategic considerations. These factors are significant and are thus discussed along ideational ones in the empirical analysis below. At the same time, the article does attempt to convey the argument that material factors alone cannot explain different national energy policies towards Russia, and that the ideational dimension is a fundamental determinant. In other words, Germany's decision to support the Nord Stream 2 project was not simply driven by economic interests, but also rested on positive political conceptualisations of energy relations with Russia. By the same token, antagonistic constructions of the Russian Other (and of German-Russian cooperation) are at least as important as strategic or economic considerations in shaping Poland's opposition to the project.

Furthermore, Russian agency also plays a role in shaping German and Polish ideas and policies, as well as concrete policy outcomes. Launching the Nord Stream 2 project was possible because the Russian side had a political and economic interest and shared a positive ideational conceptualisation of energy cooperation with its German and Western partners. On the other hand, it was aware of Polish political opposition to expanding energy cooperation (Martewicz 2018). While this remains beyond the scope of the article, it is plausible that Russian ideational constructs mirrored Polish ones (that is, they conceptualised Poland as an antagonistic Other; see BBC 2017 for an example of a contemporary dispute concerning identity and historical issues) and were not conducive to seeking further energy cooperation with Warsaw.[4]

The Nord Stream 2 project

The Nord Stream 2 project was launched in the summer of 2015 by Russia's state energy company Gazprom together with five Western European partner companies. The pipeline will have a capacity of 55 billion cubic metres of gas per year (bcm/y) and follow an offshore route from Russia to Germany via the Baltic Sea. Together with the parallel infrastructure of the already existing Nord Stream pipeline (which became operational in 2011–2), this energy corridor could carry 110 bcm/y and thus a large part of Russia's gas exports to Europe, which were approximately 180 bcm in 2017 (Henderson and Sharples 2018, 6). The Nord Stream 2 project has caused a vast debate in Europe that has numerous political, economic and legal ramifications. The following paragraphs only summarise the main political and economic aspects that are essential to the ensuing discussion, and refer to more comprehensive studies (Goldthau 2016; Henderson and Sharples 2018; Lang and Westphal 2017) for further details.

Nord Stream 2 could make EU-Russia gas trade much less dependent on transit pipelines in Ukraine. Ukrainian transit has been essential to gas flows from (Soviet) Russia to Europe since the Cold War, but has become more controversial following the 2006 and 2009 Russian-Ukrainian gas crises (which led to a temporary interruption of gas flows to Europe) and the more fundamental conflict between Moscow and Kiev that began in 2014. The future of the ageing Ukrainian transit pipelines after the expiry of the Russian-Ukrainian transit agreement in 2019 remains unclear, even if both sides have already stated that some volumes of Russian gas directed to Europe will continue to be channelled through them (Soldatkin 2018). While Nord Stream 2 creates an alternative and arguably more secure gas route than Ukrainian transit, it is seen by many in Europe and the US as highly controversial from a political standpoint. Critics argue that the pipeline would consolidate Europe's energy dependence on Russia at a time when the EU has adopted sanctions against Moscow and supported Ukraine in the conflict with Russia. The potential redirection of gas flows from Ukrainian transit to Nord Stream 2 would indeed imply an economic loss for Ukraine (which currently earns approximately $2 billion per year from transit fees) and weaken its strategic leverage vis-à-vis Russia.

Eastern European EU member states such as Poland, Slovakia and the Baltic States are particularly vocal in their criticism of Nord Stream 2 for both political reasons (the damage that it would inflict on Ukraine and the more general objection to deals with Russia) and because it would redirect gas flows and transit revenues away from their territory. Moreover, Poland is developing its own plans to import non-Russian gas, both via pipeline (through the Baltic Pipe) and LNG terminals (such as its Swinoujscie LNG terminal), and potentially re-export part of it to other East-Central European markets. Warsaw therefore sees Nord Stream 2 and additional flows of Russian gas to Germany as thwarting its energy strategy. The European Commission has criticised the project too, arguing that it contradicts the spirit of its Energy Union initiative, especially the objective of diversifying import partners (Siddi 2016). Supporters of Nord Stream 2 counter that the pipeline is a commercial project and it should not be undermined by politics. This argument is substantiated by the fact that EU market rules are based on the concept of competition, and the Commission has the power to act as a watchdog of competition, but cannot influence it for political reasons.

Other arguments that have been made in favour of Nord Stream 2 focus on stable or increasing European gas demand at a time of diminishing domestic gas production and the need to buy gas where it is cheaper for the sake of commercial competitiveness.[5] It is also argued that additional gas imports would allow reducing coal and oil consumption (which pollute more than gas) and keep gas as a backup for intermittent renewable energy production while Europe pursues the transition to a low carbon economy. In Germany, the decision to switch off nuclear power plants by 2022 puts additional pressure on the government to secure other energy sources while making sure that the country meets its decarbonisation targets.

Nord Stream 2: an articulation of the EU-Russia conflict-cooperation dichotomy?

Nord Stream 2 and conceptualisations of the Russian Other in Germany

The Nord Stream 2 debate took place against a background of high tensions in EU-Russia relations, which were related primarily to the Ukraine crisis, Russia's military intervention in Syria and allegations of Russian interference in Western electoral processes and societal debates. As a consequence of these tensions, long-standing identity-based narratives of the Russian Other were reactivated and influenced current political debates in many EU member states (see Siddi 2017b, 137–156). However, this also meant that different national articulations of the Russian Other became relevant and influenced policy debates in different ways from country to country. While the assessment of Russia became more negative throughout the EU, leading to the joint EU decision to impose sanctions on Moscow, there were different views about the nature of Russian policies and especially about how to engage the Kremlin in the future. Nowhere does this become clearer than in the divergent German and Polish approaches to energy relations with Russia. The German and Polish debate on Nord Stream 2 reflected two radically different perceptions of the Russian Other.

At the time when the Nord Stream 2 project was launched, high-ranking German officials such as then Foreign Minister Frank-Walter Steinmeier (2016) argued that the West and Russia "need[ed] each other" to resolve regional conflicts, as negotiations on the Iranian nuclear programme and Syria had shown. Despite tensions and Steinmeier's own critical assessment of Russian behaviour in the Ukraine crisis, he described Russia as "the EU's largest neighbour", arguing that "good neighbourly relations [were] in the interests of both sides". Significantly, he believed that "after the experiences of the twentieth century, we Germans in particular bear a responsibility to keep finding channels of communication and solutions to conflicts [with Russia]". This discourse reflected consolidated German narratives about guilt for the Second World War, and particularly for war crimes in Eastern Europe, which had been influential in the framing of *Ostpolitik* in the 1960s and 1970s (Siddi 2018b). In the post-2014 context, this ideational background induced German policy makers to be wary of radicalising the debate on Russia and seek instead a resolution of the crisis through dialogue, diplomacy and neighbourly cooperation.

One of the prominent articulations of this cooperation concerned trade and energy policy, much like during the *Ostpolitik* of the 1970s (Lang and Westphal 2017, 27). Steinmeier (2016) argued that

> Russia was always a reliable energy partner for us – including in difficult times. The Nord Stream 2 project is currently being discussed in depth between the companies involved and the European Commission. And of course we are also taking part in this discussion […] Our economic ties with Russia remain very close […] I am pleased that most German companies are continuing to work with Russia despite this difficult environment.

Steinmeier's views were widely shared among top officials in the German coalition government (including the centre-left Social Democratic Party and the centre-right Christian Democratic Union/Christian Social Union). This was especially true of Steinmeier's fellow Social Democrats, who often praised their former party leader Willy Brandt for crafting the *Ostpolitik*. Minister of Economic Affairs and Energy (2013–7) and then Foreign Minister (2017–8) Sigmar Gabriel argued that he was "strongly in favour of a new *Ostpolitik* and a new policy of détente", adding that "Brandt began his *Ostpolitik* in 1968 after the Soviet Union had invaded Czechoslovakia, in other words, during the most difficult times" (Gabriel 2017a). Gabriel's successor as foreign minister, Social Democrat Heiko Maas, has stated that "the only possible answer [to the crisis with Russia] is a European *Ostpolitik*" (Maas 2018).

While references to Brandt were mostly the domain of Social Democratic ministers, support of Nord Stream 2 was widely shared across party lines in the government (except for a critical and vocal minority) and even among the opposition. In parliamentary debates, only the Green Party, in opposition, consistently criticised the project. The German media debate on Nord Stream 2 was more critical, but this did not seem to alter the stance of political leaders on the project (Siddi 2020; see also Heinrich 2017, 74–79 for an analysis of media and parliamentary debates on the first Nord Stream project). Most notably, Chancellor Angela Merkel emphasised that Nord Stream 2 was a commercial endeavour and should not be undermined by politics (see for instance German Federal Government 2018a). In fact, behind this apparently neutral stance was significant political support for the project, which emerged more clearly over time, as Nord Stream 2 came under attack from Eastern European member states and particularly the US.

As Polish opposition to Nord Stream 2 became more vocal (see below), Gabriel (2017b) told Polish media that the pipeline was in the broader European interest and conformed to EU market principles: "Gas pipelines do not only transport Russian gas to Germany, but also to Poland, of course [...] We ask people to understand that we want to stand by the liberalisation of the gas supply undertaken in Europe years ago". At the same time, Gabriel and Merkel conceded that Nord Stream 2 would have an impact on gas transit in Ukraine, Poland and other Eastern European countries, and pledged that Germany would support the continuation of this transit (Gabriel 2017b; German Federal Government 2018b).

The German official response to the US was more critical. The US were seen as interfering in European energy politics and having a conflict of interests on the Nord Stream 2 question. In June 2017, the US Congress prepared a draft bill that included possible sanctions against Western companies participating in the Nord Stream 2 project. At the same time, US President Donald Trump and numerous other US politicians argued that the EU should import US liquefied natural gas rather than Russian gas. Soon after the sanctions bill was announced, Gabriel issued a joint statement with Austrian Federal Chancellor Christian Kern which criticised harshly the US stance:

> We cannot, however, accept the threat of illegal extraterritorial sanctions being imposed on European companies that are participating in efforts to expand Europe's energy supply network! The draft bill of the US is surprisingly candid about what is actually at stake, namely selling American liquefied natural gas [...] This is about the competitiveness of our energy-intensive industries, and about thousands of jobs [...] Europe's energy supply network is Europe's affair, not that of the United States of America! (Gabriel and Kern 2017).

Thus, German leaders insisted on the commercial nature of the project, as well as the fact that it respected EU market principles and laws, whereas stopping it for political reasons would counter those very principles. Arguably, the German defence of Nord Stream 2 went beyond commercial and legal issues and backed a policy line which sought a partial rapprochement with Russia on mutually beneficial contact points. The pursuit of Nord Stream 2 amidst contemporary tensions in EU-Russia relations reflected the belief that cooperation with the Russian Other was still possible, and that conflict was neither all-encompassing nor preordained. The ideational constructs that shaped relevant German discourses played an important role in the persistence of the cooperative dimension of the EU-Russia conflict/cooperation dichotomy.

The Polish view on Nord Stream 2 and the Russian Other

The Polish debate on Nord Stream 2 and the Russian Other was radically different from the German debate. The Russian Other was mostly essentialised as a security threat and all its policy initiatives – including energy projects – were seen as having negative security implications. As previously argued, antagonistic Polish narratives of the Russian Other have a long history that predates Moscow's aggressive policies in Ukraine or Syria, and are grounded in Polish experiences of Tsarist and Soviet domination (Zarycki 2004). In the realm of energy policy, these narratives had already been activated earlier, for instance in relation to the first Nord Stream project (Siddi 2017b, 76–83). In 2006, shortly after the project was announced, then Defence Minister Radoslaw Sikorski called it "a new Molotov-Ribbentrop pact" (cited in Castle 2006), thus comparing it to the 1939 Nazi-Soviet deal to partition Eastern Europe. Following the death of Polish President Lech Kaczynski in April 2010 in a plane crash in Russia, while he was *en route* to visit the Katyn memorial site, the question of the repatriation of the plane wreck to Poland has been a constant irritant in bilateral relations, and the relevant debate has often strayed off to historical disputes (Davies 2016; Sus 2018, 78, 87).

Moscow's post-2014 belligerent foreign policy contributed to reviving the most antagonistic Polish identity narratives about Russia. In this regard, Russian agency was compounded by changes in Polish domestic politics, most notably the rise to power of the nationalist and profoundly anti-Russian Law and Justice party. The electoral victory of Law and Justice in the fall of 2015 ended eight years of centre-right government under the leadership of Donald Tusk's Civic Platform. Law and Justice has a history of antagonising both Russia and Germany in political discourse (Reeves 2010). In 2016, one of its main representatives, then Foreign Minister Witold Waszczykowski, argued that Russia was an existential threat for Europe, one more dangerous than ISIS (cited in Guardian 2016). Hence, as a result of both Russian policies and Polish domestic politics, the Polish-Russian bilateral relationship took the form of a confrontational deadlock (for a full account, see Sus 2018). In the Polish domestic debate, Law and Justice politicians used the image of the antagonistic Russian Other against the political opposition, arguing that the Civic Platform and the Russian leadership had been responsible for the Smolensk plane crash and the death of Lech Kaczynski (Davies 2016).

Against this domestic and international background, the Polish parliamentary and media debates on Nord Stream 2 have been overwhelmingly negative across party lines. The project is seen as politically motivated, as well as a threat to Poland's energy security and economic and strategic interests (Sus 2018, 85–6). Many of the arguments that had been made against the first Nord Stream project have been reiterated – for instance, the notion that Poland will face political pressure from Russia after the pipeline is built (cf. Heinrich 2017, 65–73). However, as illustrated in the analysis below, the official debate has become more radicalised due to the tenser international context and the fact that Law and Justice is now in power in Warsaw.

When Nord Stream was launched, some Polish politicians still argued that the damage which the pipeline would inflict on Poland was actually limited, and Warsaw could compete with it (also) by promoting alternative routes for Russian gas (such as the Amber pipeline through the Baltic states) (Heinrich 2017, 67–68, 85). In the context of the Nord Stream 2 debate, such moderate considerations are absent: the project is seen as catastrophic for Poland. The Polish government's position on Nord Stream 2 is well summarised in the op-ed written by Minister for European Affairs Konrad Szymanski for *Financial Times* in October 2016.

> Poland has opposed Nord Stream 2 since it was first announced by Gazprom in 2015. It undermines European solidarity and the Energy Union, the EU's flagship project. The economic arguments for Nord Stream 2 were always questionable […] And given Europe's considerable dependence on Russian gas and the damage the project would cause to the Ukrainian economy (which is subsidised by the EU), the political motivations behind it seemed obvious […] [Nord Stream 2] now looks like a Trojan horse capable of destabilising the economy and poisoning political relations inside the EU […] By supporting Nord Stream 2, the EU in effect gives succour to a regime whose aggression it seeks to punish through sanctions. This contradiction is unsustainable. (Szymanski 2016)

Szymanski cited economic factors and European solidarity first, but his main argument was political: it was based on juxtaposing Nord Stream 2 to Russia's aggressive policy in the Ukraine crisis. The project was not assessed with reference to market factors, such as European demand, transit risks and competition among gas suppliers, but exclusively as a Russian instrument in the geopolitical struggle for Eastern Europe. The conceptualisation of Russia as a threatening Other provides the underlying logic for this narrative.

Szymanski's arguments were reiterated in the public statements of Poland's top leadership. President Andrzej Duda argued that Nord Stream 2 "has nothing to do with economics" and "is an investment of political nature" (Reuters 2016a). Prime Minister Beata Szydlo argued that the project represented a threat to the energy independence of the whole Central and Eastern Europe (PAP 2017). Foreign Minister Witold Waszczykowski claimed that the pipeline undermined trust among EU member states, struck "a blow against not only CEE [Central and Eastern Europe]'s security of gas supplies, but also Ukraine's stability" (2016a); it may also cause "geopolitical destabilisation in Central Europe" (2016b).

In the speeches of Polish leaders, explicit references to history were present next to the analysis of current political and energy relations with Russia. These references reflected long-standing Polish identity narratives which constructed Russia as a conflictual and threatening Other. For instance, in an interview focusing on Poland's foreign, security and energy policy, Waszczykowski explained his country's stance by arguing that "Poland has had bad experiences in its history. We want to be cautious. We have a war behind our doors right now. We have an aggressive neighbour that is openly proclaiming the redrawing of the borders of Europe" (cited in Dempsey 2016). Similarly, in his speech on Polish foreign policy tasks in 2017, he argued that "Poland will not accept such a vision [the Russian vision] of the political order in Europe, and will not condone the carving up of our continent into spheres of influence. Never again Munich or Yalta!" (Waszczykowski 2017).

Waszczykowski also used the Nord Stream 2 controversy to criticise Germany and associate the project with unrelated issues. He argued that Chancellor Angela Merkel was "working very hard on Nord Stream 2" (cited in Dempsey 2016) and that the pipeline was a way for Berlin and Brussels to punish Poland for a controversial judicial reform (which, in the view of the European Commission, undermines the rule of law in the country) (Harper 2017). In his address on Polish foreign policy tasks for 2018, Foreign Minister Jacek Czaputowicz (who succeeded to Waszczykowski after a cabinet reshuffle) juxtaposed his criticism of Nord Stream 2 to demands that Germany compensates Poland for the losses the latter suffered during the Second World War (Czaputowicz 2018).[6] Juxtapositions like this one aimed at mobilising influential Polish identity narratives of the Second World War that constructed Germany as a negative Other and use them in the current political debate.

Polish and German leaders have engaged each other in the attempt to resolve differences concerning the Nord Stream 2 project, but their visions have remained fundamentally different. In a bilateral meeting between Merkel and Polish Prime Minister Mateusz Morawiecki in February 2018, Merkel continued to defend Nord Stream 2 as an economic project and an import diversification route, whereas Morawiecki reiterated that it entails political and security risks (BiznesAlert 2018; King 2018).

As the project went ahead, Polish leaders further radicalised their rhetoric. President Andrzej Duda called Nord Stream 2 "a weapon in the hybrid war being conducted against Ukraine" (cited in Radio Poland 2018). Similarly, Morawiecki stated that the pipeline is a weapon of hybrid warfare that Moscow wants to use to undermine European energy security and EU and NATO solidarity, "a poison pill for European security" (cited in RFE/RL 2018). Thus, from a Polish perspective, the project continued to be a malign activity engineered by the threatening Russian Other for geopolitical purposes. In the discourse of Polish leaders, the only possible responses to Nord Stream 2 were efforts to block it at the European level, or counter it with alternative projects without Russian participation, such as the Baltic Pipe (see Waszczykowski 2017) and LNG deliveries from the United States (Czaputowicz 2018).[7] In stark contradiction with Germany's position, the Polish stance epitomised the conflictual dimension of the EU-Russia conflict/cooperation dichotomy in energy policy.

Including material factors in the analysis

The investigation of the German and Polish stance on Nord Stream 2 would be incomplete without an analysis of material factors, particularly economic and strategic ones. While ideas and a greater predisposition to cooperate with Russia on energy policy played a role in Germany's positive stance on Nord Stream 2, so did the material gains expected from the project. Together with the already operational Nord Stream pipelines, Nord Stream 2 would allow Germany to become the main hub for Russian gas in Europe. The pipelines create a direct link between Gazprom's gas fields and German consumers, without any transit-related risks and tariffs. From an economic perspective, this is understandable because Germany is the largest importer of Russian gas in Europe, and gas is expected to acquire a more important role in the German energy mix due to the phase-out of nuclear power plants and the need to curb coal consumption.

In addition to satisfying its own gas demand, however, Germany will probably also be in the position of managing substantial flows of Russian gas towards Western, Southern and

Central Europe (cf. Loskot-Strachota and Poplawski 2016). This can be inferred from the fact that the combined capacity of the Nord Stream pipelines (110 bcm/y) exceeds German gas consumption of Russian gas (which was 53.4 bcm/y in 2017[8]). Potentially, this also means that countries further down the pipes may have to pay slightly higher prices for gas than Berlin due to the additional transport costs. This has caused some concern in states that are industrial competitors of Germany, such as Italy (Reuters 2016b).

By the same token, material factors also play some role in Poland's opposition to Nord Stream 2. If the project is completed, the transit pipelines channelling Russian gas across Polish territory (Yamal-Europe) could lose economic and strategic relevance – although the main impact will be on Ukrainian transit pipelines, which have a much larger capacity. This would also endanger Polish revenue from transit fees, which however is very modest, around $5.5 million a year (cf. Reuters 2017a). The Polish authorities also fear that, by making large volumes of cheap Russian gas available on the Polish market, Nord Stream 2 would prevent competition and the diversification of Poland's gas imports. In fact, this argument seems to combine economic and political factors. From an economic perspective, regardless of current prices, a more diversified portfolio of suppliers prevents the emergence of a monopolist, and thus reduces the risk of higher prices in the future. At the same time, Poland's diversification away from Russian gas imports is at least partly motivated by politics, particularly at a time when gas from Russia tends to be cheaper than the alternatives envisaged by the Polish government (such as US LNG).

Warsaw's strategic arguments are grounded on the following logic. By redirecting volumes of gas away from Ukraine, Nord Stream 2 would weaken Kiev's strategic position vis-à-vis Russia and the EU (which will reduce reliance on Ukrainian transit pipelines) and decrease its income from transit fees (Loskot-Strachota 2015). The overall impact may therefore be the economic and strategic weakening of Ukraine, which Poland sees as an important geopolitical partner curbing Russian influence. However, this conceptualisation of Ukraine as an anti-Russian buffer is also grounded in long-standing Polish ideational constructs and historical narratives (Fomina 2016, 107). Similarly, Polish perceptions of Russian-German commercial deals as a threat are not simply due to possible negative economic consequences for Poland; they are also linked to negative ideational constructs of German-Russian cooperation, which are deeply entrenched in Polish identity (cf. Reeves 2010, 527–8). Thus, both the economic and the strategic factors guiding Poland's stance appear to be intertwined with ideational constructs.

Hence, it is difficult to argue that material factors were the main determinant of Poland's opposition to Nord Stream 2. Had Warsaw been guided by economic logic, it would have attempted to compete with Nord Stream 2 by securing its own supplies of cheap Russian gas, for instance through the expansion of the Yamal pipeline. In the current Polish political discourse, however, this course of action appears unthinkable because the pervasive, negative constructions of the Russian Other make further energy cooperation with Moscow highly undesirable.

The stances of other EU member states: a brief overview

While an in-depth assessment of the stances and discourses of other EU member states involved in the Nord Stream 2 debate is beyond the scope of this article, there is room to present an overview of the main positions and of how they related to the German and Polish approaches. As briefly mentioned earlier, Austria's stance on Nord Stream 2 was similar to that of Germany. While Austria does not have an *Ostpolitik* tradition with Russia as influential as that of Germany, it does have a long history of energy trade with Moscow and a national identity that is largely based on its neutral post-Second World War constitution (Kovacs and Wodak 2003). Together with its economic interests in the project, this arguably motivated the Austrian negative reaction to US extraterritorial sanctions targeting Nord Stream 2 (cited above), which could be seen as an attempt to force upon the country a choice between good relations with either Russia or the US.

Other EU member states that had a tradition of cooperative commercial relations and energy trade with Russia took a similar stance to that of Austria and Germany and criticised the US extraterritorial sanctions (Reuters 2017b). As French and Dutch companies are involved in Nord Stream 2, their interests are a factor affecting the stance of France and the Netherlands. The French and Dutch governments refrained from commenting on Nord Stream 2 and let Germany take the lead in its defence. Moreover, like Germany, France has a tradition of seeing economic cooperation with Russia positively, and the Macron government has not departed from it (Deutsche Welle 2018; cf. Cadier 2018). Italy expressed a critical perspective on Nord Stream 2 due to the fact that it concentrates EU-Russia gas trade along a northern route, as opposed to a southern one reaching Italian territory. However, Rome disapproved of the US sanctions because energy trade has been a cornerstone of Italian-Russian relations (Italy is the second largest importer of Russian gas after Germany) and Italian companies were involved in other projects that might be affected too (Bongiorni 2017; Siddi 2018c).

The United Kingdom (UK) kept a low profile towards Nord Stream 2. The new crisis in bilateral relations with Russia following the poisoning of Sergei and Yulia Skripal on British soil led some UK politicians, such as then Foreign Secretary Boris Johnson, to support a more critical stance towards the project (Wintour 2018). Nevertheless, Prime Minister Theresa May refrained from overtly criticising Nord Stream 2 (Sengupta 2018). As the potential consequences of the project are likely to be mostly positive for the UK (due to additional gas reaching the North-Western European markets, see Goldthau 2016, 30–31), no strong opposition to it has arisen in the domestic private sector. Thus, the UK could be seen as a discursive arena where perceptions of the Russian Other are predominantly negative (cf. Nitoiu 2018), but they are not pervasive in national identity and the political debate. This enables economic considerations on themes such as Nord Stream 2 to play an important role in the national debate, alongside negative identity-driven or political arguments.

Nordic members of the EU (Sweden, Finland and Denmark) are not directly affected by Nord Stream 2, if one excepts their decision on granting permission to build the pipeline in their Exclusive Economic Zones or, in the case of Denmark, in its territorial waters. While their national debates on Russia and Nord Stream 2 have become more securitised following the Ukraine crisis, environmental and legal considerations – rather than identity-driven narratives – are the key factor in the Finnish and Swedish stance. They also face the pressure of maintaining positive relations with Germany and Russia, which are key commercial and security actors in their neighbourhood. Finland also maintains a close energy relationship with Russia, including the recent decision to have Russian company Rosatom build a new nuclear plant on Finnish soil (Aalto et al. 2017). Denmark has recently passed a law that would enable it to deny permission to construct the pipeline on its territory for security reasons (Reuters 2018). However, it is unlikely that it will stop the project (for further analysis, see Gotkowska and Szymanski 2016).

The position of several Eastern European member states tends to be far more critical, if not overtly hostile to Nord Stream 2 (cf. Lang and Westphal 2017, 29–34). Apart from Poland, five more of them (the Baltic States, Romania and Slovakia) have consistently argued against the project. The position of the Baltic States is very similar to that of Poland, both in terms of official stance and of likely underlying factors. As the Nord Stream project does not divert gas transit away from their territory (and thus transit revenues), their stance is mostly due to the same strategic and political considerations as Poland's, and is similarly influenced by pervasive negative constructions of the Russian Other (for an extensive discussion, see Berg and Ehin 2009).

While Russia, and particularly its Soviet past, has been conceptualised negatively also in the national identities of other Eastern European countries, antagonising constructions of the Russian Other do not appear as dominant as in Poland or the Baltic States, particularly in current political discourse. Hence, while negative perceptions of Russia are influential also in these countries, their national debates tend to be influenced more by contextual and material factors. In the case of Slovakia, economic considerations appear to be the main reasons for its opposition to Nord Stream 2. Slovakia plays a key role in the transit of gas that reaches the EU via Ukraine and earned over €350 million annually in transit revenues in recent years. It thus stands to lose if gas flows are redirected to the Nord Stream 2 route. Romania is an important transit country for Russian gas supplies to the Balkans, and would most likely lose this function if Ukrainian transit pipelines are no longer used (Lang and Westphal 2017, 28–30; Loskot-Strachota and Poplawski 2016).

On the other hand, some other Eastern European countries have been ambivalent towards Nord Stream 2. This is the case of Bulgaria, whose population has closer cultural and linguistic ties with Russia than other regional actors, and thus a less critical conceptualisation of the Russian Other. Material factors also play a role: Sofia maintains an interest in a new Southern route for Russian gas imports, and is thus wary of undermining its relations with Russia and Gazprom (Lang and Westphal 2017, 34; Smilov and Andreev 2018). Perspectives on Russia tend to be complex, and by far not as one-sided as in Poland and the Baltics, also in the Czech Republic and Hungary. Material factors are likely to be significant in both cases. With Nord Stream 2 operational, the Czech Republic could acquire greater importance as a transit country in Central Europe and also strengthen its energy security (Groszkowski 2017). After initially voicing a critical stance, Hungary has taken a more supportive approach to Nord Stream 2. Due also to the positive relationship between President Viktor Orban and Putin, Budapest is cooperating with Russia in strategic energy projects in the nuclear field and appears interested in further cooperation with Gazprom with regard to gas trade and infrastructural projects (Aalto et al. 2017; Hejj 2018; Lang and Westphal 2017, 33).

Conclusions

Trade and cooperation have continued to shape the EU-Russia energy relationship after the Ukraine crisis, and volumes of Russian energy exports to the EU have reached new peaks in 2017 and 2018 (Siddi 2018d, 3). The energy relationship thus remains an important "contact zone" between Brussels and Moscow at a time of high political tensions.

However, largely due to these tensions and to Russian agency in the foreign policy realm, EU-Russia energy relations have become more controversial than in the past. Arguably, they evolved into another articulation of the conflict/cooperation dichotomy that characterises the broader framework of EU-Russia relations. The article exposed this through an analysis of European discourses on Nord Stream 2, with a focus on Germany and Poland. It argued that ideational factors, particularly identity-based constructions of the Russian Other, play an important role in shaping national positions, alongside material factors.

Focusing on ideational factors, the article presented a theoretical framework according to which the role and centrality of the Russian Other in national identity construction influences foreign and energy policy debates concerning Russia. Where the Russian Other is central to national identity construction, energy relations tend to be discussed with more frequent references to political and historical issues. The forms these discussions take depend on whether constructions of the Russian Other are predominantly antagonistic or cooperative. The analysis of German and Polish official discourses provided empirical evidence for these theoretical claims. In the German case, the Russian Other is partly conceptualised in non-antagonistic terms based on the *Ostpolitik* tradition and long-standing economic cooperation. This conceptualisation results in a fluid boundary between the German Self and the Russian Other. In the Polish case, the Russian Other is constructed as threatening and aggressive, which generates a solid boundary between the Polish Self and the Russian Other. As the discourse analysis has shown, these constructions shape different views on energy relations with Russia.

Ideational factors are thus important drivers of both cooperative and conflictual approaches to energy relations with Russia. At the same time, the article did not dismiss material factors as unimportant. From a theoretical perspective, it was argued that material factors play an important role – and can be even more influential than ideational factors – in shaping debates and policies where the Russian Other is not central to national identity construction. The brief overview of the stances and debates on Nord Stream 2 in other EU member states provided concrete examples of this, which could be investigated further in future studies. The Nord Stream 2 project has also led to extensive legal controversy, mostly due to the attempts of some EU member states (Poland *in primis*) and the European Commission to thwart the project through legal means (Fischer 2017; Yafimava 2019). While the legal aspects of the controversy were not the focus of this article, they are an important and still developing component of the Nord Stream 2 debate that should be explored in depth in future scholarly endeavours.

Both ideational and material factors in Western, Southern and some Eastern EU member states continue to determine a cooperative pattern in EU-Russia energy relations, despite the concomitant political crisis. However, the cooperative approach has been challenged by a number of Eastern member states, where the Russian Other is conceptualised predominantly or exclusively as a security threat due to long-standing conflictual interaction. This has resulted in a conflict-cooperation dichotomy in EU-Russia energy relations. As Poland's and the Baltic States' opposition to the Nord Stream 2 project shows, the conflictual dimension of the dichotomy is particularly strong near the geographical contact zone between the EU an Russia, whereas the energy relationship is more cooperative at the macro level. Different conceptualisations of the Russian Other have fostered conflict both in the EU's internal formulation of its energy policy towards Russia (where member states retain important competences) and in EU-Russia energy relations.

Notes

1. On the websites of the German and Polish foreign ministry, the ministry of the economy and the prime minister's office, the search function for "Nord Stream" was used to retrieve all speeches and press releases pertaining to the project.
2. In turn, a nation can be described as "a community with shared beliefs and mutual commitment, extended in history and connected to a particular territory. It is marked off from other nations by a distinct public culture, including shared political principles, social norms and cultural ideals" (Siddi 2017b, 7).
3. Gerhard Schröder vigorously supported energy trade with Russia and the construction of the first Nord Stream project. Angela Merkel's governments have supported the Nord Stream 2 project since 2015, and can also be located on the cooperative side of the axis, even though their rhetoric has been more nuanced than that of Schröder (for instance, Merkel recognised that the project would have an impact on gas transit and revenues in Ukraine).
4. Had mutual perceptions of Russian-Polish energy relations been positive, Gazprom may have considered doubling the capacity of the Yamal-Europe pipeline via Belarus and Poland together with, or rather than building Nord Stream 2.
5. See also Nord Stream 2 website, "Fact-checking myths", https://www.nord-stream2.com/project/facts-myths/.
6. Czaputowicz stated: "We consider the Nord Stream 2 project to be a threat to the whole region's energy security, and to the common EU energy market. We will also be discussing the need to compensate Poles for the losses suffered during World War Two."
7. The Baltic Pipe is a planned pipeline connecting the Polish Baltic coast to Denmark, which would allow Poland to increase imports of Norwegian gas.
8. See http://www.gazpromexport.ru/en/statistics/.

Disclosure statement

No potential conflict of interest was reported by the author.

ORCID

Marco Siddi http://orcid.org/0000-0002-5881-5574

References

Aalto, Pami, and Tuomas Forsberg. 2016. "The Structuration of Russia's Geo-Economy under Economic Sanctions." *Asia Europe Journal* 14 (2): 221–237.

Aalto, Pami, Heino Nyyssönen, Matti Kojo, and Pallavi Pal. 2017. "Russian Nuclear Energy Diplomacy in Finland and Hungary." *Eurasian Geography and Economics* 58 (4): 386–417.

Averre, Derek. 2009. "Competing Rationalities: Russia, the EU and the 'Shared Neighbourhood.'" *Europe-Asia Studies* 61 (10): 1689–1713.

BBC. 2017. "Russia Warns Poland Not to Touch Soviet WW2 memorials," 31 July. https://www.bbc.com/news/world-europe-40775355.

Belyi, Andrei. 2015. *Transnational Gas Markets and Euro-Russian Energy Relations*. Basingstoke: Palgrave Macmillan.

Berg, Eiki, and Piret Ehin. 2009. *Identity and Foreign Policy: Baltic-Russian Relations and European Integration*. Farnham: Ashgate.

BiznesAlert. 2018. "Merkel and Morawiecki: We Have Different Views on Nord Stream 2," 19 February. http://biznesalert.com/merkel-morawiecki-nord-stream-2/.

Boersma, Tim, and Andreas Goldthau. 2017. "Wither the EU's Market Making Project in Energy: From Liberalization to Securitization?" In *Energy Union. Europe's New Liberal Mercantilism? Basingstoke*, edited by S. Andersen, A. Goldthau, and N. Sitter, 99–114. Basingstoke: Palgrave Macmillan.

Bongiorni, Roberto. 2017. "Da Nord Stream a Sakhalin, a rischio 8 progetti europei". *Il Sole 24 Ore*, 26 July. http://www.ilsole24ore.com/art/mondo/2017-07-25/da-nord-stream-sakhalin-rischio-8-progetti-europei–200606.shtml?uuid=AEYMUD3B.

Cadier, David. 2018. "France's Russia Policy from Europeanisation to Macronisation." In *EU Member States and Russia: National and European Debates in an Evolving International Environment*. FIIA Report 53, edited by M. Siddi, 41–58. Helsinki: Finnish Institute of International Affairs.

Castle, Stephen. 2006. "Poles Angry at Pipeline Pact." *The Independent*, 1 May. www.independent.co.uk/news/world/europe/poles-angry-at-pipeline-pact-6102171.html.

Czaputowicz, Jacek. 2018. "Information of the Minister of Foreign Affairs on Polish foreign policy tasks in 2018," 21 March. https://www.msz.gov.pl/en/ministry/minister/speeches/information_of_the_minister_of_foreign_affairs_on_polish_foreign_policy_tasks_in_2018.

David, Maxine, and Tatiana Romanova. 2015. "Modernisation in EU–Russian Relations: Past, Present, and Future." *European Politics and Society* 16 (1): 1–10.

Davies, Christian. 2016. "The Conspiracy Theorists Who Have Taken Over Poland." *The Guardian*, 16 February. https://www.theguardian.com/world/2016/feb/16/conspiracy-theorists-who-have-taken-over-poland.

Dempsey, Judy. 2016. Interview with Witold Waszczykowski. *Carnegie Europe*, 17 March. http://carnegieeurope.eu/strategiceurope/63057.

Deutsche Welle. 2018. "French President Emmanuel Macron in Russia Proposes Joint Initiatives with Vladimir Putin", 24 May. https://www.dw.com/en/french-president-emmanuel-macron-in-russia-proposes-joint-initiatives-with-vladimir-putin/a-43920043.

Fischer, Severin. 2017. *Lost in Regulation: The EU and Nord Stream 2. Policy Perspectives 5/5*. Zurich: Centre for Security Studies, ETH Zurich.

Fomina, Joanna. 2016. "Understanding Russia? Helping Ukraine? Poles and Germans on the Russo-Ukrainian Conflict." *Historie – Otázky – Problémy (History, Issues, Problems)* 8 (2): 103–117.

Gabriel, Sigmar. 2017a. "Interview with Focus," 14 July. https://www.auswaertiges-amt.de/en/newsroom/news/170714-bm-focus/291394.

Gabriel, Sigmar. 2017b. "Interview with Gazeta Wyborcza," 8 March. https://www.auswaertiges-amt.de/en/newsroom/news/170308-bm-gazetawyborcza/288368.

Gabriel, Sigmar, and Christian Kern. 2017. "Statement on the Imposition of Russia Sanctions by the US Senate." 15 June. https://www.auswaertiges-amt.de/en/newsroom/news/170615-kern-russland/290666.

German Federal Government. 2018a. "Press Release on Polish Prime Minister's Visit," 16 February. https://www.bundesregierung.de/Content/EN/Artikel/2018/02_en/2018-02-16-morawiecki-in-berlin_en.html?nn=709674.

German Federal Government. 2018b. "Press Release on Angela Merkel's Visit to Vladimir Putin in Sochi," 18 May. https://www.bundesregierung.de/Content/EN/Reiseberichte/2018_en/2018-05-18-merkel-sotschi_en.html.

Goldthau, Andreas. 2016. *Assessing Nord Stream 2: Regulation, Geopolitics & Energy Security in the EU, Central Eastern Europe & the UK*. EUCERS Strategy Paper 10, London: King's College. https://www.kcl.ac.uk/sspp/departments/warstudies/research/groups/eucers/pubs/strategy-paper-10.pdf.

Gotkowska, Justyna, and Piotr Szymanski. 2016. "The Nordic countries on Nord Stream 2: Between Scepticism and Neutrality." *Energy Post*, 3 November. http://energypost.eu/nordic-countries-nord-stream-2-scepticism-neutrality/.

Groszkowski, Jakub. 2017. "Czech Support for Nord Stream 2." *OSW Analysis*, 29 November. https://www.osw.waw.pl/en/publikacje/analyses/2017-11-29/czech-support-nord-stream-2.

Guardian. 2016. "Russia is More Dangerous than Isis, Says Polish Foreign Minister," 15 April. https://www.theguardian.com/world/2016/apr/15/russia-more-dangerous-isis-polish-foreign-minister-witold-waszczykowski.

Hadfield, Amelia. 2016. "EU-Russia Strategic Energy Culture: Progressive Convergence or Regressive Dilemma?" *Geopolitics* 21 (4): 779–798.

Harper, Jo. 2017. "Nordstream II Gas Pipeline in Deep Water." *Deutsche Welle*, 14 November. https://www.dw.com/en/nordstream-ii-gas-pipeline-in-deep-water/a-41372833.

Haukkala, Hiski. 2015. "From Cooperative to Contested Europe? The Conflict in Ukraine as a Culmination of a Long-Term Crisis in EU–Russia Relations." *Journal of Contemporary European Studies* 23 (1): 25–40.

Heinrich, Andreas. 2017. "Securitisation in the gas Sector: Energy Security Debates Concerning the Example of the Nord Stream Pipeline." In *Energy Security in Europe*, edited by K. Szulecki, 61–91. Basingstoke: Palgrave Macmillan.

Hejj, Dominik. 2018. "Hungary Does Not Support Poland in the Area of Gas." *Biznes Alert*, 3 April. http://biznesalert.com/hejj-poland-hungary-gas-nord-stream-2/.

Henderson, James, and Jack Sharples. 2018. *Gazprom in Europe – Two "Anni Mirabiles", But Can It Continue?* Oxford: Oxford Institute for Energy Studies, March. https://www.oxfordenergy.org/wpcms/wp-content/uploads/2018/03/Gazprom-in-Europe-%E2%80%93-two-Anni-Mirabiles-but-can-it-continue-Insight-29.pdf.

Hopf, Ted. 2002. *Social Construction of International Politics: Identities and Foreign Policies, Moscow, 1955 and 1999*. Ithaca, NY: Cornell University Press.

Judge, Andrew, Tomas Maltby, and Jack Sharples. 2016. "Challenging Reductionism in Analyses of EU-Russia Energy Relations." *Geopolitics* 21 (4): 751–762.

King, Esther. 2018. "German and Polish Leaders Clash over Nord Stream 2 Pipeline." *Politico*, 16 February. https://www.politico.eu/article/nord-stream-2-german-and-polish-leaders-clash/.

Kovacs, Andras, and Ruth Wodak. 2003. *NATO, Neutrality and National Identity: the Case of Austria and Hungary*. Vienna: Böhlau.

Lang, Kai Olaf, and Kirsten Westphal. 2017. *Nord Stream 2 – A Political and Economic Contextualisation*. Berlin: Stiftung Wissenschaft und Politik.

Lebow, Richard Ned. 2008. "Identity and International Relations." *International Relations* 22 (4): 473–492.

Loskot-Strachota, Agata. 2015. "The Case Against Nord Stream 2." *Energy Post*, 23 November. http://energypost.eu/case-nord-stream-2/.

Loskot-Strachota, Agata, and Konrad Poplawski. 2016. "EUGAL: The Unknown German branch of Nord Stream 2 will Make Germany the Key Gas Hub in Europe." *Energy Post*, 6 July. http://energypost.eu/eugal-project-unknown-german-branch-nord-stream-2-will-make-germany-key-gas-hub-europe/.

Maas, Heiko. 2018. "Speech at the Tiergarten Conference of the Friedrich-Ebert-Stiftung," 27 June. https://www.auswaertiges-amt.de/en/newsroom/news/maas-fes-tiergarten-konferenz/2113728.

Martewicz, Maciej. 2018. "Poland Waves Goodbye to Russian Gas after 74 Years." *Bloomberg*, 8 February. https://www.bloomberg.com/news/articles/2018-02-08/poland-bets-on-lng-norwegian-gas-as-divorce-with-russia-looms.

Morozov, Viacheslav, and Bahar Rumelili. 2012. "The External Constitution of European Identity: Russia and Turkey as Europe-Makers." *Cooperation and Conflict* 47 (1): 28–48.

Neumann, Iver. 1998. *Uses of the Other: The East in European Identity Formation*. Minneapolis, MN: University of Minnesota Press.

Nitoiu, Cristian. 2017. "Still Entrenched in the Conflict/Cooperation Dichotomy? EU-Russia Relations and the Ukraine Crisis?." *European Politics and Society* 18 (2): 148–165.

Nitoiu, Cristian. 2018. "The United Kingdom: From Pragmatism to Conflict?" In *EU Member States and Russia: National and European Debates in an Evolving International Environment*, edited by M. Siddi, 93–105. Helsinki: Finnish Institute of International Affairs.

PAP (Polish Press Agency). 2017. "PM Szydlo Urges EU to 'Hasten Steps' on Nord Stream 2." 20 October. http://www.pap.pl/en/news-/news,1132702,i-asked-eu-for-faster-action-on-nord-stream-2—pm-szydlo-in-brussels.html.

Radio Poland. 2018. "Planned Russia-Germany Pipeline a 'Political Project': Senior EU Official," 13 March. http://www.thenews.pl/1/10/Artykul/353727,Planned-RussiaGermany-pipeline-a-%E2%80%98political-project%E2%80%99-senior-EU-official.

Reeves, Christopher. 2010. "Reopening the Wounds of History? The Foreign Policy of the 'Fourth' Polish Republic." *Journal of Communist Studies and Transition Politics* 26 (4): 518–541.

Reuters. 2016a. "Duda Says Nord Stream 2 Pipeline Undermines EU Solidarity," 18 January. https://www.reuters.com/article/poland-energy-eu-nordstream/duda-says-nord-stream-2-pipeline-undermines-eu-solidarity-idUSL8N1521RZ.

Reuters. 2016b. "ENI CEO Says Nord Stream 2 would Raise Gas Prices in Italy," 26 May. https://de.reuters.com/article/energy-nordstream-eu-idUKL5N18K4KG.

Reuters. 2017a. "Poland Not Concerned about Yamal Transit Fees –Naimski," 20 June. https://af.reuters.com/article/commoditiesNews/idAFL8N1JH27B.

Reuters. 2017b. "La France juge illicites les sanctions US contre la Russie," 26 July. https://fr.reuters.com/article/companyNews/idFRL5N1KH4LV.

Reuters. 2018. "Russia-led Nord Stream 2 Seeks New Route to avoid Danish Waters", 10 August. https://uk.reuters.com/article/uk-eu-gazprom-nordstream/nord-stream-2-seeks-alternative-route-to-avoid-danish-waters-idUKKBN1KV118.

RFE/RL (Radio Free Europe/Radio Liberty). 2018. "Polish PM Calls Nord Stream 2 'Weapon' Of Hybrid Warfare," 28 May. https://www.rferl.org/a/polish-pm-calls-nord-stream-2-weapon-of-hybrid-warfare/29255392.html.

Samokhvalov, Vsevolod. 2017. *Russian-European Relations in the Balkans and Black Sea Region*. Basingstoke: Palgrave Macmillan.

Sengupta, Kim. 2018. "Message of Defiance against Russia from UK Allies May Yet Dissolve into Inaction." *The Independent*, 15 March. https://www.independent.co.uk/news/world/europe/russia-spy-poisoning-sergei-skripal-joint-statement-uk-us-trump-putin-germany-france-a8258191.html.

Siddi, Marco. 2016. "The EU's Energy Union: A Sustainable Path to Energy Security?" *The International Spectator* 51 (1): 131–144.

Siddi, Marco. 2017a. "Identities and Vulnerabilities: The Ukraine Crisis and the Securitisation of the EU-Russia Gas Trade." In *Energy Security in Europe*, edited by K. Szulecki, 251–273. Basingstoke: Palgrave Macmillan.

Siddi, Marco. 2017b. *National Identities and Foreign Policy in the European Union. The Russia Policy of Germany, Poland and Finland*. Colchester: ECPR Press.

Siddi, Marco. 2018a. "The Role of Power in EU-Russia Energy Relations: The Interplay Between Markets and Geopolitics." *Europe-Asia Studies* 70 (10): 1552–1571.

Siddi, Marco. 2018b. "An Evolving Other: German National Identity and Constructions of Russia." *Politics* 38 (1): 35–50.

Siddi, Marco. 2018c. "Italy's 'Middle Power' Approach to Russia." *The International Spectator* 54 (2): 123–138.

Siddi, Marco. 2018d. *Russia's Evolving Gas Relationship with the European Union: Trade Surges Despite Political Crises*. FIIA Briefing Paper 246. Helsinki: Finnish Institute of International Affairs.

Siddi, Marco. 2020 (forthcoming). *National Identities, the Russian Other and Foreign Policy in the European Union*. Abingdon: Routledge.

Smilov, Daniel, and Alexander Andreev. 2018. "Bulgaria Torn between Russia and the West." *Deutsche Welle*, 31 May. https://www.dw.com/en/bulgaria-torn-between-russia-and-the-west/a-44027331.

Smith, Hanna. 2014. "Politicising Energy Security: Russia and the European Union." In *Russian Energy and Security up to 2030*, edited by S. Oxenstierna, and V. P. Tynkkynen, 77–94. Abingdon: Routledge.

Soldatkin, Vladimir. 2018. "Gazprom Says Gas Transit Via Ukraine to Europe May Fall to 10-15 bcm Per Year." *Reuters*, 10 April. https://www.reuters.com/article/us-russia-ukraine-gas/gazprom-says-gas-transit-via-ukraine-to-europe-may-fall-to-10-15-bcm-per-year-idUSKBN1HH2HL.

Steinmeier, Frank-Walter. 2016. "Interview with the Russian News Agency Interfax," 23 March. https://www.auswaertiges-amt.de/en/newsroom/news/-/279458.

Sus, Monika. 2018. "Poland: Leading Critic or Marginalized Hawk?" In *EU Member States and Russia: National and European Debates in an Evolving International Environment*, edited by M. Siddi, 77–89. Helsinki: Finnish Institute of International Affairs.

Szymanski, Konrad. 2016. "Russia's Gas Pipeline Threatens European Unity." *Financial Times*, 21 October. https://www.ft.com/content/25a17928-96c3-11e6-a1dc-bdf38d484582.

Vihma, Antto, and Mikael Wigell. 2016. "Unclear and Present Danger: Russia's Geoeconomics and the Nord Stream II Pipeline." *Global Affairs* 2 (4): 377–388.

Waszczykowski, Witold. 2016a. Op-ed for the Frankfurt Allgemeine Zeitung "The today and tomorrow of European integration: Warsaw's perspective," 4 April 2016. https://mfa.gov.pl/en/news/minister_witold_waszczykowski_for_faz___the_today_and_tomorrow_of_european_integration__warsaw_s_perspective_.

Waszczykowski, Witold. 2016b. "Interview with Die Welt," 28 May. https://www.msz.gov.pl/en/news/the_eu_should_not_aspire_to_become_a_superstate__minister_witold_waszczykowski_speaks_to_die_welt.

Waszczykowski, Witold. 2017. "Information of the Minister of Foreign Affairs on Polish Foreign Policy Tasks in 2017." https://www.msz.gov.pl/en/ministry/minister/archive_speeches/information_of_the_minister_of_foreign_affairs_on_polish_foreign_policy_tasks_in_2017.

Webber, Mark, ed. 2000. *Russia and Europe: Conflict Or Cooperation?* Basingstoke: Palgrave Macmillan.

Wendt, Alexander. 1999. *Social Theory of International Politics*. Cambridge: Cambridge University Press.

Wintour, Patrick. 2018. "Boris Johnson Joins US in Criticising Russia to Germany Gas Pipeline." *Guardian*, 22 May 2018. https://www.theguardian.com/world/2018/may/22/boris-johnson-joins-us-criticising-russia-germany-gas-pipeline-nord-stream-2.

Yafimava, Katja. 2015. *European Energy Security and the Role of Russian Gas: Assessing the Feasibility and the Rationale of Reducing Dependence*. IAI Working Papers 15/54, Rome: Istituto Affari Internazionali. http://www.iai.it/sites/default/files/iaiwp1554.pdf.

Yafimava, Katja. 2019. *Gas Directive Amendment: Implications for Nord Stream 2*. Oxford: The Oxford Institute for Energy Studies. https://www.oxfordenergy.org/wpcms/wp-content/uploads/2019/03/Gas-Directive-Amendment-Insight-49.pdf?v=f0aa03aaca95.

Zarycki, Tomas. 2004. "Uses of Russia: The Role of Russia in the Modern Polish National Identity." *East European Politics and Societies* 18 (4): 595–627.

Crisis response, path dependence, and the joint decision trap: the EU's eastern and Russia policies after the Ukraine crisis

Joan DeBardeleben

ABSTRACT
The outbreak of the Ukraine crisis has been widely seen as heralding a critical change in relations between the European Union (EU) and Russia. Both path dependence and the joint decision trap have influenced EU responses to the crisis in terms of its broader policy toward Russia, the Eastern Partnership, and energy policy. The nature of the EU's response has involved a combination of sustained crisis response and incremental change, reflecting relative continuity in the underlying principles governing the approach combined with immediate crisis response measures. The EU's approach reflects elements of both conflict and cooperation in the relationship.

With the outbreak of the Ukraine crisis in 2014, some fundamental objectives of the EU's eastern policy were undermined. The European Neighbourhood Policy (ENP), initiated in 2004, sought "to develop a zone of prosperity and a friendly neighbourhood – a 'ring of friends' – with whom the EU enjoys close, peaceful and cooperative relations" (Commission 2003, 4). The Eastern Partnership (EaP) policy, launched on the basis of the ENP in 2009 and directed at Ukraine and five other eastern neighbours, affirmed a "shared commitment to stability, security, and prosperity of the European Union, the partner countries and indeed the entire European continent" (Council 2009).

By the end of 2014, a civil war was underway in Ukraine and relations with Russia were in tatters. European leaders strongly condemned Russia's annexation of Crimea and interference in eastern Ukraine, and in March 2019 the EU High Representative for Foreign Affairs and Security Policy, Federica Mogherini, identified Russia's actions as "a direct challenge to international security, with grave implications for the international legal order that protects the territorial integrity, unity and sovereignty of all States" (Mogherini 2019). In response, the introduction of a sanctions regime, in a surprising show of EU unity, was accompanied by a freeze in most aspects of EU-Russia relations.

In the face of the crisis, one would expect the EU to engage in policy reflection on its eastern policy. Indeed, a formal review of the ENP was undertaken, with results announced in November 2015. In contrast, no major review of the EU's long-term policy toward Russia was announced. Instead, in March 2016 Mogherini proposed "five guiding principles" for dealing with Russia that were supported unanimously by the

Foreign Affairs Council of the EU (Mogherini 2016), reaffirmed in April 2018 (Council 2018) and still the apparent basis of EU policies in early 2020.

While the events in Ukraine posed a crisis moment for EU foreign policy, some of concrete objectives of the EaP were realised: three of the six EaP countries embarked upon Association Agreements (AA) with the EU in 2014. While Armenia backed away from an AA at the last minute in favour of joining the Russian-led Eurasian Economic Union (EAEU), the country concluded a Comprehensive and Enhanced Partnership Agreement with the EU in September 2017. These successes were bittersweet, however, given the broader context of civil war in Ukraine, the breakdown in relations with Russia, and the resultant assault on the European security architecture.

This article examines the EU's response to this cascading foreign policy crisis. Did the crisis provide an opening for fundamental policy reflection and learning? Has it presented a critical juncture in reshaping the EU's Russian and eastern policy? Or, on the other hand, has the EU been limited to path dependent responses and subject to policy paralysis or dynamics of a joint decision trap? The analysis contributes to this special issue by exploring whether the EU's stark reaction to Russian actions in Ukraine has been accompanied by a paradigm shift in EU policy or only by smaller-scale adjustments that reflect relative continuity involving a combination of conflict and cooperation. To explore these questions, this analysis proposes a typology of crisis response and relates it to widely used concepts to explain the dynamics of policy change and to the developing literature on the role of crisis in inducing policy reform in the EU. The article focuses on three dimensions of the EU's eastern policy: policy toward Russia, EaP, and energy policy as it relates to Russia.

After examining the theoretical and methodological approach in the first section, the second section examines the nature of change in policy in each of the three policy areas in terms of the typology. The third section assesses the dynamics of policy change and explanatory power that the concepts of path dependence, joint decision trap, and paradigm shift offer in explaining the role of crisis in inducing significant foreign policy learning, followed by a conclusion.

Theory and methodology

A growing body of literature suggests that crisis may trigger EU policy change; it is argued that crisis situations have the potential to interrupt or disrupt patterns of "path dependence", which usually serve to restrict the choices available to policy makers. Falkner (2016, 955) argues that crises can even "propel the EU out of a joint-decision trap", which Scharpf (1988) and others (Müller 2016) have identified as often resulting in suboptimal policy choices in multilevel governance systems. Laffan (2016, 916) sees crises as "'open moments' that impact on rulers and ruled, testing existing paradigms, policies, institutional roles and rules".

Path dependence and the joint decision trap are often identified as obstacles to effective policy change. The notion of path dependence has been adapted from economics to policy studies in conjunction with the idea of critical junctures. The basic notion is that decisions, even small ones, made at some point in the past can create a strong bias in favour of policy continuity; the costs of major policy change are often high, and key constituencies and institutions may present powerful obstacles to such shifts. While fundamental change in direction is not impossible, it is relatively unlikely.

Pierson (2000, 252) identifies a dynamic of "increasing returns": "the relative benefits of current activity compared with other possible options increase over time." This does not mean, however, that the chosen approach produces the optimal outcome; "in the long-run, the outcome that becomes locked in may generate lower pay-offs than a foregone alternative would have" (253). One possible exit point from path dependence occurs at so-called critical junctures when constraints on change are reduced, thus providing an opportunity for a radical change in direction, possibly setting the trajectory for a new path-dependent process; however, continuity may also result (Capoccia and Daniel Kelemen 2007). Hogan (2019, 180) notes that "the failure of extant policies provides a window of opportunity for change agents to contest the viability of the underlying paradigm." Djelic and Quack (2007, 181) observe that the generation of new path policy paths may occur over an extended period of time and that crisis can contribute to the process, particularly when "external pressures and solutions are connected to local stakeholders and their traditions."

Scharpf's concept of the "joint decision trap" further clarifies potential obstacles to significant policy change in multi-level systems such as the EU. In a seminal article, Scharpf (1988, 239) observed that "the fact that member governments are participants in central decisions, and that there is a de facto requirement of unanimous decision, will systematically generate sub-optimal policy outcomes unless a 'problem-solving' (as opposed to a 'bargaining') style of decision-making has prevailed." He concludes that for change to occur, "the system might be jolted out of its present equilibrium by external interventions or by a dramatic deterioration of its performance" (271). However, the analysis of Kamkhaji and Radaelli (2017) raises doubts about whether crisis situations provide fertile ground for policy learning. While Falkner (2016, 257) argues that "extreme time pressures" raise the potential to overcome blockages, Kamhhaji and Radaelli suggest that a compressed time frame is less amenable to deliberative policy reflection and therefore real policy learning is not likely to occur until later, as result of, rather than a cause of, the immediate crisis response. They argue that, nonetheless, new policy paradigms can arise from this process, but these are "not the fruit of reflexive lesson drawing (for which time and knowledge accumulation are critical)" but rather are an "associative response" to the demands of the immediate crisis. (722). This might suggest that the type of "problem-solving" approach referred to by Scarpf may be difficult to achieve in a crisis context.

Alecu de Flers, Chappell, and Müller (2011) suggest mechanisms through which the joint decision trap can be overcome in the EU; these involve the emergence of common norms, building of institutions to facilitate foreign policy cooperation, and mechanisms to build consensus (810). Such processes, combined with critical events like EU policy failure, may produce socialisation and "thick learning" that reinforce adherence to shared norms. Nonetheless, Müller (2016) sees little evidence that the EU has overcome the joint decision trap in the foreign policy arena, despite multiple crises in recent years, due to member state divisions and concerns about foreign policy sovereignty. In fact the joint decision trap may be particularly powerful in the foreign policy sphere because member states retain the freedom to act on their own in this arena and therefore reaching a joint position is not so critical. Accordingly, the ability of crises to induce policy change seems stronger in policy areas where unanimity is not required and where EU competencies are stronger, i.e. for some types of internal EU matters. Examples would be responses to the Eurozone crisis (Clime 2018; Foster 2018) and the refugee crisis (Zaun 2018; Niemann and Speyer 2018). While the Eurozone and refugee crises had exogenous roots (Laffan 2016, 916), the challenges they posed were primarily internal.

Whether crisis-induced changes are as likely in the foreign policy arena, where EU competencies are weaker and unanimity is often required, is open to question. D'Erman and Verdun argue that external challenges can also invoke policy change, citing the collapse of the Soviet Union, which finally triggered the large EU enlargements of 2004 and 2007. The weak response of the EU to violent conflict in West Balkans policy in the 1990s was a clearer case of crisis triggering foreign policy change, in this case enhanced efforts on the part of major EU member states (Britain and France, with the St. Malo Declaration) to set in motion the development of the European Security and Defense Policy, later transformed into the Common Security and Defense Policy (Jopp and Diedrichs 2009, 97; Ross 2011, 37). This example provides evidence that external crises can lead to responses that enhance the scope or depth of EU foreign policy integration, even though conditions to overcome the joint decision trap seem to be weak or absent. Cross and Karolewski (2017, 11) look more specifically at the EU's response to the Ukraine crisis. They argue that while "international crises create openings in terms of the way in which the EU might become more constrained or enabled," the actual impact of crisis on policy change is dependent on a variety of factors. These include how other actors respond, available resources, and internal discord (13). Falkner sees little reform in EU foreign policy as a result of the Ukraine crisis; she explains this in part by NATO responses, by the fact that only some member states were more critically affected by the crisis, and by the absence of extreme time pressure (Falkner 2016, 261). Ikani (2019, 14) also concludes that the Ukraine crisis brought a combination of continuity and change in the ENP – a significant rhetorical shift but "minimal reforms in terms of policy tools and targets."

Like the Balkan wars and Kosovo crisis, the Ukraine events of 2014 challenged a fundamental objective of the EU, namely the establishment of peace and stability in Europe. However, unlike that case, which had demonstrated the *inability* of the EU *to respond* to an external challenge, in the 2014 Ukraine crisis the EU was arguably *implicated as a contributor* to the outbreak of instability and conflict because its Eastern Partnership policy did not take adequate account of the likely Russian reaction. In the most proximate sense, the crisis was triggered by Ukrainian President Viktor Yanukovych's decision not to sign an Association Agreement (AA) and Deep and Comprehensive Free Trade Area (DCFTA) with the EU at the Vilnius summit in 2013. In a more fundamental sense, the objective of the EU's EaP itself had, according to some analysts, already set the EU on a collision course with Russia (e.g. Korosteleva 2016). The policy sought "to create the necessary conditions to accelerate political association and further economic integration between the European Union and interested partner countries" (Council 2009), thus intervening in an arena that Russia considered it "privileged sphere of influence" (Medvedev 2008). The outbreak of the crisis challenged fundamental assumptions that had driven the EU's eastern policy, namely the idea that offering closer relations with the EU as a reward for liberalising and market reforms would create conditions for peace and stability in the region.

Types of crisis response

The analysis in this article builds on an four-part categorisation of crisis response that the author has developed: sustained crisis response, business as usual, incremental adaptation, and paradigmatic adaptation.[1] (See Table 1).

Sustained crisis response involves acknowledgement of the reality of the crisis; here, however, immediate crisis responses become institutionalised, with a nearly exclusive focus on short-term reactions such as sanctions, rhetorical interventions, or a freeze in relations. Such an approach may appear as inertia, reflecting an inability to process the larger implications of the crisis or to adopt a revised strategic approach.

A second type of response, *business as usual*, involves minor (often technical) adjustments to existing policy, reflecting an effort to "normalize" the situation, keeping it within the framework of existing policy practice, norms, and assumptions. In contrast to *sustained crisis response,* this approach deemphasises the crisis nature of the situation. Similar to Allison's (1969) "standard operating procedures", this response is situated within an "organizational process" that relies on learning that is constrained by existing practices and approaches.

A third response category is *incremental adaptation*, where the underlying norms and assumptions are not challenged, but particular policy instruments are evaluated and adapted. Unlike *business as usual*, there is an acknowledgement of a need for change, but only particular tools, mechanisms and vehicles are adapted. Like *business as usual*, this response seeks to "normalize" the situation, but with a recognition that current practices have substantial deficiencies. The incremental approach also allows change to be tested in iterations, to avoid unexpected consequences.

The fourth, most radical, response is *paradigmatic adaptation.* Adapting Thomas Kuhn's (1970) notion to policy studies, Peter Hall (1993, 279) defines paradigm change as involving "radical changes in the overarching terms of policy discourse." Underlying goals, assumptions, or normative values of the previous policy approach are challenged; reconsideration of how to frame fundamental interests or a radical shift in policy instruments may take place. This differs from *incremental adaptation* because it places in question the very foundations of the previous strategy. The initiation of paradigmatic adaptation may be hard to identify in the immediate aftermath of the crisis or as the crisis is ongoing, but may first be indicated by a far-reaching policy debate that occurs in decision-making circles and that raises fundamental questions about the policy approach. Following Kamkhaji and Radaelli (2017), *paradigmatic adaptation* may follow the initial crisis response. It also is the only one of the four responses to a crisis situation that charts a new strategic direction or a fundamental rethinking of the policy that is most indicative of the type of "open moment" referred to by Laffan.

Table 2 relates these categories of crisis response to the concepts of path dependence and joint decision trap. Three of the categories (except *business as usual*) meet the conditions for viewing the Ukraine crisis as a potential critical juncture, i.e. a situation where constraints on change are reduced, opening the door to the possibility of radical policy revision. *Business as usual* involves no escape from path dependence or the joint decision trap, while *sustained crisis response* suggests at least a temporary exit from path dependence. However, without subsequent paradigmatic adaptation path dependence is likely to prevail in the longer term. *Incremental adaptation* has the markings of path dependence

Table 1. Types of crisis response.

Crisis response	Policy failure acknowledged?	Fundamental assumptions challenged?	Decision-making	Venue-of decision-making/authority	Nature of policy change	Time frame
Business as usual	No	No	Routine	Bureaucracy	Minor, technical, normalising	Continuity of past policy
Sustained crisis response	Yes	Not immediately	Urgent, extra-ordinary	Top political/executive authority	May be significant, but intended to be temporary	Short- to medium-perspective
Incremental adaptation	Yes	No	Following policy review and input	Usual decision-making bodies	Tools and mechanisms adapted; iterative	Medium-term
Paradigmatic adaptation	Yes	Yes	Following fundamental debate (possibly experimentation)	Venue may shift	Strategic	Long-term

Table 2. Types of crisis response and obstacles to policy learning.

	Meets conditions as a potential critical juncture	Involves escape from ….	
		path dependence	joint decision trap
Business as usual	No	No	No decision taken
Sustained crisis response	Yes	Maybe temporarily	Maybe temporarily
Incremental adaptation	Yes	No	Possibly on smaller issues
Paradigmatic adaptation	Yes	Yes	Probably

if pressure from key constituencies and existing commitments make fundamental change too costly. Finally, the joint decision trap is likely to be a powerful inhibition to *paradigmatic adaptation* but might be overcome in achieving *incremental adaptation*. Whether either of these responses represents an optimal policy outcome is open to debate.

Methodology

This study does not seek to examine in depth the process that led to policy changes since February 2014 but rather focuses on outcomes, as expressed in official policy positions. The methodology involves a qualitative analysis of EU documents in the period following inception of the Ukraine crisis, compared to earlier policy positions. The analysis compares terminology describing the policy as well as priorities and key principles underlying it. Determining the reference point from the pre-2014 period to assess whether change has occurred involves a reliance on the broad body of primary and secondary literature that documents the EU's EaP and Russia policies during that period. There is no single document that provides an authoritative summary of EU policy toward Russia up to 2014; the Common Strategy of the European Union Russia of 1999 (European Council 1999) has not been updated since; a multitude of agreements between the EU and Russia, including the 1997 Partnership and Cooperation Agreement (Agreement 1997), the Four Common Spaces and their Road Maps (European Commission 2005), and the Partnership for Modernisation (European Commission 2010) provide guidance. The websites of the European Commission and European External Action Service also document various aspects of the EU's Russia policy. A clear official delineation of the principles of the Eastern Partnership policy exists in declarations of the EaP summits of 2009, 2011, and 2013 (Council 2009, 2011, 2013).

For the period following the eruption of the Ukraine crisis in 2014 the study relies on key documents and positions of EU officials, the European Council, the Foreign Affairs Council of the Council of the European Union, the European External Action Service (EEAS), and the European Commission, as well speeches and press releases relating to actions and positions of these bodies and figures. In addition, policy statements of selected EU member state leaders are examined to supplement research on this aspect carried out by other scholars that is documented in a rich secondary literature.

Results: EU policy directions since the Ukraine crisis began

This section examines three issues: the bilateral relationship with Russia, and those aspects of the EaP and energy policy that affect Russia. This analysis evaluates where policy development fits in the crisis response typology and identifies the main elements of change, compared to pre-2014 policy.

The EU's Russia policy

The EU's relations with Russia were fraught even before the Ukraine crisis. A period of optimism in the 1990s saw the signing of a Partnership and Cooperation Agreement (PCA) that went into effect in 1997. In 2003, the EU and Russia agreed on Four Common Spaces of cooperation and in 2005 Four Roapmaps were developed to realise the objectives. In 2003–2004, when the Wider Europe and then the ENP were announced, the EU hoped to include Russia in a larger process of regional integration and to promote joint efforts at regional security (Delcour 2018). Russia, presumably irritated by the secondary status this implied, rejected the EU's invitation to be part of the ENP. This set the EU on a path dependent process that resulted in two-track approach to its eastern neighbours. (DeBardeleben 2011). Russia was defined as a strategic partner, with the relationship cloaked in a discourse of equality and mutual interests; with the launching of the EaP in 2009 other eastern neighbours were encouraged to accept EU guidance in their reform processes while being offered enhanced incentives for closer integration with EU norms and policies. The EU did not intend for the EaP to produce competition with Russia and continued to promote cooperation in a wide range of areas, resulting in a highly institutionalised set of interactions through multiple vehicles such as the Energy Dialogue, Visa Dialogue, biannual summits, and numerous working groups. Nonetheless, developing tensions were reinforced by Russia's intervention in Georgia in 2008. Russian spokespersons repeatedly expressed resentment of EU criticism of its human rights and governance approaches; the Russian leadership was also frustrated by delays in realising a visa-waiver agreement and by EU energy competition rules. On the other side, the EU saw slow progress in many Russian reform efforts and regression in political liberalisation. Efforts to negotiate a successor to the PCA, which formally ended in 2007, faltered. With the EaP, Russia became increasingly concerned about perceived EU intrusions into its proclaimed sphere of geopolitical influence. Russia's intervention in Crimea and eastern Ukraine brought a radical and dramatic worsening in the relationship.

Most internal EU discussions regarding Russia in the period after 2014 dealt with the sanctions regime introduced by the EU, Russia's continuing involvement in eastern Ukraine, disinformation, cyberattacks, or the Salisbury poisonings (e.g. European Council, 2018, 2019), or with issues not directly involved in the EU-Russia relationship, such Syria or Turkey (e.g. European Council 2016; Council 2020). The sanctions regime, part of the EU's crisis response, was successfully extended every six months by unanimous agreement of the member states, despite indicators of discontent from certain member states such as Austria, Italy, and Greece. The first move to try to chart a broader policy direction toward Russia occurred, however, on March 14, 2016, when the Foreign Affairs Council gave unanimous support to "five guiding principles" for the EU's relation with Russia that were presented by High Representative Federica Mogherini. When presenting the five principles, Mogherini emphasised that the discussion was "not a focus on sanctions … , but on our bilateral common policy of EU-Russia relations" (Mogherini 2016).

Alongside the sanctions, these principles represent the clearest statement of the EU's policy toward Russia in the post-2014 period. The principles are:

(1) "demand the full implementation of Minsk agreements, as a key element for any substantial change in EU-Russian relations;"

(2) "strengthen relations with the EU's Eastern partners and Central Asia countries;"
(3) "strengthen EU resilience to Russian threats … ;"
(4) "engage selectively with Russia on foreign policy issues … where there is a clear EU interest;"
(5) "support Russian civil society and engage in people-to-people contacts … ." (Council, 2018)

On the face of it, the principles fall into the categories of *sustained crisis response* and *incremental change*. Points one and three reflect the continuing crisis context. EU leaders have consistently identified the Russia's compliance with the Minsk agreements "as a key element of any substantial change in our relations," in other words, a condition for moving out of the crisis phase. The third point evokes a defensive reaction to security threats, with specific mention, by Mogherini, of "energy security, hybrid threats, and strategic communication. . . ." (Mogherini 2016). Points 2, 4, and 5, on the other hand, involve a mix of continuity and incremental adaptation from pre-2014 policy. Point 2 commits to a continuation of EaP (discussed further below), but with increased attention to Central Asia. Point 3 reflects an incremental adjustment both from the pre-2014 partnership and the post-2014 freeze in relations by suggesting *selective* engagement with Russia. The fifth point reflects continuity with past policy, but suggests a higher priority for youth contacts.

Just as important is what is missing from the five principles, as this reveals nuances of continuity and change. First, there is no mention of shared values with Russia. In fact, over time, in response to Russian objections, the EU had, even previously, muted its value discourse with Russia, so this change reflects continuation of an existing trajectory. Second, the five principles, supported by other statements by EU officials (Euraktiv 2014, Baltic News Network 2019, European Parliament 2019), omit any affirmation of a "strategic partnership" with Russia, which was a fundamental precept of past policy. Furthermore, the turn from strategic partnership toward a language of threat could be indicative of an incipient *paradigmatic adaptation* in the underlying assumptions about the relationship, However, the full context does not yet suggest a paradigm shift; the possibility of partnership is still contained in points 1 (Minsk agreements), 4 (selective engagement), and 5 (civil society links) even if a much more constrained relationship compared to the previous broad-ranging "strategic parntership". A third point of omission relates to the EaP. Because the principles are presented as addressing "our bilateral common policy on EU-Russian relations" (Mogherini, 2016), the absence of a reference to Russia in point 2 is significant. However, in April 2018, a statement on behalf of Mogherini (EEAS 2018) did indicate that "we will pursue a policy of transparency with Russia on our cooperation with our eastern partners, exploring cooperation in areas of mutual interest"; this echoes previous approaches where Russia was eligible for cooperation in the context of specific projects through the ENP Instrument (ENPI).

Overall, one can read the five points as reflecting a continuation of the *sustained crisis response*, with some attempt to suggest a way to "manage" the relationship (EEAS 2018) through small steps; these include, for example, cross-border cooperation projects, meetings of the EU-Russia Joint Science and Technology Committee, periodic meetings between Mogherini and Russian Foreign Minister Lavrov, informal consultations on issues such as counter-terrorism, and the initiation, in 2018, of trilateral talks between Russia, Ukraine, and the EU on long-term gas transit to Europe.

Eastern Partnership policy

As noted above, the EaP was launched in 2009 as an amendment to the ENP, addressed specifically to six countries of Eastern Europe and the Caucasus region. Even before the Ukraine crisis there were numerous criticisms of the policy, most prominently the inadequate incentives for reform offered, particularly the absence of a membership perspective. However, since 2009 partner countries had been offered the prospect of association agreements (AA) with the EU, including DCFTAs, as well a process leading to a visa-waiver regime. Various EaP partners had demonstrated varying levels of interest and commitment to the reform processes, with Ukraine the frontrunner, already having initialed the AA in 2012 and expected to sign it at the Vilnius summit in November 2013. Georgia, Armenia, and Moldova were expected to initial the agreement at that time and sign shortly thereafter. Plans were disrupted when Ukrainian president Viktor Yanukovych stepped back from the agreement shortly before the summit, followed by Armenia.

In response to the unsettling developments that followed in Ukraine (and others in the Southern neighbourhood), the EU did undertake a formal review of the ENP. In November 2015 the European Commission and the High Representative of the Union for Foreign Affairs and Security Policy released a document with results of that review (EC and HR 2015), which followed an extensive internal EU and public consultation. In May 2017, the two institutions issued a report regarding implementation of the approach outlined in the review (EC and HR 2107). Other key documents are joint declarations from the EaP summits in Riga in May 2015 and in Brussels in November 2017 (European Council 2015; Council 2017b). In addition, in December 2016 staff of the Commission and of the High Representative issued a working document that identified 20 key "deliverables" to serve as a work plan up to the year 2020 (EC and HR 2016). Finally, the EaP is referenced in a few of the "Outcomes" documents of meetings of the Council of the European Union and the Foreign Affairs Council of the EU. These, for the most part, reiterate points made in the documents referred to above and stress the "strategic importance the EU attaches to the EaP" (Council 2016a, 5; Council 2017a, 5), or mention meetings with EaP and EU foreign affairs ministers (Council 2016b, 8)

These documents, collectively, indicate that revisions to the EaP fall into the category of *incremental adaptation*. Three main challenges seem to have driven policy adaptation. First it had become evident by that time that the six EaP partner countries were taking divergent paths and facing a varied mix of challenges. On the one hand, Belarus and Armenia had joined the Russian-dominated EAEU. Belarus was already a founding member of the Eurasian Customs Union formed in 2010, and, as noted above, Armenia signed an agreement to join the EAEU in late 2014. On the other end of the spectrum are Ukraine, Georgia, and Moldova, each having signed AAs and DCFTAs with the EU in 2014. However, each of these three countries faces particular challenges and degrees of domestic contestation over the choice. Finally, Azerbaijan has so far abstained from pursuing deep integration with either union, favouring a multi-vector policy. In response to these increasingly distinct responses of partner countries, the ENP policy review emphasised the importance of "differentiation" and the necessity to respond to the "different aspirations" of partners (EC and HR 2015, 2-4). While the ENP and EaP previously also included a strong bilateral element, this element is identified as of increasing importance in the review.

A second challenge relates to security. Specific security challenges emanating from the southern neighbourhood as well as Russian actions in the east elicited elevated awareness among key partners and in the EU itself of the importance of having more robust measures to deal with new security threats, including energy security issues, cybersecurity, and the need for security sector reform in partner countries. The 2017 document notes that "increasing security is a shared objective relevant to all ENP countries" (EC and HR 2017, 19), referencing "terrorism, violent extremism, and various forms of organized crime", but also more specific issues in the eastern neighbourhood such as frozen conflicts, the need for security sector reform, and border issues. However, no specific mention is made of Russia, except in the most general context of human rights violations (13). Cooperation in the area of strategic communications to counteract misinformation is also referenced (EC and HR 2015, 21), reinforced in the 2017 document regarding implementation of the review, noting the creation of a new *East Strategic Communications (StratComm) Task Force* (EC and HR 2017, 9).

A third challenge relates to ineffective incentives for reform in EaP countries. This issue has been on the EU agenda since earlier reviews of the ENP, but took on increased salience with the signing of the AAs and DCFTAs, where the degree of reform measures required to implement these agreements is higher. The 2015 review document highlights that "the incentive-based approach ('More for More') has been successful … where there is a commitment by partners to such reforms. However, it has not proven a sufficiently strong incentive to create a commitment to reform, where there is not the political will" (EC and HR 2017, 5).

In addition to responding to these key challenges, the documents highlight specific sectoral arenas of intensified attention, including the energy sector, digital connectedness, the environment, market development, and youth programmes. The twenty key deliverables forming the the workplan for the EaP up to the year 2020 (EC and HR 2016) are organised around four subject areas, which largely parallel those emerging from the 2015 EaP summit (European Council, 2015): (a) "economic development and market opportunities"; (b) "strengthening institutions and good governance"; (c) "connectivity, energy efficiency, environment, and climate change"; and (d) "mobility and people-to-people contacts." In addition three "cross-cutting" areas are included; "civil society", "gender equality", and "communication" (EC and HR 2016). There is an important element of country differentiation drawn out in the ENP review, while for planning purposes there appears to be a similarity of objectives in relation to the various partner countries. Furthermore, security issues are mainly addressed under the "good governance" heading, emphasising societal resilience, as well as energy security concerns, rather than hard security measures.

In summarising the results of the 2015 review, the 2017 implementation report states that the review

> introduced a new approach that encompasses greater respect for the diverse aspirations of the EU's partners; more effective pursuit of areas of mutual interest; new working methods to support a greater sense of ownership by the partners and greater involvement and shared responsibility by the Member States; as well as greater flexibility in the way the EU conducts its policies and its development funds (EC and HR 2017, 3).

COOPERATION AND CONFLICT BETWEEN EUROPE AND RUSSIA 111

This summary statement reflects only incremental change in terms of the previous approach of the EaP. As expected, the documents and statements continue to reflect a two-track policy, one track for the EaP countries and one for Russia. Closer ties between the EU and the EaP countries will progress without trilateral negotiations involving Russia, except in the area of gas transit, with additional cooperation possible on an ad hoc basis to "[address] common challenges . . . when conditions allow" (EC and HR 2015, 19). The EaP review charts a middle course that largely avoids direct engagement with Russia over the EaP and, likewise, avoids a rhetoric of competition, reflecting overall policy continuity from before the 2014 period.

EU energy policy

Energy policy is a complex field in the EU; therefore this section takes a narrow focus on the potential impact of the Ukraine crisis on post-2104 change. The EU and Russia had developed a deeply institutionalised set of energy relations prior to 2014, beyond trade relations that originated in the Soviet period. An EU-Russian Energy Dialogue was established in 2010, with a wide-ranging mandate involving energy security, investment and commercial relations, infrastructure, and energy efficiency (European Commission DG Energy 2011). An important achievement was the development of an early warning system in 2009, in the wake of the 2009 Ukraine-Russia energy dispute, to prevent future supply disruptions; in 2013 the *Roadmap on Russia-EU Energy Cooperation until 2050* was agreed, reflecting "both parties' commitment to the long term strategic energy cooperation," which would result in a "Pan-European Energy Space" (Roadmap 2013, 4-5). However, some analysts assess the achievements of the Energy Dialogue as limited (Georgiou and Rocco 2017). Russia's failure to ratify the Energy Charter Treaty, which the EU hoped would provide a multilateral framework for energy relations, left many issues unresolved in terms of mutual rights and obligations, particularly regarding transit. Other issues of tension were also evident. Already in 2012 the European Commission began formal proceedings regarding possible breaches of the EU's competition rules by Gazprom in Central and Eastern Europe (European Commission, 2012), an issue which also raised difficulties with Russia's favoured South Stream pipeline project, according to EU officials in December 2013 (Lewis 2013).

EU concerns about energy interdependence with Russia precede the Ukraine crisis, particularly given the high dependence of some countries (such as the Baltic states) for their gas supply and the disruptions that occurred in some EU countries in 2006 and 2009 as a result of Ukraine-Russian disputes. It is widely acknowledged that the 2006 and 2009 disruptions contributed to increased concern in the EU about energy security. However, as the 2013 *Roadmap* makes clear, complex "weaning" from Russian energy supplies was not on the agenda. Nonetheless the EU took a variety of actions before 2014 to address dependence on Russian gas, including increased diversity of supply sourcing, sometimes involving new gas pipelines; more robust reserve supplies; strengthening cross-border energy supply systems within the EU; and reduced reliance on fossil fuels through improved energy efficiency and an increased reliance on renewable sources. The last measures were, however, primarily related to concerns about greenhouse gas emissions and climate change. Because all of these policy directions were in place before the 2014 Ukraine crisis erupted, they cannot be seen as attributable to that situation. The question is whether the Ukraine crisis was a threshold event that marked a further shift in policy.

In terms of energy interdependence, the fundamental position of the EU, summarised above, did not change following 2014. However, elements of *crisis response* have affected the relationship and undermined the operation of many of the institutional mechanisms established earlier (Romanova, 2018); thus, the path outlined in the *Roadmap* was largely placed in abeyance. Nonetheless, the fundamental thrust of EU policy, i.e. continued cooperative interdependence with Russia, was not reversed even though concerns about energy security increased. Doubters about Russia's reliability as an energy partner were increasingly vocal in some circles (see Buck 2018), with conflict over the Nordstream 2 pipeline, involving Gasprom and European co-financers, at the epicentre in EU discussions. Critics, including voices from Baltic member states and in the European Commission, depicted the pipeline as potentially undermining EU energy security by assuring continuing and possibly increasing dependence on Russian sources, as well as reducing Ukraine's receipts from transit fees due to diverted supplies through the new pipeline. Objections also arose over the terms of the European Commission's settlement of the anti-trust dispute with Gazprom in May 2018, with Polish objections to the absence of a fine (Reed and Schreuer 2018).

Policy developments after the Crimean annexation reinforced the EU's attention to energy security and to development of a more coherent, unified approach to external energy relations. On May 28, 2014, the European Commission announced the Energy Security Strategy (European Commission 2014), the foundations of which, however, were evidently laid before the Ukraine crisis erupted. Following this was creation of the Energy Union in February 2015 (European Commission 2015). The overriding goal of the Energy Union is "security of supply, sustainability, and competitiveness" (European Commission 2015), and, in its external dimension, to increase the coherence of EU policy. In relation to external partners and supply issues, the Energy Union is intended to make the EU "more resilient to supply disruptions." This requires a more coordinated, less fragmented policy approach: "The EU will use all external policy instruments to ensure a strong, united EU engages constructively with its partners and speaks with one voice on energy and climate" (Energy Commission 2015). A particularly important provision involves the requirement that member states concluding inter-governmental energy agreements (IGAs) with external partners undergo ex ante assessments by the European Commission to determine compliance with EU law (Decision [EU] 2017/684). While security is an important theme in the Commission's 2015 Communication (mentioned 49 times), other concepts such as efficiency (65 mentions), climate (35), price (28), and competitiveness (25) are also emphasised, indicating the broad-reaching scope of the Energy Union strategy (European Commission 2015). Thus, the trajectory of the Energy Union is over-determined by a range of motivations that all push policy in the same direction. In this context it is difficult to identify the unique contribution of the Ukraine crisis to policy development.

Despite this emphasis on reduced vulnerability to external disruption, Energy Union documents do not reference Russia as specific threat. In the Commission's 2015 Communication on the Energy Union, Russia is mentioned only once: "When the conditions are right, the EU will consider reframing the energy relationship with Russia based on a level playing field in terms of market opening, fair competition, environmental protection and safety, for the mutual benefit of both sides" (European Commission 2015). In line with this and a continuing commitment to cooperative interdependence, trilateral talks between Ukraine, Russia, and the EU regarding gas transit to the EU through Ukraine were initiated in July 2018 (Šefčovič 2018).

These developments reveal two contradictory tendencies since early 2014: on the one hand, an increased effort to increase coherence of EU policy, and, on the other, increasingly politicised conflict over energy initiatives, such as Nordstream. While the Commission has proposed a framework to try to mitigate the impact of such policy differences, this effort is still plagued by many of the same issues that existed prior to the Ukraine crisis. However, as the Energy Union is gradually implemented, the capacity of the Commission to reign in contradictory trajectories of individual member states may be reinforced, even if just to assure that member states' actions do not contravene EU regulations and laws.

Discussion

The analysis suggests that thus far the EU's Russia policy has exhibited little evidence of significant policy learning but involves an immediate and continuing crisis response. In relation to the EU's EaP and energy policies incremental change has occurred. However, for the EaP, no serious change in policy direction has taken place (Ikani 2019). Changes in the field of energy policy have been more assertive, but they are over-determined by a number of explanatory variables so it is difficult to isolate a clear influence of the Ukraine crisis.

Reasons for minimal change in all of these various arenas likely reflect different factors. For the EaP, path dependence is a strong determinant of continuity. With the signing of AAs and DCFTAs with three EaP partners, it would have been highly politically costly for the EU to change its course. Furthermore, strong institutional mechanisms and forces in the European Commission gravitate toward continuity. Finally, key member states differed on the overall direction of a more substantial shift in policy (e.g. strengthened or weakened conditionality, more or less engagement with Russia) (Ikani 2019). A shift toward a greater accommodation with Russia in the "shared neighbourhood" or toward an explicit membership perspective for EaP members would elicit strong objections from certain member states. Thus, the joint decision trap also posed an obstacle to more significant change.

Likewise, EU energy policy has also seen incremental change since the Ukraine crisis, but no shift in strategic direction that could be attributable to the Ukraine crisis. The fundamental precept that has driven the EU's policy, namely that energy interdependence can promote peace and stability, remains. Policy change that projects a shift to differentiation and reduced reliance on fossil fuels has been driven by a variety of factors, notably climate change considerations, that predated the Ukraine crisis of 2014. In this sphere path dependence may play a role as a range of institutional interests support a continuation of EU-Russia energy interdependence, including the positions of key member states and firms.

Regarding strategic policy toward Russia a more complex picture emerges. Because the crisis response froze many of the existing institutional bases of the previous policy, path dependence is a less powerful factor here. The crisis surely represents a critical juncture for EU-Russia relations, but not necessarily one that will bring paradigm change. Two obstacles are particularly inhibitory to the charting of a new strategic approach to

Russia. First is the difficulty of gaining member state agreement on an alternative strategy. Second is the absence of a viable alternative that is consistent with the EU's fundamental value commitments and interests. A continuum of responses around three broad alternative strategic trajectories can be mapped. One end of the continuum would involve an attempt at reengagement with Russia based on an explicit recognition of Russia's legitimate interests in the shared neighbourhood. A second, at the other end of the continuum, would be to explicitly define Russia as a regional adversary. A third middle position, reflected in the current incremental approach, involves small steps toward reengagement, building on past cooperation in some areas and attempting to use these to restore trust, while at the same time maintaining current commitments to EaP partners.

Neither of the first two trajectories was, or is, likely to gain acceptance among EU member states. Regarding the first option, the EU as a whole was neither ready to share authorship of its own regional policy with Russia, nor to abandon its commitment to EaP partners' sovereign choice. This approach would imply acceptance of a trilateral format of regional decision-making (involving Russia, EU and partner states) or explicit concessions to Russia in the form of a reduced EU priority on the EaP partnerships. Countries such as the Baltics states and Poland would resist any concessions on Ukraine and EaP partners for the sake of normalising relations with Russia (Republic of Estonia 2019; Republic of Poland 2019; Republic of Latvia, Ministry of Foreign Affairs 2020).

The second alternative is equally problematic for some EU member states including Germany and France, which have taken on an enhanced leadership role in dealing with Russia through the Normandy format; Germany has strong historic reasons and both Germany and France have strong economic interests for avoiding an explicitly adversarial relationship with Russia. Leaders of other countries including Italy, Austria, Hungary, and Bulgaria have argued for "a balanced policy" with Russia (*Sofia Globe* 2019) and cooperative engagement (Euraktiv 2019; Karnitschnig 2018; Plucinska 2019) rather than an adversarial relationship.

The third approach, small steps and selective engagement, combined with strong support for the "European choice" of EaP partners, does not represent a strategic shift, but a pragmatic approach that might allow the EU to maintain unity and eventually move from a crisis response mode. Even leaders of the more Russosceptic countries affirm the necessity of dialogue and cooperation with Russia in areas of mutual interest (Government Offices of Sweden 2019) and praise cooperation where it exists (Latvian Public Broadcasting. 2019). On the other side, while some EU countries are resistant to a continuation of sanctions and would like to see the shift toward reengagement occur more quickly, so far unanimous support for the sanctions has not been shattered due to normative consensus on the unacceptability of the Russian actions in Ukraine (Sjursen and Rosén. 2017). There appears to be a path dependent dynamic that produces repeated confirmation of the sanctions, despite objectors. The five principles represent a compromise position by supplementing the continued crisis response (i.e. sanctions) with possible steps toward a new "normalization" of the relationship. So far this compromise approach seems to have the support of all member states, as evidenced by unanimous approval in the Foreign Affairs Council. Countries like Germany have played a critical role in forging compromise (Fix 2018; Siddi 2016; Daehnhardt 2018) and most other member states have taken account of other countries' positions (Sjursen and Rosén 2017; Natorski and Pomorska 2017). Courted by Russia, some member states have pursued bilateral deals with Russia at the same time (Orenstein and Keleman 2017); unlike Scharpf's expectation, this has not necessarily increased their unwillingness to support a common EU position, at least on sanctions, but might make it difficult to find a shared longer-term strategy. Should one or more member states break rank and veto the continued sanctions prior to Russia meeting the stated conditions, this would present a new decision point. On the one hand, the path of small steps might be continued or even accelerated, posing the possibility of a return to a new "normal" representing incremental change from the pre-2014 approach. Or, on the other hand, such a development could open the door to more intense contestation and deliberation among EU member states about the EU's Russia policy, as Khamkaji and Radaelli suggest can follow the immediacy of a crisis response. Finding a viable alternative strategy toward Russia would face divided member states and an intrinsic difficulty due to the incompatibility of Russian actions with shared EU values, on the one hand, and the importance of establishing cooperation with a key neighbour, on the other. The difficulty is intensified by additional sources of conflict with Russia that have emerged since February 2014 (e.g. Russia's role in the Syrian crisis, the overall arms buildup, alleged Russian election interference, the alleged Skripal poisonings in the UK).

Finally, while EU policy has so far changed only incrementally, a certain discursive shift does, however, appear to be underway. First is the abandonment of talk about strategic partnership with Russia. Second is the inclusion of geopolitical considerations in EU policy deliberation. Third, EU normative discourse in the region emphasises more strongly the notions of stability and security, resilience, territorial integrity, and international law rather than human rights and democracy. The EU's discursive shifts have gotten cool reception in Moscow. This is ironic, since Russian leaders have long advocated a relationship based on interests rather than values.

Conclusion

What does this analysis tell us about the explanatory power of the concepts of path dependence, critical junctures, and joint decision trap? Path dependence seems to be a highly important factor in explaining the lack of real change in the EU's EaP and the direction of change in the EU's energy policy. While the Ukraine crisis was arguably a critical juncture for the EU's Eastern policy (Ikani 2019), and did in fact trigger a major policy review, the outcome was one based on the same premises as the previous policies, with some incremental changes such as a greater emphasis on differentiation and a higher concern with security matters. This case confirms the notion that critical junctures do not necessarily mitigate the impact of path dependence. Proposals for more fundamental change would likely have also confronted the joint decision trap, which itself can reenforce path dependence.

For the EU's strategic policy toward Russia the joint decision trap appears to be much more important than path dependence because the crisis itself did disrupt past patterns of response and interaction. While the crisis no doubt represents a critical juncture for the EU's relations with Russia, it has thus far not ushered in a paradigm shift, but rather a sustained crisis response. This response may involve a temporary suspension of the joint decision trap, but the failure to agree on a longer-term strategic approach suggests that this mechanism is still at play These findings suggest the difficulty of achieving paradigmatic policy change in EU foreign policy, even in the face of a significant crisis. However, this finding should be tested in relation to other foreign policy crises. This study is also not able to identify the factors that may, in the future, make it more likely that a sustained crisis response will engender a longer-term paradigmatic shift, or the degree to which the joint decision trap may continue to inhibit agreement on a longer-term strategy. As Khamkaji and Radaelli argue, paradigmatic change can be introduced gradually, presumably even over a period of years. So, an eventual shift in the policy paradigm cannot be excluded, especially if the crisis continues over an extended period of time (DeBardeleben 2018). The immediate crisis response measures (especially sanctions) could also take on a path dependence of their own that could set that relationship on a longer-term adversarial trajectory.

Another limitation of this study is that the process through which the joint decision trap operates has not been examined, rather the outcomes of policy. Clarifying the decision-making process would require deeper examination of the positions and inter-actions of particular member states in shaping EU responses to the crisis. However, it is well known that, particularly since the 2004 enlargement, agreement on a broader strategic policy toward Russia has been hard to achieve within the EU. Up until 2014, differences between member states resulted in a compromise position that many observers considered sub-optimal for a variety of reasons. When that path was interrupted by Russia's annexation of Crimea, the moment for a reversal in strategy became available, the type of "open moment" that Laffan refers to. However, the first order of business was to respond to the crisis situation. Unanimous agreement on the sanctions was achieved and sustained due to Russia's egregious and obvious breach of EU norms. Remaining in a sustained crisis mode has allowed the EU to delay the difficult task of escaping the joint decision trap and charting a longer-term strategy. Determining whether sustained crisis response provides a way to circumvent difficult decisions on long-term strategy in other cases will require further research.

Note

1. In contrast to the typology developed in this article, Krotz and Maher (2016) identified three types of responses as being breakdown, adaptation, or transformation.

Acknowledgements

This research was supported by the Social Sciences and Humanities Research Council of Canada. It is also an associated activity of the Jean Monnet Chair in EU Relations with Russia and the Eastern Neighbourhood, co-funded by the Erasmus+ Programme of the European and located at Carleton University. European Commission support for the Chair does not constitute an endorsement of the contents of this publication, which reflects the views only of the author, and the European Commission cannot be held responsible for any use which may be made of the information contained therein. I am grateful to the anonymous reviewers for their very helpful comments on an earlier version of this article.

Disclosure statement

No potential conflict of interest was reported by the author(s).

Funding

This work was supported by European Commission: [grant number 574775-EPP-1-2016-1-CA-EPPJMO-chair]; Social Sciences and Humanities Research Council of Canada: [grant number 435-2016-1009].

ORCID

Joan DeBardeleben ⓘ http://orcid.org/0000-0003-1978-2623

References

"Agreement on Partnership and Cooperation establishing a partnership between the European Communities and their Member States, of one part, and the Russian Federation, of the other part". 1997. *Official Journal of the European Communities*, 40 (28 November, L327/3). https://eur-lex.europa.eu/legal-content/EN/TXT/?uri=OJ:L:1997:327:TOC.

Alecu de Flers, Nicole, Laura Chappell, and Patrick Müller. 2011. "The EU's Foreign and Security Policy." In *The EU's joint decision traps: comparing EU policies*, edited by Gerda Falkner, 162–180. Oxford: Oxford University Press. https://www.oxfordscholarship.com/view/10.1093/acprof:oso/9780199596225.001.0001/acprof-9780199596225-chapter-10

Allison, Graham T. 1969. "Conceptual Models and the Cuban Missile Crisis." *The American Political Science Review* 63 (3): 689–718.

Baltic News Network. 2019. "Tusk kept reminding EU of Russia being a 'strategic problem', not partner," Nov. 19. https://bnn-news.com/tusk-kept-reminding-eu-of-russia-being-strategic-problem-not-partner-207508.

Buck, Tobais. 2018. "Nord Steam 2: Gas pipeline from Russia that's dividing Europe," *Irish Times*, July 21. https://www.irishtimes.com/news/world/europe/nord-stream-2-gas-pipeline-from-russia-that-s-dividing-europe-1.3571552.

Capoccia, Giovanni, and R. Daniel Kelemen. 2007. "The Study of Critical Junctures: Theory, Narrative, and Counterfactual in Historical Institutionalism." *World Politics* 59 (April): 341–369.

Clime, Cameron. 2018. "The European Stability Mechanism and the IMF: From the Enhanced Cooperation to Embedded Supervisor." *Review of European and Russian Affairs* 12 (1): 1-16. doi:10.22215/rera.v12i1.1232.

Commission of the European Communities. 2003. "Communication from the Commission to the Council and the European Parliament. Wider Europe—Neighbourhood: A New Framework for Relations with Our Eastern and Southern Neighbours." Brussels, 11 March, COM (2003) 104 final, http://eeas.europa.eu/archives/docs/enp/pdf/pdf/com03_104_en.pdf.

Council of the European Union. 2009. "Joint Declaration of the Prague Eastern Partnership Summit, 7 May 2009". Brussels, 7 May, 8435/09 (Presse 78).

Council of the European Union. 2011. "Joint Declaration of the Eastern Partnership Summit, Warsaw, 30 September 2011". Warsaw 14983/11 PRESSE 341.

Council of the European Union. 2013. "Joint Declaration of the Eastern Partnership Summit, Vilnius, 28-29 November 2013, Eastern Partnership: the Way Ahead." Vilnius, 29 November, 17130/13 (OR.en) PRESSE 516.

Council of the European Union. 2016a. "Outcome of the Council Meeting, 3460th Council meeting, Foreign Affairs." Luxembourg, April 18-19, 8022/16 (OR. en) PRESSE 20 PR CO 19.

Council of the European Union. 2016b. "Outcome of the Council Meeting, 3466th Council meeting, Foreign Affairs." Brussels, 23 May, 9300/16 (OR. en) PRESSE 26 PR CO 25.

Council of the European Union. 2017a. "Outcome of the Council Meeting, 3535th Council meeting, Foreign Affairs." Brussels, 15 May, 9226/17 (OR.en) PRESSE 23 PR CO 23.

Council of the European Union. 2017b. "Joint Declaration of the Eastern partnership summit" Brussels, Nov. 24. http://www.consilium.europa.eu/media/31758/final-statement-st14821en17.pdf.

Council of the European Union. 2018. "Outcome of the Council Meeting", 3613rd Council Meeting, Foreign Affairs, Luxembourg, April 16, 7997/18 (OR.en) PRESSE 23 PR CO 23.

Council of the European Union. 2020. "Statement of the Foreign Affairs Council," March 6, https://data.consilium.europa.eu/doc/document/ST-6657-2020-INIT/en/pdf.

Cross, Mai'a K. Davis, and Ireneusz Pawel Karolewski. 2017. "What Type of Power has the EU Exercised in the Ukraine– Russia Crisis? A Framework of Analysis." *Journal of Common Market Studies* 55 (1): 3–19. doi: 10.1111/jcms.12442.

Daehnhardt, Patricia. 2018. "German Foreign Policy, the Ukraine Crisis and the Euro-Atlantic Order: Assessing the Dynamics of Change." *German Politics* 27 (4): 516–538. doi: 10.1080/09644008.2018.1448386.

DeBardeleben, Joan. 2011. "Revising the EU's European Neighbourhood Policy: The Eastern Partnership and Russia." In *Russia Foreign Policy in the 21st Century*, edited by Roger E. Kanet, 246–265. Houndsmill: Palgrave Macmillan.

DeBardeleben, Joan. 2018. "Alternative Paradigms for EU-Russian Neighbourhood Relations." In *EU-Russia Relations in Crisis: Understanding Diverging Perspectives*, edited by Tom Casier, and Joan DeBardeleben, 115–136. London: Routledge.

"Decision (EU) 2017/684 of the European Parliament and of the Council of April 5, 2017". 2017. *Official Journal of the European Union*, April 12. https://eur-lex.europa.eu/legal-content/EN/TXT/?uri=celex:32017D0684.

Delcour, Laure. 2018. "Dealing with the Elephant in the Room: the EU, its 'Eastern Neighbourhood' and Russia." *Contemporary Politics* 24 (1): 14–29. doi: 10.1080/13569775.2017.1408169.

D'Erman, Valerie, and Amy Verdun. 2018. "Introduction: Integration Through Crisis." *Review of European and Russian Affairs* 12 (1): 1-16. https://ojs.library.carleton.ca/index.php/rera/article/view/1230.

Djelic, Marie-Laure, and Sigrid Quack. 2007. "Overcoming Path Dependency: Path Generation in Open Systems." *Theory and Society* 36 (2): 161–186. DOI 10.1007/s11186-007-9026-0.

EC and HR (European Commission and High Representative of the Union for Foreign Affairs and Security Policy). 2015. "Joint Communication to the European Parliament, the Council, the European Economic and Social Committee and the Committee of the Regions: Review of the European Neighbourhood Policy." JOIN (2015) 50 final. Brussels, Nov. 18. https://ec.europa.eu/neighbourhood-enlargement/sites/near/files/neighbourhood/pdf/key-documents/151118_joint-communication_review-of-the-enp_en.pdf.

EC and HR (European Commission and High Representative of the Union for Foreign Affairs and Security Policy). 2016. "Joint Staff Working Document: Eastern Partnership – Focusing on key priorities and deliverables." SWD (2016) 467 final, Brussels, Dec. 15. https://ec.europa.eu/neighbourhood-enlargement/sites/near/files/near-eeas_joint_swd_2016467_0.pdf.

EC and HR (European Commission and High Representative of the Union for Foreign Affairs and Security Policy). 2017. "Joint Report to the European Parliament, the Council, the European Economic and Social Committee and the Committee of the Regions: Report on the Implementation of the European Neighbourhood Policy Review." JOIN (2017) 18 final, Brussels, May 18. https://eur-lex.europa.eu/legal-content/EN/TXT/?uri=CELEX:52017JC0018

EEAS. 2018. "Speech on behalf of High Representative/Vice-President Federica Mogherini at the European Parliamentary plenary session on the situation in Russia," Delivered by Christos Stylianides, April 18, https://eeas.europa.eu/delegations/russia/43152/speech-behalf-high-representativevice-president-federica-mogherini-european-parliament-plenary_en.

Euraktiv. 2014. "Mogherini: Russia is no longer the EU's strategic partner." Sept. 3. https://www.euractiv.com/section/global-europe/news/mogherini-russia-is-no-longer-the-eu-s-strategic-partner/.

Euraktiv. 2019. "Hungary's Orban defends Russia cooperation at Putin visit." Oct. 31. https://www.euractiv.com/section/politics/news/hungarys-orban-defends-russia-cooperation-at-putin-visit/.

European Commission. 2005. "EU/Russia: The four 'Common Spaces'." Brussels, 18 March, Memo/05/103, https://ec.europa.eu/commission/presscorner/detail/en/MEMO_05_103.

European Commission. 2010. "EU and Russia launch new partnership for modernization". Brussels, 1 June, Press release, https://ec.europa.eu/commission/presscorner/detail/en/IP_10_649.

European Commission. 2012. "Antitrust: Commission opens proceedings against Gazprom." Brussels, 4 September, Press release. http://europa.eu/rapid/press-release_IP-12-937_en.htm.

European Commission. 2014. "Communication from the Commission to the European Parliament and the Council, European Energy Security Strategy, " May 28. COM/2014.0330final. https://eur-lex.europa.eu/legal-content/EN/ALL/?uri=CELEX:52014DC0330&qid=1407855611566.

European Commission. 2015. "Communication from the Commission to the European Parliament, the Council, the European Economic and Social Committee, the Committee of the Regions and the European Investment Bank: A Framework Strategy for a Resilient Energy Union with a Forward-Looking Climate Change Policy." COM/2015/080 final. https://eur-lex.europa.eu/legal-content/EN/TXT/?qid=1449766536658&uri=CELEX:52015DC0080.

European Commission DG Energy (European Commission, Directorate-General Energy). 2011. "EU-Russia Energy Dialogue: The first ten years." Brussels. https://ec.europa.eu/energy/sites/ener/files/documents/2011_eu-russia_energy_relations.pdf.

European Council. 1999. "Common Strategy of the European Union on Russia" 3-4 June." *Official Journal of the European Communities* (OJ L 157, 24.6.1999), 1–10.

European Council. 2015. "Joint Declaration of the Eastern Partnership summit (Riga 21-22 May 2015)." https://www.consilium.europa.eu/media/21526/riga-declaration-220515-final.pdf.

European Council. 2016. 'European Council, 20-21 October 2016: Main results." Brussels. October 20-21, http://www.consilium.europa.eu/en/meetings/european-council/2016/10/20-21/.

European Council. 2018. "European Council Meeting, 22-23 March 2018." Brussels. https://www.consilium.europa.eu/en/meetings/european-council/2018/03/22-23/.

European Council. 2019. "European Council meeting (20 June 2019) - Conclusions." Brussels. https://www.consilium.europa.eu/media/39922/20-21-euco-final-conclusions-en.pdf.

European Parliament News. 2019. "Russia can no longer be considered a 'strategic partner', say MEPS." March 12. https://www.europarl.europa.eu/news/en/press-room/20190307IPR30737/russia-can-no-longer-be-considered-a-strategic-partner-say-meps.

Falkner, Gerda. 2016. "The EU's Problem-Solving Capacity and Legitimacy in a Crisis Context: a Virtuous or Vicious Circle?" *West European Politics* 39 (5): 953–970. doi: 10.1080/01402382.2016.1186386.

Fix, Liana. 2018. "The Different 'Shades' of German Power: Germany and EU Foreign Policy During the Ukraine Conflict." *German Politics* 27 (4): 498–515. doi: 10.1080/09644008.2018.1448789.

Foster, Chase. 2018. "Economic Patriotism After the Crisis: Explaining Continuity and Change in European Securities." *Review of European and Russian Affairs* 12 (1): 1–23. doi:10.22215/rera.v12i1.1233.

Georgiou, Natasha A., and Andrea Rocco. 2017. "The Energy Union as an Instrument of Global Governance in EU-Russia Energy Relations: From Fragmentation to Coherence and Solidarity." *Geopolitics, History, and International Relations* 9 (1): 241–268.

Government Offices of Sweden, Ministry of Foreign Affairs. 2019. "The Government's Statement of Foreign Policy 2018." Feb. 13. https://www.government.se/speeches/20192/02/the-governments-statement-of-foreign-policy-2019/.

Hall, Peter. 1993. "Policy Paradigms, Social Learning, and the State: The Case of Economic Policymaking in Britain." *Comparative Politics* 25 (3): 275–293.

Hogan, John. 2019. "The Critical Juncture Concept's Evolving Capacity to Explain Policy Change." *European Policy Analysis* 5 (2): 170–189. doi: 10.1002/epa2.1057.

Ikani, Nikki. 2019. "Change and Continuity in the European Neighbourhood Policy: The Ukraine Crisis as a Critical Juncture." *Geopolitics* 24 (1): 20–50. doi: 10.1080/14650045.2017.1422122.

Jopp, Mathias, and Udo Diedrichs. 2009. "Learning From Failure: the Evolution of the EU's Foreign, Security and Defence Policy in the Course of the Yugoslav Crisis." In *Crises in European Integration.*

Challenges and Responses, 1945–2005 edited by Ludger Kühnhardt, 95–107. New York, Oxford: Berghahn Books.

Kamkhaji, Jonathan C., and Claudio M. Radaelli. 2017. "Crisis, Learning and Policy Change in the European Union." *Journal of European Public Policy* 24 (5): 714–734. doi: 10.1080/13501763.2016.1164744.

Karnitschnig, Matthew. 2018. "Austria and Putin's mutual appreciation society," *Politico*, June 5, https://www.politico.eu/article/austria-and-putins-mutual-appreciation-society/.

Korosteleva, Elena. 2016. "The EU, Russia and the Eastern Region: The Analytics of Government for Sustainable Cohabitation." *Cooperation and Conflict* 51 (3): 365–383.

Krotz, Ulrich, and Richard Maher. 2016. "Europe's Crises and the EU's 'Big Three'." *West European Politics* 39 (5): 1053–1072. DOI 10.1080/01402382.2016.1181872.

Kuhn, Thomas. 1970. *The Structure of Scientific Revolutions*. 2nd ed. Chicago: Chicago University Press.

Laffan, Brigid. 2016. "Europe's Union in Crisis: Tested and Contested." *West European Politics* 39 (5): 915–932. doi: 10.1080/01402382.2016.1186387.

Latvian Public Broadcasting. 2019. "Latvian Foreign Minister talks up 'positive trend' in economic relations with Russia." June 3. https://eng.lsm.lv/article/politics/diplomacy/latvian-foreign-minister-talks-up-positive-trend-in-economic-relations-with-russia.a321186/.

Lewis, Barbara. 2013. "New Gazprom pipeline faces long wait for EU legal clearance." *Reuters*, December 3. https://www.reuters.com/article/eu-gazprom-idUSL5N0IX4AN20131204.

Medvedev, Dmitry. 2008. "Interview given by Dmitry Medvedev to Television Channels, Channel One, Rossiia, NTV." August 31. http://en.kremlin.ru/events/president/transcripts/4830.

Mogherini, Federica. 2016. "Remarks by High Representative/Vice-President Federica Mogherini at the press conference following the Foreign Affairs Council." European External Action Service, March 14. https://eeas.europa.eu/headquarters/headquarters-homepage/5490_en

Mogherini, Federica. 2019. "Declaration by the High Representative Federica Mogherini on behalf of the EU on the Autonomous Republic of Crimea and the City of Sevastopol." Press Release, European Council/Council of the European Union, March17. https://www.consilium.europa.eu/en/press/press-releases/2019/03/17/declaration-by-the-high-representative-federica-mogherini-on-behalf-of-the-eu-on-the-autonomous-republic-of-crimea-and-the-city-of-sevastopol/.

Müller, Patrick. 2016. "EU Foreign Policy: No Major Breakthrough Despite Multiple Crises." *Journal of European Integration* 38 (3): 359–374. doi: 10.1080/07036337.2016.1140157.

Natorski, Michael, and Karolina Pomorska. 2017. "Trust and Decision-Making in Times of Crisis: The EU's Response to the Events in Ukraine." *Journal of Common Market Studies* 55 (1): 54–70. doi: 10.1111/jcms.12445.

Niemann, Arne, and Johanna Speyer. 2018. "A Neofunctionalist Perspective on the 'European Refugee Crisis': The Case of the European Border and Coast Guard." *Journal of Common Market Studies* 56 (1): 23–43. doi: 10.1111/jcms.12653.

Orenstein, Mitchell A., and R. Daniel Keleman. 2017. "Trojan Horses in EU Foreign Policy." *Jounal of Common Market Studies* 55 (1): 87–102. doi: 10.1111/jcms.12441.

Pierson, Paul. 2000. "Increasing Returns, Path Dependence, and the Study of Politics." *The American Political Science Review* 94 (2): 251–267.

Plucinska, Joanna. 2019. "Poland sees limited room for Russia diplomacy, despite Macron overture" *Reuters*, Dec. 13. https://fr.reuters.com/article/us-poland-russia-macron-idUSKBN1YH1YA

Reed, Stanley, and Milan Schreuer. 2018. "EU Settles With Russia's Gazprom Over Antitrust Charges." New York Times, May 24, https://www.nytimes.com/2018/05/24/business/energy-environment/eu-gas-gazprom.html.

Republic of Estonia, Ministry of Foreign Affairs. 2019. "Reinsalu called on his EU colleagues to extend sanctions on Russia." June 18. https://vm.ee/en/news/reinsalu-called-his-eu-colleagues-extend-sanctions-russia.

Republic of Latvia, Ministry of Foreign Affairs. 2020. "Edgars Rinkēvičs underlined the importance of maintaining a common and shared EU Policy towards Russia." March 7. https://www.mfa.gov.lv/en/news/latest-news/65679-edgars-rinkevics-underlined-the-importance-of-maintaining-a-common-and-shared-eu-policy-towards-russiar.

Republic of Poland, Ministry of Foreign Affairs. 2019. "Minister Jacek Czaputowicz attends a Foreign Affairs Council meeting in Luxembourg." June 18, https://www.gov.pl/web/diplomacy/minister-jacek-czaputowicz-attends-a-foreign-affairs-council-meeting-in-luxembourg.

Roadmap EU-Russia Energy Cooperation until 2050. 2013. https://russiaeu.ru/sites/default/files/user/2013.03.22_Roadmap%20Russia%20-%20EU%20Energy%20Cooperation%20until%202050.pdf.

Romanova, Tatiana. 2018. "EU-Russia Energy Relations: Do Institutions Stand the Test?" In *EU-Russia Relations in Crisis: Understanding Diverging Perspectives*, edited by Tom Casier, and Joan DeBardeleben, 72–92. London: Routledge.

Ross, George. 2011. *The European Union and Its Crises: Through the Eyes of the Brussels Elite*. Houndsmill: Palgrave Macmillan.

Scharpf, Fritz W. 1988. "The Joint-Decision Trap: Lessons From German Federalism and European Integration." *Public Administration* 66: 239–278. c:10.1111/j.1467-9299.1988.tb00694.x.

Siddi, Marco. 2016. "German Foreign Policy Towards Russia in the Aftermath of the Ukraine Crisis: A New Ostpolitik?" *Europe-Asia Studies* 68 (4): 665–677.

Sjursen, Helene, and Guri Rosén. 2017. "Arguing Sanctions. On the EU's Response to the Crisis in Ukraine." *Journal of Common Market Studies* 55 (1): 20–37. doi: 10.1111/jcms.12443.

Sofia Globe. 2019. "Bulgarian PM: We strive to pursue a balanced policy towards Russia." Sept. 20, sofiaglobe.com/2019/09/20/bulgarian-pm-we-strive-to-pursue-a-balanced-policy-towards-russia/.

Šefčovič, Maroš. 2018. "Statement on the Ist round of trilateral talks with Russia and Ukraine" EEAS website, July 6, https://eeas.europa.eu/delegations/russia/48060/statement-1st-round-trilateral-talks-russia-and-ukraine_en.

Zaun, Natascha. 2018. "States as Gatekeepers in EU Asylum Politics: Explaining the Non-Adoption of a Refugee Quota System." *Journal of Common Market Studies* 56 (1): 44–62. doi: 10.1111/jcms.12663.

Index

Note: Page numbers in italics refer to figures, in bold refer to tables and followed by n refers to notes.

Aalto, P. 52
Allison, Graham T. 104
Allseas 74
Ansip, Andrus 19
Anti-Ballistic Missile Treaty 57
Arab spring 39
Arctic cooperation 1
Armenia 101, 109
Association Agreement (AA) 26, 57, 101, 103, 109
Atlantic Alliance 8
Azerbaijan 109

balanced policy, with Russia 114
Balkan wars 103
Baltic Hong Kong *see* Kaliningrad
Baltic Pipe 90, 95n7
Baltic sea 15; environmental management 1
Baltic states 21, 57, 93, 114
Barinov, Aleksander 22
Barroso, J. 19
Baxendale, J. 52
Belarus 109
Belova, Anna 24
besieged fortresses narrative 45
Brandt, Willy 86–7
British-Dutch Shell 73
Bronze Soldier statue, removal of 18–19
Brussels 69
Bulgaria 93
business as usual response 104, **105**, **106**

Casier, Tom 3, 4, 8
Central and Eastern Europe (CEE) 37, 43–4
Chisinau 25, 27–8
circles of influence strategy 26
citizens, *privileged categories* of 54–5
classical/traditional geopolitics 39–40; *vs.* hybrid geopolitics 41–2
Cohen, Saul Bernard 41
Cold War 4, 36–7
collective identity 82

Collective Security Treaty Organisation (CSTO) 72
Common European Home project 37
Common Foreign and Security Policy, Global Strategy for 60
Common Strategy of the European Union Russia of 1999 106
Comprehensive and Enhanced Partnership Agreement 101
conflict/cooperation, in EU-Russia relations 36–8; during 1991 and 2016 4, *5*; ambiguous coexistence 65–76; persistence of 35–46
Construal-Level Theory (CLT) 65, 69–70, 71, 75
Consultative Group of the Treaty of Conventional Armed Forces in Europe 51
contested boundary 6
Crimea, annexation of 1, 20, 21, 100, 112
crisis response 101, 112; discussion 113–14; types 104–6, **105**, **106**
CSCE summit in Helsinki communiqué (1992) 17
culture, common space for 66
cyber-attacks 107; in Estonia government websites 18–19
Czaputowicz, Jacek 90
Czech Republic 93

DeBardeleben, Joan 3, 4, 9, 69, 100
Deep and Comprehensive Free Trade Area (DCFTA) 103, 109
Dembińska, Magdalena 1, 4, 7, 13
demilitarization, of Estonia 16–17
Denmark 92
Diener, Alexander 52
disputed symbolic boundary 6, 14; Moldova 24–8
Djelic, Marie-Laure 102
Dodon, Igor 27
Dodon, Ion 25
Domaniewski, Stanislaw 52–3
domestic politics 68, 76n3, 88
Donbas conflict, Russia's involvement in 20
Donnelly, Chris 56

INDEX

Duda, Andrzej 89, 90
Dunnett, Chris 3

Eastern Partnership (EaP) policy 26, 100, 106, 109–11
East Strategic Communications (StratComm) Task Force 109
economic profitability, of energy policy 84
economic space 66
education, common space for 66
education, in EU-Russia relations 67
education system, symbolic boundaries through 14
elites, symbolic boundaries through 14
energy and trade, in EU-Russian relations 27–8
energy crisis 1
Energy Dialogue 107, 111
energy policy 82–4, 111–13; material determinants of 84
energy relations 1, 68; EU-Russia 67, 80–95
Energy Union 112–13
Engie 73
Erasmus programme 67
Estonia 4; demilitarisation of 16–17; energy security 19–20; *hidden sanctions* economic pressure 19; minority issues and removal of Bronze statue 18–19; new citizenship policy 18; Nord stream 2 19–20; relocation of Russian military cemetery 19; *returning to Europe* aim 15; Russian-speakers 17–18; solid symbolic boundary 16–20; withdrawal of Russian troops 17
Eurasian Economic Union (EAEU) 37, 101
European Commission 106; anti-trust dispute with Gazprom 112; criticism of Nord Stream 2 project 85; Energy Security Strategy 112; facilitated transit document (FTD) 54; Future of Europe White Paper 60; technical assistance in Kaliningrad 23
European External Action Service (EEAS) 55, 60, 106
European Neighbourhood Policy (ENP) 26, 100, 107; 2015 revision 38
European security system 51
European Union (EU) 17; *circles of influence* strategy 26; crises 35, 39, 43; Eastern Partnership policy 109–11; Energy policy 111–13; foreign trade in Kaliningrad 23; Local Border Traffic Regulation 55; member states 91–3; policies after Ukraine crisis 106–13; promotion of norms in post-Soviet space 2–3; rapprochement with NATO and 15; resilience 67; Russia's policy 107–9
Euro-Russian conflicts 3
Euro-Russia relations 1; ambiguous coexistence of conflict/cooperation 65–76; approach to hybrid geopolitics 42–5; coexistence 4–6; conflict/cooperation dichotomy 36–8; conflictual dynamics from high to low

politics 72–5; cooperative practices from low to high politics 71–2; deterioration of 13; energy and trade 27–8; energy relations 80–95; Estonia 16–20; geopolitical fields 6–7, 65–6; geostrategic debate 2–4; hybrid geopolitics 35–46; Kaliningrad 20–4; local autonomy 13–29; low *vs.* high politics 68–71; Moldova 24–8; new visa regime 23; Nord Stream 2 project 85–93; paradox 66–8; persistence of conflict/cooperation in 35–46; rise of geopolitics 38–41; Russian Other and energy policy 82–4; shared neighbourhood 36, 40, 45, 46; Strategic Partnership 66, 75; theorising cooperation and conflict 1–9; traditional *vs.* hybrid geopolitics 41–2; unidimensional leadership 4
Eurozone crisis 35, 38, 103
EU-Russian contestation 51; over human transit 52
EU-Russian Visa Facilitation Agreement 54
external security, common space for 66

facilitated transit document (FTD) 54
Falkner, Gerda 101–3
Feklyunina, Valentina 4
Ferrero-Waldner, Benita 26
Finland 92
fluid symbolic boundary 6, 7, 14, 36; Kaliningrad 20–4
Foreign Affairs Council 109, 114
foreign policy, and national identity 82
Forsberg, Tuomas 54
Four Common Spaces and their Road Maps 106, 107
freedom, common space for 66

Gabriel, Sigmar 87
Gagauzia 25, 26
Gazprom 28, 93, 95n4, 112; German consumers for 90; international expansion strategy 19–20
geopolitical fields 2, 68; crises EU experienced in 35, 39; of EU-Russia relations 65–6; vertical and horizontal dimension of 7
geopolitical frames 14
geopolitical wrapping 77n12
Georgia 109
Georgian-Russian war of 2008 40, 46n3, 57
Germany: conceptualisations of Russian Other 86–8; US nuclear weapons in 58
Global Strategy 2016 38
good governance 110
Gorbachev, M. 2, 37
Götz, E. 3
governmentality 45
Great Russia 2
Grenell, Richard 74
Grigas, Agnia 20
Grønbjerg, L. 51
Grybauskaite, Dalia 57

Hagen, Joshua 52
Hall, Peter 104
Haukkala, Hiski 54
high politics 65; conflictual dynamics 72–5; cooperative practices 71–2; *vs.* low politics 68–71
Hill, William H. 59
Hogan, John 102
Holtom, P. 52
Hopf, Ted 4
Horris, James 23
Hungary 93
hybrid geopolitics 7; approach of EU and Russia in 42–5; Euro-Russian relations 35–46; *vs.* traditional geopolitics 41–2

ideational factors 81–2, 84, 94
identity crises 41–4
Ikani, Nikki 103
incremental adaptation 104, **105**, **106**, 108, 109
initial crisis response 104
interdependence and insecurity 71
inter-governmental energy agreements (IGAs) 112
Intermediate-Range Nuclear Forces Treaty (INF) 58
international relations 43
Iranian nuclear programme 67, 86
Iskander missiles 8, 56, 58
issue area typology 70
issue politics paradigm 68
Italian-Russian relations 92

Jean Monnet projects 67
Johnson, Boris 92
Joint Comprehensive Plan of Action (JCPOA) *see* Iranian nuclear programme
joint decision trap 101–2, 104, 113
justice, common space for 66

Kaczynski, Lech 88; death of 88
Kaliningrad 4, 8, 14; *bridge* between Russia and Europe 20, 22; demilitarisation of 21, 56; dual shift in cooperation/conflict 51–62; EU-Russian contention over human transit 52; EU-Russian diplomacy 54–6; evolving borders 53–4; fluid symbolic boundary 20–4; foreign trade by EU 23; migration 1; mobility issues cooperation 21–4; SBT agreement (2012) 24; shifting transit regulations to security concerns 56–61; visa-free transit 52; weapon market 21
Kamkhaji, Jonathan C. 102, 104, 115, 116
Karabeshkin, L. 54
Kiev, and Moscow conflicts 85
Kissinger, Henri A. 3
Kneissl, K. 67
Konashenkov, Igor 57
Kosovo crisis 103

Kosovo war 1
Kozak plan 27
Kozyrev, Andrei 17
Kremlin, Moscow 2, 27, 43; foreign policy 38
Krickovic, A. 71
Kuhn, Thomas 104
Kunertova, Dominika 1

Laffan, Brigid 101, 103, 104, 116
Larson, Deborah Welch 4
Lavrov, Sergei 54–5, 59, 74, 108–9
liberal democracy 37
Linkevicus, Linas 57
Liquefied Natural Gas (LNG) 74
Lithuania: accession to EU 51; Kurshsky gulf navigation agreement with Russia
low politics 65; conflictual dynamics from higher politics domain 72–5; cooperative practices to higher politics domain 71–2; *vs.* high politics 68–71
Luik, Juri 16–17

Maas, Anna-Sophie 8, 51
Maas, Heiko 87
macro-variables, explaining cooperation/conflict coexistence 14
Mankoff, Jeffrey 2
mass media, symbolic boundaries through 14
Matochkin, Yurii 20, 22
May, Theresa 92
Mearsheimer, John 2–3
Medvedev, Dmitrii 57–8
Melvin, Neil J. 18, 21
memory wars 18
Mérand, Frédéric 1, 4, 7, 13
Meri, Lennhart 16
Merkel, Angela 19, 87, 90, 95n3
migrant crisis 39
migration 18
Milner, H. V. 68
minority rights, controversies concerning in Estonia 18
Minsk agreements 67, 107–8
Mobility Partnership 2008 26
Mogherini, Federica 100–1, 107–8
Moldova 4, 109; disputed symbolic boundary 24–8; dual identity of 25; energy and trade 27–8; EU-Russia contest over 26; Russian speakers 25–6
Montesano, Francesco S. 27
Morawiecki, Mateusz 90
Morozov, Viacheslav 42
Moscow 3, 69; embassy blockade 19; foreign policy 88; and Kiev conflicts 85; Russian interests/humiliation in 1990 2

Narva region (Estonia), Russian-speakers in 18
National Defence Authorization Act 74
national identity, and foreign policy 82

NATO: enlargement of 2–3; rapprochement with EU and 15
NATO-Russia Council 1
NATO-Russia Founding Act 1997 59
NATO-Russian relations 51, 58–9
natural gas 67, 74; import of 65
near abroad policy 15, 18
Neumann, Iver B. 3–4
9M729 missile 58
Nitoiu, Cristian 7, 35
Nordic Council 17
Nord Stream 2 project 19–20, 73–4; articulation of EU-Russia conflict/cooperation 86–93; and conceptualisations of Russian Other in Germany 86–8; French and Dutch companies 92; material factors 90–1; Polish view of Russian Other and 88–90; stances of EU member states 91–3
Nord Stream Gas Pipeline (NSGP) project 19–20
Normandy format 67
nuclear missiles, Russia's deployment of 51
nuclear weapons 58

Obama administration 74
OMV 73
open economic zone 22
open moments, crises as 101, 104, 116
Ostpolitik tradition 8, 83, 86–7, 92

Paet, Urmas 19
paradigmatic adaptation 104, **105, 106**, 108
Partnership and Cooperation Agreement (PCA) 66, 106, 107
Partnership for Modernisation 66, 106
Partnership for Peace (PfP) programme 26
Pasatoiu, Florin 35
path dependence 101–2, 104, 115
Perry, Rick 74
Peskov, Dimitry 58
Poland 21, 93, 114; accession to NATO 51; SBT agreement (2012) 24; view of Russian Other and Nord Stream 2 project 88–90
Pouliot, Vincent 3–4
power, and space 41–2
privileged categories, of citizens 54–5
Prodi, Romano 54
Putin, Vladimir 3, 54, 58, 67

QDA Miner 15
Quack, Sigrid 102

Radaelli, Claudio M. 102, 104, 115, 116
refugee crisis 103
regional conflicts, between West and Russia 86
research, common space for 66
Romania 93
Romanianism 25
Romanova, Tatiana 71
Rome 92

Rosenau, J. 70
Rozhkov-Yurevsky, Yuriy 22
Russia: balanced policy with 114; collapse of 21; crises 39, 43; disintegration period between 1991-2016 15; embassy blockade in Moscow 19; ethnic minorities 40; EU policy 107–9; foreign policy 39; and Italy relations 92; Kurshsky gulf navigation agreement with Lithuania 23; minority issues/removal of Bronze statue in Estonia 18–19; and NATO relations 51, 58–9
Russian-European relations 13; varying according to symbolic boundaries 14 (*see also* Euro-Russian relations)
Russian financial crisis 23
Russian Other 8, *83*; conceptualisations in Germany 86–8; and energy policy 82–4; Polish view of Nord Stream 2 project and 88–90

Sakwa, Richard 51, 60
Salaru, Anatolie 27
Salisbury poisonings 107
Samara summit 19
Scharpf, Fritz 101–2, 115
Schengen zone 24, 51, 54
Schevchenko, Alexei 4
Schmidt-Felzmann, Anke 51
Schröder, Gerhard 84, 95n3
security, common space for 66
Shtaltovna, Anastasiya 4, 7, 13
Siddi, Marco 8, 80
Sikorski, Radoslaw 55, 88
Skripal (Sergei and Yulia) poisoning 92
Slovakia 93
Small Border Traffic (SBT) agreement 24
Smolensk plane crash 88
social mobility, Russian language as 18
solid symbolic boundary 6, 14; Bronze Soldier statue case 18–19; Estonia 16–20
Sovietisation/Russification campaign 16
Soviet Union: collapse of 2; dissolution of 37, 43 (*see also* Russia)
space, power and 41–2
special economic zone (SEZ): in Kaliningrad 22–3
Steinmeier, Frank-Walter 19, 86
Stoltenberg, Jens 56, 61–2
strategic considerations, of energy policy 84
Strategic Partnership, EU-Russia relations 66, 75, 108
Studzińska, Dominika 52–3
sustained crisis response 104, **105, 106**, 108
Sweden 92
Swinoujscie LNG terminal 85
symbolic boundaries: conceptual framework of 65; disputed 6, 14, 24–8; through elites/education system/mass media 14; fluid 6, 7, 14, 20–4, 36; and geopolitical fields 6–7; solid 6, 14, 16–20

Syria 86
Syrian crisis 115
Szydlo, Beata 89
Szymanski, Konrad 89

Tallinn: rapprochement with NATO 16; relocating of Russian military cemetery 19
Tingley, D. 68
Tiraspol 25–6
trade: in EU-Russia relations 27–8, 66–7; foreign trade by EU 23
Transnistria 26; frozen conflict 25–6; sanctions and military support 15; support to join Russia 25
Trenin, Dimitri 2
Trump, Donald 74, 87
Tsygankov, Andrei 4
Tusk, Donald 88

Ukraine: conflict 1; geopolitical fault line 2; Russia's involvement in Donbas conflict 20
Ukraine crisis (2014) 3, 35, 36, 39, 55, 60, 80, 100, 103
Ukrainian affair 9
Uniper 73
United Kingdom (UK) 92; Sergei and Yulia Skripal poisoning in 92
United States (US): Germany nuclear weapons in 58; LNG deliveries from 74, 90; missile defense plan 1; State Department 17

van der Togt, Tony 27
Vasquez, J. A. 70
Victory Day 18; clash on 9 May 2006 19
Vilnius summit 28, 103, 109
Vinokurov, E. Y. 52
visa free dialogue 55
visa-free transit 52–3
visa liberalization 54–5
vision and division principles 6, 14
Volovoj, Vadim 26
Voronin, Vladimir 27

War Graves Protection Act 19
Warsaw 84, 89, 91
Waszczykowski, Witold 88, 89
Wellmann, C. 54
West: open-arms policy 3; and Soviet Russia 37
Wider Europe 76, 107
Wintershall 73
Wolff, S. 3

Yamal pipeline 91
Yanukovych, Viktor 103, 109
Yegorov, Vladimir 56
Yeltsin, B. 17, 22
Youngs, Richard 67

Zweers, Wouter 27